Cambridge Opera Handbooks

W. A. Mozart
Le nozze di Figaro

W. A. Mozart
Le nozze di Figaro

TIM CARTER

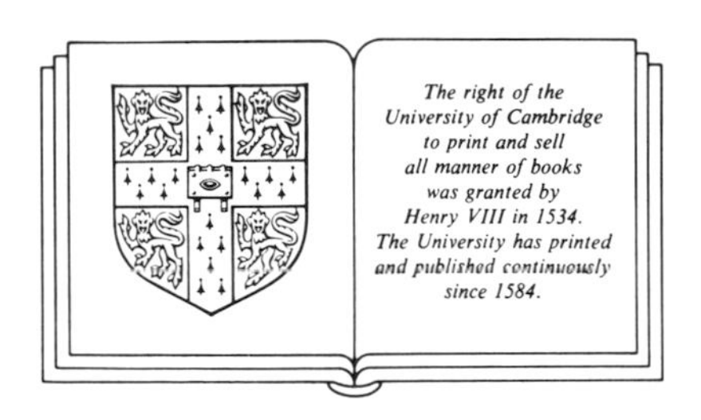

CAMBRIDGE UNIVERSITY PRESS

Cambridge
New York   New Rochelle   Melbourne   Sydney

Published by the Press Syndicate of the University of Cambridge
The Pitt Building, Trumpington Street, Cambridge CB2 1RP
32 East 57th Street, New York, NY 10022, USA
10 Stamford Road, Oakleigh, Melbourne 3166, Australia

First published 1987

Printed in Great Britain at
the University Press, Cambridge

British Library cataloguing in publication data

Carter, Tim
W. A. Mozart: Le nozze di Figaro.
(Cambridge opera handbooks).
1. Mozart, Wolfgang Amadeus. Nozze di
Figaro
I. Title
782.1'092'4 ML410.M9

Library of Congress cataloguing in publication data

Carter, Tim.
W. A. Mozart, Le nozze di Figaro.
(Cambridge opera handbooks)
Bibliography.
Discography.
Includes index.
1. Mozart, Wolfgang Amadeus, 1756–91. Nozze di
Figaro. I. Title. II. Title: Nozze di Figaro.
III. Series.
ML410.M9C33 1987 782.1'092'4 87–11

ISBN 0 521 30267 6 hard covers
ISBN 0 521 31606 5 paperback

ME

CAMBRIDGE OPERA HANDBOOKS

General preface

This is a series of studies of individual operas written for the opera-goer or record-collector as well as the student or scholar. Each volume has three main concerns: historical, analytical and interpretative. There is a detailed description of the genesis of each work, the collaboration between librettist and composer, and the first performance and subsequent stage history. A full synopsis considers the opera as a structure of musical and dramatic effects, and there is also a musical analysis of a section of the score. The analysis, like the history, shades naturally into interpretation: by a careful combination of new essays and excerpts from classic statements the editors of the handbooks show how critical writing about the opera, like the production and performance, can direct or distort appreciation of its structural elements. A final section of documents gives a select bibliography, a discography, and guides to other sources. Each book is published in both hard covers and as a paperback.

CAMBRIDGE OPERA HANDBOOKS

Published titles

Richard Wagner: *Parsifal* by Lucy Beckett
W. A. Mozart: *Don Giovanni* by Julian Rushton
C. W. von Gluck: *Orfeo* by Patricia Howard
Igor Stravinsky: *The Rake's Progress* by Paul Griffiths
Leoš Janáček: *Káťa Kabanová* by John Tyrrell
Giuseppe Verdi: *Falstaff* by James A. Hepokoski
Benjamin Britten: *Peter Grimes* by Philip Brett
Giacomo Puccini: *Tosca* by Mosco Carner
Benjamin Britten: *The Turn of the Screw* by Patricia Howard
Richard Strauss: *Der Rosenkavalier* by Alan Jefferson
Claudio Monteverdi: *Orfeo* by John Whenham
Giacomo Puccini: *La bohème* by Arthur Groos and Roger Parker
Giuseppe Verdi: *Otello* by James A. Hepokoski
Benjamin Britten: *Death in Venice* by Donald Mitchell
W. A. Mozart: *Die Entführung aus dem Serail* by Thomas Bauman

Contents

General preface		*page* v
List of illustrations		viii
Preface		ix
1	Introduction	1
2	Mozart and the *opera buffa* tradition *by Michael F. Robinson*	11
3	Beaumarchais, da Ponte and Mozart: from play to opera	33
4	Synopsis	49
5	Verse and music in *Le nozze di Figaro*	75
6	*Opera buffa* and the Classical style: the Act I trio	88
7	Music and drama in *Le nozze di Figaro*	105
8	*Le nozze di Figaro*: a brief performance history	122
Notes		148
Select bibliography		163
Discography *by Malcolm Walker*		168
Index		174

Illustrations

1 *Le nozze di Figaro*, Act IV finale: engraving in *Orphea Taschenbuch für 1827* (Leipzig, Ernst Fleischer, 1826) *page* 69
2 *Le nozze di Figaro*, libretto (Vienna, G. de Kurzbek, 1786), p. 67 70
3 *Le nozze di Figaro*, Act III, No. 19: London, British Library, R.M. 22.i.5, fol. 70r 127
4 Henry Bishop, *The Marriage of Figaro*: London, British Library, Add. MS 27712, fol. 63r 128
5 *Le nozze di Figaro*, Act II scene 3: set by Oliver Messel, Glyndebourne 1955 141
6 *Le nozze di Figaro*, Act II Scene 8 (above), Act III scene 5 (below): production and set by Jean-Pierre Ponnelle, Salzburg 1972 143
7 *Le nozze di Figaro*, Act III scene 5: production by Peter Hall, Glyndebourne 1973 144

The illustrations appear by permission of the following: The British Library (Plates 1, 3 and 4), The Library of Congress (Plate 2), Glyndebourne Opera House (Plates 5 and 7), Pressebüro Salzburger Festspiele and *Opera* (Plate 6).

Preface

Le nozze di Figaro (1786) was Mozart's first mature *opera buffa.* It was also the first of his three major collaborations with the librettist Lorenzo da Ponte. Unlike *Don Giovanni* (1787) and *Così fan tutte* (1790), *Figaro* has few obvious problems, and even if it is not without flaws, it nevertheless contains a remarkable mixture of all those elements that go to produce a good opera: a sound plot, a well-structured text and fine music. Moreover, by being an adaptation of a pre-existing play, *Figaro* allows us to explore fundamental issues concerning the nature of opera and the various roles of a playwright, librettist and composer in producing a true *commedia per musica.*

Mozart and da Ponte based their opera on a recent play by the French playwright Pierre-Augustin Caron de Beaumarchais, *La folle journée ou Le mariage de Figaro* (written by 1781, performed 1784). There was nothing new in adapting a play for an opera: indeed, in 1782 Giovanni Paisiello had done the same for Beaumarchais's first 'Figaro' play, *Le barbier de Séville ou La précaution inutile* (written 1772, performed 1775). However, *Le mariage* was a daring choice: it had created a scandal in Paris and across Europe because of its apparently subversive political content. Nevertheless, Beaumarchais's play had several advantages – strong issues, clear-cut characters and a fast pace – that made it an ideal subject for an *opera buffa*: his contribution to *Figaro* should not be underestimated.

Da Ponte's task was to rework the play to suit the requirements of sung rather than spoken drama. He was a good librettist with a fine sense of the stage and could produce well-crafted verse that captured a dramatic situation with economy and wit. Moreover, he seems to have known full well the capabilities of Mozart's music. If anyone can counter the tendency of current operatic criticism to devalue the librettist, it is da Ponte. Indeed, his importance for the success of *Figaro* is one of the major points to emerge from this study.

Five years before *Figaro,* Mozart had moved from a provincial town, Salzburg, to a cosmopolitan capital, Vienna, that was perhaps the centre of the current musical world. The musical excitement of Vienna and Mozart's own increasing emotional and compositional maturity are felt in many of the works composed during his early years in the city: witness the first 'mature' piano concertos or the six 'Haydn' quartets. However, his letters to his father make it clear that he was drawn first and foremost to opera, and in particular *opera buffa*. Laying aside the mixed experiences of *Idomeneo* (1781), he searched avidly for a good libretto, produced a fine if idiosyncratic German Singspiel, *Die Entführung aus dem Serail* (1782), and made at least two false starts on an Italian *opera buffa* before settling down to work on *Figaro*. The sheer joy of having found a subject and a librettist to match his talents is apparent throughout Mozart's score.

The layout of this study needs little explanation. Chapter 1 places *Figaro* in the context of Mozart's early years in Vienna, and in Chapter 2, Michael Robinson ventures into the hitherto little-explored terrain of *opera buffa* from the 1760s onwards to give the opera an all-important historical perspective. Chapter 3 discusses the way in which Beaumarchais's play was turned into an opera, and Chapter 4 gives a detailed synopsis with commentary. Chapter 5 deals with an aspect of da Ponte's libretto which is often ignored, its poetic structure and the way in which this structure might be said to have influenced Mozart's setting. Chapters 6 and 7 are concerned with the music, looking at specific features of the score in detail as well as offering an overview of what I deem to be the most important musico-dramatic considerations in the opera. Chapter 8 surveys some performances of *Figaro* in the late eighteenth and early nineteenth centuries, partly to illuminate particular performing traditions and partly to examine how these traditions cast light on the work itself. The Handbook concludes with a discography, and a Select Bibliography that aims to be useful rather than exhaustive.

Three points remain before concluding on procedural matters. First, I have been unable to discuss an important new trend in Mozart scholarship, the use of manuscript studies to illuminate the compositional process. The autograph manuscripts of *Figaro* are not easily accessible (Acts I and II are in the Deutsche Staatsbibliothek, East Berlin, and Acts III and IV in the Biblioteka Jagiellońska, Kraków). Some questions on the order of numbers in the opera and the revisions that occurred in the course of its composition are raised here at the end of Chapter 4 and in Chapter 8, but the broader issues are best left to the major study of Mozart manuscripts (including a discussion of *Figaro*) by Alan Tyson that is to appear shortly. Second, it has been impossible to cover every aspect of *Figaro*, or to discuss every note of Mozart's music. Nor was I interested in providing just a narrative account of the opera. Thus I have had to be selective, if only to be able to go into the kind of detail that this rich opera demands. Third, it is only fair to warn the reader that some parts of the Handbook are more technical than others. It is entirely possible to talk seriously about music without lapsing into high-flown analytical jargon, but to ignore the deeper levels of the opera is to do Mozart an injustice. Chapters 5 and 6 in particular may seem 'difficult' at first. However, the issues should be clear, even if the detail is not.

Three editions of the opera have been used (see the Select Bibliography): the full score edited by Ludwig Finscher as part of the *Neue Mozart-Ausgabe*, the miniature score edited by Rudolf Gerber (published by Eulenburg Editions), and the vocal score, with a splendid English translation, edited by Edward J. Dent (published by Boosey & Hawkes). Finscher's edition is the most scholarly and reliable, but Gerber's and Dent's will be more generally available and reference is made to these whenever possible. Bar numbers are taken from Gerber: readers wishing to make detailed reference to the vocal score will need to add bar numbers themselves (each aria or ensemble should have its own set of numbers extending into the succeeding recitative; in the case of Nos. 17, 19, 26 and 27, the bar numbers should start at the preceding accompanied recitative). Pitches given in roman capitals as C, D, etc., are to be understood as having no reference to a particular octave: pitches given in italics as *C* (*D*, etc.), *c*, *c′*, *c″*, etc., use the Helmholtz system whereby c′ = 'middle' C. Keys are generally stated in full (F major), although sometimes in examples it has been useful to abbreviate them according to convention (F = F major, f = F minor). The standard roman numerals are used for chord and key relationships (I = tonic, IV = subdominant, V = dominant). Quotations from the libretto are taken from the edition by Lecaldano (see the Select Bibliography), although I have sometimes added punctuation and made other editorial changes to clarify the sense. Music examples from Mozart's operas are adapted where possible from the editions in the *Neue Mozart-Ausgabe*. All translations are my own unless indicated otherwise.

It gives me great pleasure to thank my contributors, Michael Robinson and Malcolm Walker. I am grateful to Rosemary Dooley, formerly of Cambridge University Press, for her help in the initial stages of this project, and to Penny Souster and Michael Black for bringing it to fruition. Eric Cross, Nigel Fortune, Denis McCaldin, Anthony Pople and Julian Rushton made perceptive comments on my early drafts; Frederick Sternfeld generously shared his notes on *Figaro* with me; I have benefited from contact with Daniel Heartz and Alan Tyson; and Robert Meikle is owed my deep gratitude for our long conversations on Mozart, *opera buffa* and the Classical style. Present and former music students of the University of Lancaster will no doubt realise the extent to which they have been treated as guinea-pigs for most of the ideas presented here. This book is dedicated to them.

TIM CARTER

Lancaster
Summer 1986

1 *Introduction*

Mozart arrived in Vienna from Munich on 16 March 1781 to take his place in the entourage of Archbishop Colloredo of Salzburg, who was on an official visit to the city. His position as the Archbishop's court organist was a respectable one, but he complained of being ranked only just above the cooks and below the valets,[1] and he was clearly dissatisfied with his lot. One can see why. During his precocious childhood he had been fêted throughout Europe. But now he was no longer a novelty, and despite the staunch efforts of his father he felt that he had not yet found a post to match his abilities. Attempts to secure a position at Munich and Mannheim had failed, and his recent trip to Paris was fraught with personal sadness – the death of his mother – and professional neglect. Even the success of *Idomeneo*, K366, in Munich (it was staged there on 29 January 1781) was scant compensation for his uncertain prospects.

Above all, Mozart could not bear the thought of spending any more time in his native Salzburg. Not only did he dislike working for the Archbishop, but he also loathed what he felt was the provinciality of this small city in northern Austria. Even amid the disappointments of Paris he could not see himself returning there. In mid-1778 he wrote to the Abbé Bullinger that 'Salzburg is no place for my talent':

> In the first place, professional musicians there are not held in much consideration; and, secondly, one hears nothing, there is no theatre, no opera; and even if they really wanted one, who is there to sing? For the last five or six years the Salzburg orchestra has always been rich in what is useless and superfluous, but very poor in what is necessary, and absolutely destitute of what is indispensable. . .[2]

A lack of respect for musicians, the absence of a theatre and opera, and a poor-quality orchestra scarcely made Salzburg attractive to a young composer for whom so much had been promised. It is small wonder, then, that Mozart seems to have been thoroughly seduced by the bright lights of Vienna. According to Michael Kelly:

the Court of Vienna was, perhaps, the most brilliant in Europe. The theatre, which forms part of the Royal Palace, was crowded with a blaze of beauty and fashion. All ranks of society were doatingly fond of music, and most of them perfectly understood the science. Indeed, Vienna then was a place where pleasure was the order of the day and night.[3]

Things came to a head for Mozart in Vienna when the Archbishop prevented him from playing before the Emperor and moreover from earning the equivalent of half his Salzburg salary in one evening. On 9 May Mozart asked for his dismissal, and it was eventually granted a month later 'with a kick on my arse'. He was now on his own.

Mozart was optimistic about the possibilities of earning a living in Vienna by teaching, playing and the support of noble patrons, and his early years in Vienna were indeed successful. Moreover, he was able to hear the music of and meet the leading composers of the age, such as Joseph Haydn, and to take advantage of the interests of noble dilettantes to explore the music of the past, as with Baron van Swieten's taste for the music of J. S. and C. P. E. Bach and Handel. Mozart also fell in love and married. But above all he felt that here in 'the land of the clavier'[4] he was among people who could appreciate his talents.

Mozart's repeated complaints about the lack of a theatre in Salzburg emphasise just how much he valued sung and spoken drama. Opera, in particular comic opera (*opera buffa*), was especially close to his heart. One can see why Mozart liked *opera buffa* – his first full-length work for the stage, *La finta semplice* (1768, composed at the age of twelve), was a comic opera – for even if he was able and willing to write *opera seria* ('serious' opera) when required, both his musical style and his own inclinations leant towards comedy. The stereotyped characters and fixed, static forms of late Baroque *opera seria* may have held the stage for almost a century, but *opera buffa* was a rising star, a true product of the Age of Enlightenment. Italian composers of the early eighteenth century had begun to turn away from the epic heroes and the plots concerned with honour, virtue and glory typical of *opera seria* to focus on real people with human needs and emotions from all levels of society. These composers were inspired by contemporary developments in spoken comedy, in particular under the influence of the *commedia dell'arte*, with its fast-moving, improvisatory plots, its slapstick comedy, and its down-to-earth humour. Giovanni Battista Pergolesi's famous *La serva padrona* (1733) was just one of many works that reflected this new spirit of comedy, and the new genre reached its first peak in the operas of Baldassare Galuppi to the libretti of that great comic writer of the eighteenth century, Carlo Goldoni.

These new comic plots inevitably affected the musical forms and styles available to the opera composer. The static da capo (ABA) aria, with its emphasis on vocal display, no longer reigned supreme, and composers were free to explore, indeed invent, musical processes that would match this new kind of drama. First Pergolesi and Galuppi, and then Niccolò Piccinni, Domenico Cimarosa and Giovanni Paisiello, were all composers who forged new musical techniques in their attempts to come to terms with the demands of *opera buffa*. They had to develop a kind of music that would match the wit and pacing of the drama, and express the human emotions of the characters. Mozart was eager to follow their example.

He had already cut his teeth on both comic and serious operas, and *Idomeneo* had allowed him to prove what he could do with opera as a mature composer. It is not surprising that his thoughts soon turned to writing an opera for Vienna. But if he was to do so, then it would have to be in German rather than Italian, for in 1776 the Emperor Joseph II had dismissed his Italian opera company at the Burgtheater and replaced it with a German company in a move to develop a German-language Nationaltheater.[5] From 1778, the sung offerings of the Nationaltheater consisted of so-called Singspiels, spoken plays with songs, many of which were translations of French *opéras comiques*. As Mozart's later letters reveal, he was not averse to opera in German, indeed he sometimes claimed to prefer it, and by the end of July 1781 he had received a libretto by Gottlieb Stephanie Jr., *Belmonte und Konstanze* or *Die Verführung* [later *Entführung*] *aus dem Serail*. Mozart's setting was eventually performed on 16 July 1782.

Mozart's correspondence on *Die Entführung*, K384, like that on *Idomeneo*, suggests just how well-formed his operatic instincts now were. It also reveals how much he liked writing opera, and he bubbled with enthusiasm to tell his father exactly what he was planning to do:

> Osmin's rage is rendered comical by the use of the Turkish music. In working out the aria ['Solche hergelauf'ne Laffen', No. 3] I have. . .allowed Fischer's beautiful deep notes to glow. The passage 'Drum beim Barte des Propheten' is indeed in the same tempo, but with quick notes; and as Osmin's rage gradually increases, there comes (just when the aria seems to be at an end) the allegro assai, which is in a totally different metre and in a different key; this is bound to be very effective. For just as a man in such a towering rage oversteps all the bounds of order, moderation and propriety and completely

forgets himself, so must the music too forget itself. But since passions, whether violent or not, must never be expressed to the point of exciting disgust, and as music, even in the most terrible situations, must never offend the ear, but must please the listener, or in other words must never cease to be *music*, so I have not chosen a key foreign to F (in which the aria is written) but one related to it – not the nearest, D minor, but the more remote A minor. Let me now turn to Belmonte's aria in A major, 'O wie ängstlich, o wie feurig' [No. 4]. Would you like to know how I have expressed it – and even indicated his throbbing heart? By the two violins playing octaves. This is the favourite aria of all those who have heard it, and it is mine also. I wrote it expressly to suit Adamberger's voice. You see the trembling – the faltering – you see how his throbbing breast begins to swell; this I have expressed by a crescendo. You hear the whispering and the sighing – which I have indicated by the first violins with mutes and a flute playing in unison.[6]

All this reflects important preoccupations of Mozart the opera composer: the importance of writing with the capabilities of particular singers in mind and with an eye and ear for stage effect, and the dramatic and expressive possibilities of tonality and of instrumental writing. They have a bearing on all his subsequent dramatic works, and not least, as we shall see, on *Le nozze di Figaro*.

The success of *Die Entführung* in Vienna in 1782 opened up other possibilities, as Mozart wrote to his father on 21 December:

On the 10th my opera was performed again with the greatest applause. It was the fourteenth time and the theatre was as full as on the first night, or rather it was as packed as it has invariably been. Count Rosenberg himself spoke to me at Prince Galitzin's and suggested that I should write an Italian opera. I have already commissioned someone to procure for me from Italy the latest opere buffe texts to choose from, but as yet I have not received any, although I myself wrote to Ignaz Hagenauer about it. Some Italian male and female singers are coming here at Easter.[7]

These plans for an Italian, not German, opera, and the reference to the imminent arrival of Italian singers, suggest that something new was in the air. Indeed, Joseph II must have finally realised that his experiments with a German theatre had failed, largely, it seems, through a lack of good poets and musicians willing to write for it. His ambassador to Venice, Count Giacomo Durazzo, was asked to recruit singers, and Durazzo in turn approached Michael Kelly, an Irish tenor currently working in Italy. According to Kelly:

One morning I received a message from His Excellency the Austrian Ambassador, desiring me to go to him in the evening. I waited on His Excellency, who informed me that he had received a letter from Prince Rosenberg, Grand Chamberlain of His Majesty Joseph the Second, Emperor of Germany, directing him to engage a company of Italian singers for a comic opera to be given at the Court of Vienna; that no expense was to be spared, so that the artists were of the first order; that no secondary talent would be received among them, and that characters were to be filled by those engaged, without distinction, according to their abilities; and the will of the director appointed by the Emperor.[8]

The new Italian *buffo* company was established in the Burgtheater by April 1783. As well as Kelly, it included Stefano Mandini (baritone), Francesco Bussani (bass) and, as the 'stars' of the group, the bass Francesco Benucci (the first Figaro) and the soprano Nancy Storace (the first Susanna). According to Johannes Pezzl, writing in 1787:

The singers at the opera are select and well paid. Mandini and Benucci are the most accomplished *buffo* actors one can see. The chief idol in this comic Pantheon was, up to the present, La Storace, of Italian descent, but born in London. She earned over 1000 ducats yearly. To tell the truth, she sang very well but her figure was not advantageous: a thick little head, without any feminine charm, with the exception of a pair of large and nearly expressionless eyes.[9]

The company made its début with Antonio Salieri's *La scuola degli gelosi* (first performed in Venice in 1778), revised by the composer, the director of the new company, and by the newly appointed poet to the Italian theatre, Lorenzo da Ponte.

Da Ponte's rather chequered career had led him to Vienna by a roundabout route. Born Emmanuele Conegliano at Ceneda (now Vittorio Veneto) in Italy on 10 March 1749, he had taken the name of the Bishop of Ceneda, Lorenzo da Ponte, when his father, a Jewish tanner, converted to Christianity in 1763. Da Ponte's early training at seminaries in Ceneda and Portogruaro had prepared him either for the priesthood or for teaching – he was subsequently employed in both capacities – although his penchant both for liberal and politically suspect ideas and for married women subsequently led to a ban on teaching in the Veneto and then enforced exile from Venice. Like his friend Casanova, he was something of a rake and fortune-hunter. A visit to Dresden as a guest of the librettist Caterino Mazzolà encouraged him to foster his talent for dramatic poetry, and Mazzolà's recommendation to Salieri gave him an entrée to Vienna, where he arrived by 1781. He seems to have quickly attracted the favour of Joseph II more through his good manners than his achievements to date, and as poet to the Italian theatre he worked with all the leading opera composers in Vienna – including Salieri, Vicente Martín y Soler and, of course, Mozart – whether adapting pre-existing libretti or writing them anew. After the death of Joseph II in 1792, cliques forced da Ponte to leave Vienna: he moved first to

London, where he was employed as poet of the King's Theatre, Haymarket, and then to America, where he spent his last years as a grocer and then as a teacher of Italian, most notably at Columbia College, New York. He died on 17 August 1838.[10]

Mozart repeatedly reminded his father about his requests for opera libretti, despite his apparent doubts about the likely success of the new company: 'I do not believe that the Italian opera will keep going for long, and besides, I hold with the Germans.'[11] But after the company's début Mozart seems to have been more convinced of its potential, and on 7 May 1783 he asked his father to approach the Salzburg poet, Giambattista Varesco, who had provided the libretto of *Idomeneo*:

Well, the Italian opera buffa has started again here and is very popular. The buffo is particularly good – his name is Benucci. I have looked through at least a hundred libretti and more, but I have scarcely found a single one with which I am satisfied; that is to say, so many alterations would have to be made here and there, that even if a poet would undertake to make them, it would be easier for him to write a completely new text – which indeed it is always best to do. Our poet here is now a certain Abbate da Ponte. He has an enormous amount to do in revising pieces for the theatre and he has to write *per obbligo* an entirely new libretto for Salieri, which will take him two months. He has promised after that to write a new libretto for me. But who knows whether he will be able to keep his word – or will want to? For, as you are aware, these Italian gentlemen are very civil to your face. Enough, we know them! If he is in league with Salieri, I shall never get anything out of him. But indeed I should dearly love to show what I can do in an Italian opera! So I have been thinking that unless Varesco is still very much annoyed with us about the Munich opera, he might write me a new libretto for seven characters. Basta! You will know best if this can be arranged. In the meantime he could jot down a few ideas, and when I come to Salzburg we could then work them out together. The most essential thing is that on the whole the story should be really *comic*; and, if possible, he ought to introduce *two equally good female parts*, one of these to be *seria*, the other *mezzo carattere*, but both parts equal *in importance and excellence*. The third female *character*, however, may be entirely buffa, and so may all the male ones, if necessary. If you think that something can be got out of Varesco, please discuss it with him soon. . .Tell him too that his share will certainly amount to 400 or 500 gulden, for the custom here is that the poet gets the takings of the third performance.[12]

Benucci does indeed seem to have been the mainstay of the company – certainly Joseph II regarded him as perhaps the most valuable member of it – and operas to be performed in Vienna were chosen at least partly with him in mind. His presence was surely one reason why Joseph II was so eager to perform Paisiello's *Il barbiere di Siviglia* at the Burgtheater (it was premièred on 13 August 1783), and of course Benucci's talents must have been responsible to no small degree for Mozart's idea of setting Beaumarchais's sequel to *Le barbier de Séville*, *Le mariage de Figaro.*

Mozart's specification for the cast of a new libretto from Varesco presumably reflects the composition of the new company in 1783, and his request for two equally good female parts, one *seria* and the other *mezzo carattere* (a 'mixed' character, see below, pp. 14–15), and a third perhaps *buffa*, naturally makes one think of the Countess, Susanna and Marcellina in *Figaro.*[13] He kept reminding his father about an approach to Varesco in his letters of May and early June ('the chief thing must be the comic element, for I know the taste of the Viennese'),[14] and by mid-June the poet seems to have sent at least an outline of a possible opera, *L'oca del Cairo.* Its rather improbable plot turns on an old fool of a father, his daughter and her companion locked in a tower, and an ingenious mechanical goose to smuggle in the inevitable star-crossed lovers. However, Varesco seems to have had unspecified doubts about the opera. Moreover, if he feared a repetition of the trouble he had experienced with Mozart over *Idomeneo* – the composer had incessantly requested alterations and revisions – he did so with good cause:

> Why, I consider it a great insult to myself that Herr Varesco is doubtful about the success of the opera. Of one thing he may be sure and that is, that his libretto will certainly not go down if the music is no good. For in the opera the chief thing is the music. If then the opera is to be a success and Varesco hopes to be rewarded, he must alter and recast the libretto as much and as often as I wish and he must not follow his own inclinations, for he has not the slightest knowledge or experience of the theatre. You may even give him to understand that it doesn't much matter whether he writes the opera or not. I know the story now; and therefore anyone can write it as well as he can. Besides, I am expecting today four of the latest and best libretti from Italy among which there will surely be one which will be some good. So there is plenty of time.[15]

Mozart worked slowly on the opera. Perhaps he did so because he wanted to do his best in his first *opera buffa* for Vienna – he was careful to assure his father that 'in all the operas which are to be performed until mine is finished, not a single idea will resemble one of mine'[16] – but he also seems to have been less than enthusiastic about the plot. It is clear, too, that Mozart had other irons in the fire and was working on at least one other libretto as well as considering others. He continued to set parts of *L'oca del Cairo* until the end of 1783 – in December he reported that he was three arias short of finishing the first act and that he was pleased by a *buffo* aria, a quartet and a finale – but he must have abandoned the project soon thereafter.[17]

Seven pieces for *L'oca del Cairo*, K422, survive in sketched-out form (the vocal line, bass line and some indications for the accompaniment). The opening duet for Auretta and Chichibio is, as Alfred Einstein says, 'worthy, in its freshness and charm, of Susanna and Figaro'.[18] This is followed by an aria for Auretta with shades of Donna Anna's 'Or sai chi l'onore' in *Don Giovanni*, the *buffo* aria for Chichibio which pleased Mozart, another duet for Auretta and Chichibio, and an incomplete aria for Don Pippo (which hints at Bartolo's 'La vendetta, oh la vendetta!' in Act I of *Figaro*). Then there is a fine quartet in two sections, which again contains ideas to be developed in *Figaro*. The last piece to survive is a large-scale sectional finale. It is carefully judged both in terms of contrasts in tempo and of tonal structure and is full of the musical gestures that Mozart was to put to such effect in the magnificent finales of *Figaro*, *Don Giovanni* and *Così fan tutte*. It is not surprising that *L'oca del Cairo* remained unfinished – the plot is far too trite to merit serious consideration – but there is no doubt that working on the opera gave Mozart the chance to come to terms with the comic techniques of his contemporaries and to explore how to give them an individual voice.

At the same time as Mozart was working on *L'oca del Cairo*, he also had plans for another opera. On 5 July 1783 he wrote to his father: 'An Italian poet here has now brought me a libretto which I shall perhaps adopt, if he agrees to trim and adjust it in accordance with my wishes.'[19] Presumably this was *Lo sposo deluso*, K430/424a, and it is generally assumed that the librettist was Lorenzo da Ponte, who had promised to write a libretto for Mozart (see Mozart's letter to his father of 7 May 1783 quoted above) and who had probably completed the libretto 'per obbligo' for Salieri, *Il ricco d'un giorno* (first performed on 6 December 1784). Of *Lo sposo deluso*, only an overture leading to a quartet, two arias and a trio survive. The overture is designed as if in ternary form with a slow middle section (like the overture to *Die Entführung* and the planned overture to *Figaro*, see below, p. 49), and the quartet begins at the return of the opening section. The second aria has shades of Fiordiligi's 'Come scoglio immoto resta' in *Così fan tutte*, while the trio is another fine ensemble that would not be out of place in one of the three later da Ponte operas.

As well as these two abortive attempts at full-length operas, Mozart put his foot in the door of the Burgtheater, as it were, by composing three arias (K418, 419, 420) to be inserted in Pasquale Anfossi's *Il curioso indiscreto* (staged on 30 June 1783; only two of the added arias were performed). But in the absence of a viable libretto to set himself, and perhaps possible complications from the rivalry of more established opera composers in Vienna, Mozart was forced to bide his time. Of course, he was still composing instrumental music that would stand him in good stead for the experience of *Figaro.* No doubt he also had the opportunity to get the measure of the modern *opere buffe* performed at the Burgtheater and learn accordingly. There seems little doubt that the works of one such modern composer, Giovanni Paisiello, were to have a great influence on *Figaro*: Paisiello's *Il barbiere di Siviglia* was first performed there on 13 August 1783, and his *Il re Teodoro in Venezia* on 23 August 1784. According to Einstein, *Il re Teodoro,* with its real, human characters instead of *commedia dell'arte* stereotypes must have struck Mozart and da Ponte 'like a bolt of lighting'.[20]

During 1785 and early 1786 Mozart continued to flex his operatic muscles in public. For Francesco Bianchi's *La villanella rapita,* performed at the Burgtheater on 28 November 1785, he composed a quartet, 'Dite almeno in che mancai', K479, and a trio, 'Mandina amabile', K480. 'Mandina amabile' is in large part a 'seduction'-duet in the manner of 'Crudel! perchè finora' in *Figaro* and 'Là ci darem la mano' in *Don Giovanni* (Act I, No. 7) – all three share the key of A major – while the quartet is almost a study in the comic techniques to be found in the ensembles of *Figaro.* Then in early 1786 Mozart produced a brief entertainment, *Der Schauspieldirektor,* K486 (performed on 7 February), with a splendid overture, two arias, a trio and a final *vaudeville,* and a plot that pokes fun at opera singers and impresarios.

But by now *Figaro* was well in hand. Although we lack documentary evidence on the early stages of the opera, it seems clear that Mozart and da Ponte were at work on it by mid-1785, if not before. In early November, Mozart was, according to his father, 'up to the eyes' in composing the score, although 'no doubt according to his charming habit he has kept on postponing matters and has let the time slip by. So now he must set to work seriously, for Count Rosenberg is prodding him.'[21] Rumours of its composition had reached Paris by late December, and it is possible that the first performance was planned for after Christmas during the Carnival season.[22] In the end, however, the new opera in Carnival was Martín y Soler's *Il burbero di buon cuore* (performed on 4 January; the libretto was by da Ponte). In February and March Mozart was occupied first with *Der Schauspieldirektor*, and then with a revival of *Idomeneo* (performed on 13 March), for which he had to revise the score and compose a new duet and aria (K489, 490). *Figaro* was now planned for the end of April, or so Mozart's father thought:

> 'Le Nozze di Figaro' is being performed on the 28th for the first time. It will be surprising if it is a success, for I know that very powerful cabals have ranged themselves against your brother. Salieri and all his supporters will again try to move heaven and earth to down his opera. Herr & Mme Duschek told me recently that it is on account of the very great reputation which your brother's exceptional talent and ability have won for him that so many people are plotting against him.[23]

In the event, however, the dress rehearsal was held on 29 April in the presence of the Emperor, and the first performance on 1 May. The cast was: Count Almaviva, Stefano Mandini; Countess Almaviva, Luisa Laschi; Susanna, Nancy Storace; Figaro, Francesco Benucci; Cherubino, Dorotea Bussani; Marcellina, Maria Mandini; Bartolo and Antonio, Francesco Bussani; Basilio and Don Curzio, Michael Kelly; Barbarina, Anna Gottlieb.

2 *Mozart and the opera buffa tradition*

MICHAEL F. ROBINSON

The decision by the Austrian Emperor Joseph II to disband his German opera troupe in March 1783 brought to an end an era in the history of opera at Vienna. Regarding his previous attempts to promote opera in German as failures (and in truth among the many German operas staged at the court theatre, the Burgtheater, before 1783 only Mozart's *Die Entführung aus dem Serail* had been of good quality), Joseph hereafter wanted works by Italian composers instead. After March 1783 German composers who had not had a long apprenticeship in Italy and who were not recognised by the Italians as one of themselves stood a rather poor chance of obtaining commissions for the Burgtheater. Indeed it speaks well for Mozart's talent and persistence that he obtained any commissions at all from the Emperor and the new Italian company; his first such commission was of course *Le nozze di Figaro*. Overall he fared better than other German composers in respect of the number of commissions and number of performances of his operas performed in the theatre. His comparative standing among opera composers in Vienna during the mid to late 1780s can be judged from Table 1, which gives the total number of operas, and the total number of performances of operas, by each composer staged at the Burgtheater between 22 April 1783, when the theatre reopened, and 25 January 1790, the eve of the première of Mozart's *Così fan tutte*. The table gives the full names of non-Italian composers so as to distinguish them from the native Italians. It shows that the one non-Italian who was pre-eminently successful in Vienna during the decade was the Spaniard Vicente Martín y Soler. Soler, however, is often considered a member of the Italian school in view of his particular career.

All 59 operas accounted for on this list belonged to the same genre, Italian comic opera (*opera buffa*). The Emperor's dislike of Italian 'serious' opera (*opera seria*) explains why no serious operas were then produced at the Burgtheater. Most of the works performed

Table 1 *Performances at the Burgtheater, Vienna, 22 April 1783 – 25 January 1790*

Name of composer	Number of operas	Total number of performances
G. Rust	1	2
Ditters von Dittersdorf	1	2
Josef Barta	1	3
F. Piticchio	1	8
[pasticcio]	1	8
V. Righini	1	8
Franz Seydelmann	1	10
Joseph Weigl	1	13
F. Bianchi	2	13
F. Alessandri	2	14
G. Gazzaniga	2	20
Stephen Storace	2	33
Wolfgang Amadeus Mozart	2	35
P. Guglielmi	2	39
P. Anfossi	5	51
G. Sarti	4	97
Vicente Martín y Soler	3	105
D. Cimarosa	8	124
A. Salieri	8	138
G. Paisiello	11	166

were by Italian composers. The single most popular opera, in terms of the number of performances it received over the period covered by the list, was Paisiello's *Il barbiere di Siviglia*, premièred on 13 August 1783, with 60 performances. Other popular works were Sarti's *Fra i due litiganti il terzo gode*, first heard on 28 May 1783, with 58 performances; Martín y Soler's *Una cosa rara*, produced on 17 November 1786, with 45; Salieri's *Axur, Re d'Ormus*, premièred on 8 January 1788, with 42; Martín y Soler's *L'arbore di Diana*, first staged on 1 October 1787, with 41; and Paisiello's *Il re Teodoro in Venezia*, premièred on 23 August 1784, with 36. By comparison Mozart, the most successful among the German composers, achieved 20 performances of *Le nozze di Figaro* and 15 of his later opera *Don Giovanni* on the stage of the Burgtheater during the same period.[1]

Armed with these facts we can readily guess one aspect of Mozart's strategy. In the existing cultural and political climate of

Vienna, he was an outsider, a man who although recognised as possessing exceptional talent did not have the right qualifications (because not an Italian and not recognised by the Italian musical world as its equal) to become pre-eminent among the opera composers commissioned by the court. How was he to establish his rightful place among them? Naturally he had to show that he understood all the conventions of Italian comic opera and work within these conventions. But this was not enough. Not only had he to compose like an Italian; he had to do better than most Italians to obtain equal status with them.

The conventions surrounding the music of *opera buffa* governed the general structure (the number of acts, the number and position in each act of the various musical items), the structure of the individual items, and the styles used within them. Those governing operatic structures were both changing and becoming more relaxed during Mozart's lifetime. Styles were changing too. However, the conventions governing musical characterisation were altering but little. Throughout the second half of the eighteenth century composers continued to employ certain well-tried stylistic formulas which both they and the public accepted as symbols of different types of dramatic character. Mozart was aware of all these factors, for he had been an observer of the Italian opera scene for over twenty years before he composed *Figaro* and had himself already contributed two operas to the genre, *La finta semplice*, written in Vienna in 1768 but first staged in Salzburg the following year, and *La finta giardiniera*, produced in Munich in 1775. The point of this chapter is to provide some more detailed comments about these changing and fixed conventions and to show how Mozart, ever gaining in experience between 1768, the year of *La finta semplice*, and 1786, the year of *Figaro*, used them to produce results which were uniquely his own.

What were the structural elements of a typical *opera buffa* of the late 1760s? At that time all Italian comic operas, except those of very limited size, were in three acts, the last act being the shortest. Most of the music, exclusive of the recitative, consisted of arias. But there was usually a short canzonet or two; there were usually two or three duets; and each act by custom ended with a finale, an ensemble for all the cast. It was normal practice to create extensive pieces out of the finales of Acts I and II, but not out of that of the last act. The function of these finales therefore varied according to the act they were in. In Acts I and II they were ensembles incorporating a large slice of the action; in Act III, on the other hand, they provided a perfunctory, brief finish after the action was over. Composers worked on the general principle that action-pieces like the Acts I and II finales should be composed in an *ad hoc* number of sections, the change from one section to the next being determined by the course of the drama and often musically defined by a change of tempo. On the other hand, pieces with a contemplative function – and most arias came into this category – were usually set according to some structural formula like binary or ternary form.

Choice of form, and choice of style too, were also affected by another consideration. Some of the characters of *opera buffa* were descended from the traditional characters of the *commedia dell'arte*; these included, for example, idiosyncratic, middle-class gentlemen reminiscent of Pantalone, and cunning servants resembling Columbine and Harlequin. But alongside these were others of a more serious and noble disposition drawn from the ranks of the upper-middle class and the aristocracy: some of these roles were clearly modelled on characters within *opera seria*. The cast of an average *opera buffa* therefore tended to split into 'serious' and 'comic' groups along class lines. Different musical forms and gestures went with each group. Let us take some examples. In comic opera of the 1760s it is noticeable how only those characters with the most 'serious' dispositions express themselves through the medium of a da capo aria. Any simple, strophic songs in the score are by contrast allocated to the 'comic' characters. There are stylistic differences too. Broad, legato phrasing and finely wrought embellishment (which includes vocalisations) are features associated with a 'serious', upper-class part. Music in $\frac{4}{4}$ 'Allegro' time with a strong rhythmic stress likewise has 'serious' connotations. Short phrasing, simple, folk-like tunes, dance rhythms (in fast triple time especially), patter-song, are by contrast hallmarks of the 'comic' characters of the middle and lower social orders.

This categorisation of course emphasises only certain extremes; it does not incorporate all the forms and styles of *opera buffa*. Many arias are in fact in binary form, which had no particular 'serious' or 'comic' association. Furthermore, the musical gestures and symbols of many an item fail to fit any of the above categories either because they are different or because they are confusingly mixed. This mixing of symbols was in fact a useful dramatic as well as purely musical technique. Italian librettists of the middle of the century introduced a number of 'mixed characters' (*mezzi caratteri*) into the cast with the object of unifying their plots and linking the serious and comic groups together. The 'mixed' characters of particular significance are the heroes and heroines at the centre of the action whose high-class origins conflict with their lower-class behaviour. What might be described as ambiguity of behaviour by a person of high social status is apparent in the plot of one of the most successful of all *opere buffe* of the 1760s, Niccolò Piccinni's *La buona figliuola* (first performed in Rome, 6 February 1760), to a text by Carlo Goldoni. Mozart certainly knew this opera: it was being performed in Vienna at the time he was there completing his score of *La finta semplice*. In the Piccinni opera the Marchese della Conchiglia 'demeans' his social status by falling for and courting a servant girl, Cecchina. The complexity of his 'mixed' character is brought out in his first aria, 'È pur bella la Cecchina', with its three very different moods marked by changes of time signature and speed. Cecchina's role might also be said to be ambiguous: she is serving as a gardener and is unaware until the end of the opera that she is of high birth (which disclosure conveniently permits her to marry the Marchese). Moreover, her music is complex, varying in style from the folkloristic (a style also adopted by the peasant girl Sandrina) to the sophisticatedly serious (as found also in the arias of the two haughty, upper-class characters, the Marchesa Lucinda and the Cavalier Armidoro).

Mozart's *La finta semplice*, completed in 1768 when he was twelve years old, is a competent, orthodox *opera buffa* of its period. The text is once again by Goldoni, though altered in several places specifically for Mozart by the Viennese court poet Marco Coltellini. The one surprising structural feature in the opera is the third-act finale, which embraces the last part of the action and its dénouement. As was said earlier, most third-act finales do not contain dramatic action, so this case is unusual. For the rest, neither the libretto nor, for that matter, Mozart's own limited experience encouraged him to compose much else of an unconventional kind. The plot centres on the actions of a shrewd middle-class heroine, Rosina, who assumes the role of a simple-minded lady (hence the title of the opera, *La finta semplice*), to test the qualities and the sincerity of her two suitors, the brothers Cassandro and Polidoro (she chooses Cassandro at the end). Neither brother can be described as 'serious'. There are, however, two other characters, Giacinta and Fracasso, who fit readily into this category. Then there are two servants, Ninetta and Simone, who are 'comic', as their social status leads us to expect. Mozart had enough knowledge to provide some of these characters with suitable, if stereotyped, gestures. Rosina, for example, has the most elaborate vocal lines, Fracasso the only da capo arias in the opera,[2] and Simone the conventional patter-song. However, the characterisation is generally rather feeble. About the best thing to be said for the young Mozart is that he constantly demonstrates his anxiety to illustrate any nuance or change of sense in the words by changing the mood and tempo of the music. He does this not only in the ensembles, where such changes are to be expected, but in many of his solos with formalised structures too (in binary-form arias, for example, the contrasting sections alternate).

Mozart's next *opera buffa*, *La finta giardiniera* (composed in 1775), has many more signs of that individuality that marks his mature works.[3] We can easily gauge his indebtedness to his Italian contemporaries in the case of *La finta giardiniera* and understand the ways in which he was beginning to develop his art in a manner different from theirs, because the same text had been conventionally set about a year before by one of the leading Italian composers of the age, Pasquale Anfossi (whose name, incidentally, appears prominently in Table 1 above). The extent to which Mozart borrowed his ideas from Anfossi has been slightly exaggerated;[4] nonetheless there are sufficient similarities between the two scores to show that Mozart knew Anfossi's and was trying to improve on the latter's example. Each is a three-act opera, and the number of solo items (23) and ensembles (6) is the same in both works. The structure of many of the solo items is the same too. Most of the structures which Anfossi and Mozart adopt are the old ones found in *opera buffa* of the previous decade. But we notice some changes. There are no longer any da capo arias (da capo form went completely out of fashion during the late 1760s and early 1770s). Mozart employs simple rondo form in two arias. Both composers use AAB bar form, easily distinguished by its last B section which is in a different, and usually faster, tempo than the preceding sections (the significance of this will become clear later).

It is when we consider the details of the music, however, that the differences between Mozart and Anfossi's settings become apparent. The point can be illustrated by comparing extracts from the aria 'Si promette facilmente' in Act I scene 7, as set by the two composers (Ex. 1). The aria is for the leading 'serious' lady Arminda; in both settings it is in binary form, the two halves of which are joined by a short bridge passage. The two music examples quote the bridge passage, which in both cases ends with a pause, and the start of the second section (recapitulation).

Ex. 1 (a) Anfossi, *La finta giardiniera*, I.7, 'Si promette facilmente' (London, British Library, Add. MS 15985); (b) Mozart, *La finta giardiniera*, I.7, 'Si promette facilmente'

Ex. 1a (*cont.*)

85
- dì; e la sem - pli - ce _ zi - tel - la se _ lo _ cre - de, po - ve -
mf
p

- rel - la, e _ si _ fi - da a _ dir _ di _ sì, io pe - rò non fo co -
mf
p

90
- sì, non fo co - sì.
f

Ex. 1b

65
[Allegro]
ARMINDA
Si pro - met - te, si pro -
vln. 1
vln. 2
vla.
vc. (db. all' 8va bassa)
- met - te fa - cil - men - te
70
vlns.
vla.
da - gl'a - man - ti, da - gl'a - man - ti d'og - gi - di; ma se mai, co - m'è l'u -
75
- san - za, mi man - ca - ste, m'in - gan - na - ste, io le ma - ni a - do - pre -
vlns.

Ex. 1b (*cont.*)

80
- rò, a - do - pre - rò, sì, sì. Si pro -
f
p
cresc.
f
p

85
- met - te fa - cil - men - te da - gl'a - man - ti d'og - gi - di; e la
vlns.
f
p

90
sem - pli - ce zi - tel - la se lo cre - de, po - ve - rel - la, e si
p

fi - da a dir di sì, a dir di sì, si fi - da,

Ex. 1b (*cont.*)

The similarities between these two passages are very obvious. The key, the tempo and the instrumentation are identical. Furthermore, Mozart has obviously taken a clue from Anfossi about how to shape particular musical phrases. Anfossi's phrase beginning 'Si promette facilmente' (Ex. 1a, bars 78–82) consists of four bars. He follows this with a two-bar phrase ('e la semplice zitella'), and then with a series of further phrases totalling six bars until a satisfactory close is reached at bar 90 ('non fo così'). Mozart's procedure is very similar: his opening phrase is also four bars in length, his subsequent section also covers eight bars (ending this time on a half close, see Ex. 1b, bars 82–94). There are striking similarities between the vocal figures at the cadence (Ex. 1a, bars 89–90; Ex. 1b, bars 93–4); both figures have four notes, both rise and fall a minor third, and both are detached from the preceding vocal phrase. But there are many differences in the two settings of this passage. One concerns the layout of the words: Anfossi uses all the words of the strophe but Mozart leaves out the last line, 'Io però non fo così'. This he holds in reserve for a further four-bar phrase which extends the music and brings it to an even more satisfying conclusion with a full close in the tonic (bars 95–8). The change in the mood and the quality of the texture of this last phrase is interesting too. The text contrasts two different attitudes to love. The distinction between the smooth advances of the young man and the ready acceptance of him by the average young woman on the one hand and Arminda's more cynical view of men on the other is well brought out by Mozart in the changed mood, the bare octaves, the non-legato of this final phrase. Anfossi, by comparison, makes nothing of the point and simply carries on to the end of the strophe in the same style.

The greater originality of Mozart's setting over Anfossi's becomes even more apparent if we compare their settings of the bridge passage (Ex. 1a, bars 71–8; Ex. 1b, bars 65–82). Anfossi selects for this passage the particular words taken from the aria's text which reflect the singer's adoration of her one true love, her 'idol mio'. Mozart on the other hand chooses quite different lines (taken from both strophes of the text in fact), lines which state how angrily the singer will react to any lover who jilts her. The differences in the meaning have their effect upon the music of the two passages. Anfossi's is dull: it has no outstanding qualities of its own; it is merely a means to get from the previous dominant cadence to the tonic. The interjection in the violins (bars 73–4) dividing the first and second phrases creates a slight irregularity in the phrasing which is to be welcomed, but the violin figure itself is uninspired and in no way links with the vocal line. The quality of Mozart's passage by comparison is evident. The music is better shaped and contains greater contrasts. It also displays a more imaginative use of the instruments. The violins do not merely come into prominence when filling in the gaps between vocal phrases, as in Anfossi's case. They start a phrase (see the second violins in bars 65 and 70, to which the voice and first violins respond in simple imitation). They also carry the phrase forward, taking the melodic line over from the voice (see bars 78–82). Instruments and voice therefore come into partnership during this passage and together mould the music. Such interactions are of course common in Mozart's later operas and their appearance here and in other places in *La finta giardiniera* are signs of his growing maturity as a composer.

No one, of course, should judge Mozart's early achievement as a composer of *opera buffa* solely against one or two other Italian operas. But in so far as Piccinni's and Anfossi's operas are representative of their respective periods we can still make some genuine observations about what Mozart learnt from the Italian environment and what, by 1775, was becoming apparent as his own style and method. As regards the overall plan of individual arias and ensembles he was clearly taking what hints he could about the general direction in which developments were going; and the trend was gradually towards a greater variety of available forms. In the selection of musical notes he was showing a tendency to choose combinations with a particular profuseness of technical detail. He was also giving the orchestra an extra, expressive dimension. But above all he was turning the conventional 'serious' and 'comic' character-types of the Italians into true human beings because he had the flair to imagine how a character behaves in a given dramatic situation and to translate his/her gestures and tone of voice into suitable music.

Of course, all these properties of Mozart's music are even more in evidence in a mature work like *Figaro.* The superiority of this work over an immature one like *La finta giardiniera* is obvious and is in major part the result of the improvement of his own creative skills between 1775 and 1786. No one, however, should disregard certain changes in the conventions of *opera buffa* during the late 1770s and early 1780s that also had their effect upon the shape and style of his later operas. The coincidence of his growing maturity and the emergence of new practices creating extra opportunities for composers within the genre of *opera buffa* improved the chances of a masterpiece such as *Figaro* turned out to be.

The major change in the structure of *opera buffa* emerging at this time was the contraction in the number of acts from three to two. During the 1770s librettists and composers had been gradually reducing the size of the third act till it became totally redundant. The new format of two large acts, each ending with an imposing action-finale, was neater and dramatically much more effective than the old one. The dénouement, previously left till the third act, had always (exclusive of a few rare cases like Mozart's *La finta semplice*) left an impression of anticlimax because it did not coincide with an impressive musical item. From now on it was always incorporated within the second-act finale, where a composer had the full musical resources to make the most of it.

The loss of the third-act finale did not mean that there were fewer ensembles in opera thereafter. The proportion of ensembles/choruses to solo items in new operas produced at the Vienna Burgtheater during the 1780s is actually much higher than in older operas like, say, *La finta giardiniera.* Edward Dent points out that for example the proportion of arias to ensembles/choruses in Martín y Soler's *Una cosa rara* of 1786 is just under two to one (19 to 11); he uses this fact to make a rather depreciatory comparison with *Figaro*, in which the arias and ensembles are equal in number (14 to 14).[5] But the fact that there are eleven ensembles (four duets, two trios, a sextet, two choruses and two finales) in *Una cosa rara* is itself of some significance. The increase in the number of ensembles meant of course a decrease in the number of solo items. The main musical gain was the increased richness of texture and variety of colour provided by the extra ensembles, all of which were naturally distributed within the course of each act (as opposed to at the end of it).

The liking for ensembles also affected opera in other ways. Many arias were now acquiring a formal feature commonly associated with the large ensemble, namely bipartite or multi-sectional design. We have already mentioned bar form (AAB) in relation to Mozart's *La finta giardiniera*. The B section of most of the bar-form arias in that opera is comparatively short: musically it seems to act more as a coda than as a substantive section. But in certain arias it is more expansive, and in the exceptional case of the Contino's Act II aria 'Già divento freddo' the AA section has so contracted and the B section so expanded that we have in effect a genuine AB bipartite structure that has more in common with the sectional ensemble than with the old-fashioned type of aria in binary or ternary form.[6] The major differences between the two halves of 'Già divento freddo' result in music without a strong sense of recapitulation; the music sounds ongoing and the dramatic argument, such as it is, moves forward too. The appearance of such non-recapitulatory structures in arias of the 1770s and 1780s suggests that composers were getting out of the frame of mind of believing that formalised returns of musical material or of text were necessary in solo items. This new attitude is reflected even in the many arias and short ensembles that remain throughout in one tempo. 'Returns' of one kind or another in these items there may be, but these formalised gestures are less heavily emphasised than they used to be, and the structures have a flexibility that also permits some sense of dramatic progress during the course of the music. Indeed, it seems so natural to present-day commentators of *Figaro* that each major item in that opera should be 'ongoing', even if it has an element of repetition, that Mozart has been criticised for composing his Act I duettino 'Via resti servita' (No. 5) in a more or less exact binary form, thus making the same words and the same action go round twice.[7]

The particular opera by an Italian composer that da Ponte and Mozart most had in mind when creating *Figaro* was undoubtedly Paisiello's *Il barbiere di Siviglia*, first produced in St Petersburg on 26 September 1782. Paisiello's text was based on Beaumarchais's well-known play *Le barbier de Séville*. Mozart's desire to emulate Paisiello, the most popular opera composer among the Viennese (see Table 1 above), was clearly the prime reason why *Figaro*, based on Beaumarchais's next play, *Le mariage de Figaro*, came into being. To understand the choices da Ponte and Mozart had in front of them as they set about their task, we have first to examine certain dramatic and musical precedents created by *Il barbiere* of which they must have been aware. By the norms of the early 1780s it was a most extraordinary opera. In 1782 Paisiello, then chief composer to the Empress Catherine II, was under the obligation to compose a new opera for her and found that he had no suitable libretto to set. There was no Italian librettist in St Petersburg to whom he could turn, and his appeals to correspondents in his home town of Naples for new comic libretti had produced no satisfactory result.[8] He therefore hit upon the idea of making a libretto out of Beaumarchais's play *Le barbier de Séville*, which was a favourite with the Empress. But his method of fashioning the libretto was curious. He did not adapt the plot of the play to fit normal operatic requirements, such as that an opera should be in two or three acts. Rather he retained the four acts of the original play, and within each act retained exactly the main course of the original action (even to the extent of preserving Beaumarchais's instruction for a storm interlude between Acts III and IV; his storm music is the first of its kind in Italian comic opera). The arias and ensembles are therefore inserted not necessarily where they would go according to Italian operatic convention but where the dramatic situation and the presence on stage of the relevant characters allowed them to be fitted in. In fact, there is no proper aria for the male hero, the Conte d'Almaviva, the conventional upper-class 'mixed' character, whose solos are all short pieces. Act I ends with a duet and Act II with a solo. Proper finales are reserved for the ends of the last two acts. There is no attempt to balance the amount of music in one act with that in another, and indeed the whole arrangement seems rather casual. An interesting balance though is contrived between the total number of ensembles and the total number of solo items. There are eight of the former and ten of the latter (though one of these is so short that it should barely be taken into consideration).

Il barbiere di Siviglia in short seemed to create a precedent for librettists and composers to use unaltered plots of plays as bases for operas and to fit in the musical items as best they could. But the precedent was too radical for others to follow. Even da Ponte and Mozart drew back from following it. Their problems in any case were slightly different from those which Paisiello had experienced. *Le mariage* was a longer play (in five acts) than *Le barbier* and had a more controversial subject. For both reasons they cut out some incidents and modified others. While doing this they also arranged their material in such a manner as to equalise the number of solo items and ensembles/choruses (as Paisiello more or less did) and to distribute the musical items equitably over the length of the opera (as

Paisiello did not). Their decision, by the way, to divide *Figaro* into four acts was obviously based upon the precedent of Paisiello's work. But whereas Paisiello's finales occur at the ends of Acts III and IV, da Ponte and Mozart put theirs at the ends of Acts II and IV instead. The four acts of *Figaro* can in fact be regarded as two acts each multiplied by two. The close of the first half of the opera (i.e. the end of Act II) is marked by one large finale, and the close of the second (the end of Act IV) by the other. Therefore *Figaro*, unlike *Il barbiere*, fits exactly into the category of 'two-act' operas that were becoming fashionable in the 1780s.[9]

Many of the politically controversial incidents and speeches in the play which caused such scandal when Beaumarchais first tried to stage it in France in 1782–3, and which displeased the Emperor Joseph II sufficiently to cause him to forbid a German production of it in Vienna in the first months of 1785, are not in the opera. But the kernel of the story remains. It is possible that Mozart wanted to create an opera out of the play because of the newsworthiness and scandal attached to it; and we should remember that Mozart in 1786 wished to attract attention to himself with a work somehow different from the other Italian operas which the Viennese were seeing. But da Ponte's libretto also gave him some unusual musical opportunities. The chief male figure in all the other operas so far mentioned (by Piccinni, Anfossi, Paisiello, and by Mozart himself) is a middle-to-upper-class 'mixed' character whose amorous desires are hindered by chance or by others of equal or approximately equal rank. This idea is also, by the way, central to the plot of Mozart's later comic opera, *Don Giovanni*, in which we see the hero Don Giovanni thwarted in his various love schemes by the other noble characters, Donna Anna, Donna Elvira and Don Ottavio (but he is supported by his 'comic' servant Leporello). *Le nozze di Figaro* is different in the sense that its principal characters play roles that are the reverse of the norm. It is the servant Figaro, not the Count, who is the chief male character here. He is prevented from marrying by the Count, who is his master, not his equal. In the circumstances Mozart did not make Figaro's music sound like a parody of an Italian *buffo* part (in the way that Leporello in *Don Giovanni* is an obvious parody). Figaro's music becomes progressively more 'serious' as the opera continues. The music of his fiancée, Susanna, and of his mother, Marcellina, likewise gradually 'improves' its status. Some of the conventional 'comic' and 'serious' gestures are therefore used here to impart a kind of political message: the lower classes are rising to the (musical) level of their superiors. The same types of gesture are also adopted by Mozart, though in a deliberately more obvious way, to produce the opposite result, namely, to debunk those whom he imagines are acting above their true station. For example, the musical gesture at the start of Bartolo's Act I aria 'La vendetta, oh la vendetta!' (No. 4), the move in bare octaves up the arpeggio of D major, is a characteristic 'serious' gambit. Similarly, the three-bar phrase with its snatched ending, 'l'obliar l'onte e gli oltraggi' (bars 15–17), presents a rhythm which once again often occurs in 'serious' music (Mozart himself uses it again in the Count's aria in Act III, 'Vedrò mentre io sospiro', No. 17, bars 92–7).[10] By the middle of his aria, however, Bartolo has relapsed, if this is the word, into patter-song, one of the hallmarks of the 'comic' style and of the lower classes. By deliberately mixing the styles in this aria Mozart seems to be suggesting that Bartolo imagines himself of higher status than he in fact is.

Musical characterisation is affected not merely by style and gesture but also by form. When referring to the structures of *Figaro*, we have to remember that the conventions of *opera buffa* were by now permitting an ever greater variety of structures within individual items. It is therefore no surprise that the items of *Figaro* exhibit both a variety and a freedom of design that is not apparent in those of *La finta giardiniera*. The wider choice of structures allowed all composers to highlight the actions of their characters in an increasing number of ways. Mozart's choice sometimes seems particularly complicated, yet apt for the character(s) concerned. Take for instance Cherubino's well-known arietta 'Voi che sapete' (No. 11). Da Ponte's text consists of seven short quatrains: presumably he thought that since Cherubino had obvious 'comic' characteristics Mozart would set the arietta in strophic form. But Mozart had other ideas. In his setting the music is through-composed (save for a return to the opening strophe at the ending). What is most extraordinary about it is the key scheme, which between bars 21 and 58 passes rapidly through the keys of the dominant, dominant minor, flattened leading note, supertonic, submediant, subdominant, dominant again, submediant, before returning to the tonic in bars 58–61. No aria by an Italian contemporary of Mozart has yet come to light with such a complicated key scheme as this. In context this middle section of 'Voi che sapete' sounds both playful and disorientated, which is obviously Mozart's intent. In the arietta Cherubino expresses two contrary emotions: his growing awareness of love and his desire to feel it on the one hand, and his confusion about whom he wants to love on the other. He is in fact just old enough to know what love is, yet too young to experience mature passion as a result of it. The music, ordered yet disordered, expresses a similar ambiguity.

Did Mozart imitate individual tunes by particular Italian composers? There are moments in other operas performed in Vienna sufficiently similar to passages in *Figaro* to make one wonder whether Mozart was consciously or subconsciously influenced by them. Dent published several short excerpts from Sarti's *Fra i due litiganti il terzo gode* which reminded him of *Figaro*; he also, and perhaps with some justice, pointed to the serenade from Paisiello's *Il barbiere* as the source of inspiration for Mozart's 'Voi che sapete'.[11] But even in the cases when Mozart did consciously or unconsciously use a phrase similar to that by another Italian composer, his treatment usually transformed it. The phrase may be transformed because set in a different context, because it has a more complex harmony or texture, or because it contains more complex melodic details. (The observation made after the comparison of the Mozart and Anfossi excerpts earlier that Mozart's train of musical thought preferred combinations of notes with a 'particular profuseness of technical detail' is equally true of *Figaro*.) For example, the short excerpt from the introductory ensemble to Cimarosa's *Giannina e Bernardone* (first performed in Vienna, 24 September 1784) in Ex. 2a seems to foreshadow a catchy little phrase taken from the quite different context of Mozart's Act II finale (Ex. 2b). However, the

Ex. 2 (a) Cimarosa, *Giannina e Bernardone*, Introduzione to Act I (Vienna, Gesellschaft der Musikfreunde, MS 20892); (b) Mozart, *Le nozze di Figaro*, finale to Act II (No. 15)

Ex. 2a (*cont.*)

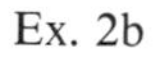
Ex. 2b

differences between the Cimarosa and Mozart excerpts are as interesting as the similarities. The two passages have the same general line, the same length, and the same cadence. Even certain details of the instrumentation are the same; for example, the dividing of the violas, and the entry of the wind and the lower strings for the second phrase. Yet Mozart opts for a more complicated way of treating the melody, the harmony and the texture. His use of accented appoggiaturas on beats one and three of the melody of bars 267–8 and 270, his different articulation of the violins and violas in bars 267–8, his change of harmony on each beat of bar 270, are all peculiarities of his setting which taken together help to give it a quality that the Cimarosa extract does not possess.

It must be said that Mozart occasionally relies upon an obviously Italianate musical gesture at moments when he seems less inspired than usual; perhaps the gesture is used as a means of rekindling his imagination. This is the final factor to be considered in any discussion of Mozart's debt to his Italian contemporaries. Siegmund Levarie has pointed out that Susanna's Act II aria 'Venite, inginocchiatevi' (No. 12) fails to project her emotions, unlike her other music;[12] the singer playing Susanna in the 1789 revival of the opera in Vienna made Mozart change it for another aria, perhaps because it seemed too cool and detached. The music does in fact have a certain charm, but this is primarily due to the recurrence of a single melodic phrase first heard in full in the first violins and first bassoon in bars 10–14 (Ex. 3). The reliance on one, or at most two, short, catchy phrases which recur at various points to maintain the music's interest is also an Italian trait; incidentally, it was a technique particularly favoured by Paisiello.[13] Mozart fills up much of the remainder of his aria in a manner of which Paisiello would have approved, namely by using short, recurring instrumental figures which create a characteristic pattern over a number of bars (see bar 14 onwards), the vocal part then being stretched across them. One of the innovatory features of the latest Italian style (i.e. the style of the 1780s) copied by Mozart was the use of cross-rhythms between the various instrumental parts: note how from bar 14 in Ex. 3 the first-violin figure alternates and overlaps with that of the lower strings, while the figure used by each pair of woodwind instruments overlaps with its repeat. This is a much more delightful way of treating rhythmic patterns than the more stodgy repetitions adopted by earlier *opera buffa* composers.

However, even in 'Venite, inginocchiatevi', which is uninspired by

Ex. 3 *Le nozze di Figaro*, 'Venite, inginocchiatevi' (No. 12)

the general standards of *Figaro*, Mozart shows traces of his individual genius. One of the many conclusions drawn from the comparison of Anfossi's and Mozart's music in Ex. 1 above is worth remembering here: Mozart's vocal and instrumental melodic lines intermingle and overlap in a supple way not noticeable in the Italian's score. The same suppleness is apparent in 'Venite, inginocchiatevi'. Mozart does not let the instrumental patterns which he began in bar 14 of this aria continue uninterrupted for long. After nine bars the flute enters with a new melody line above the figures in the strings; the bassoon soon joins the flute; then the voice line also becomes part of the melody and extends it to the cadence (see bars 23–36 of the aria). Voice and instruments are here working together in that easy partnership that is such a characteristic of Mozart's operatic music. That partnership is important. To Mozart, thinking like an instrumental as well as dramatic composer, music always had to satisfy on its own account as well as support the drama. To Anfossi and other Italians, Paisiello included, who did not have to write instrumental music to provide a living for themselves and who thought almost exclusively in terms of the theatre, music had a simpler, mainly dramatic role. Part of Mozart's superiority resides in the fact that he combined the talents of the true instrumental composer with a particular understanding of the motives and actions of dramatic characters. He was thus able to use the structures and the musical idioms of the Italian music theatre and yet make of them something all his own.

3 *Beaumarchais, da Ponte and Mozart: from play to opera*

Pierre-Augustin Caron de Beaumarchais (1732–99) lead a chequered career as a clockmaker, harp teacher, financier, gun-runner, secret agent, diplomat, satirist, publisher, playwright and librettist.[1] His first dramatic efforts were rather licentious *parades* for the French court, followed by two plays, *Eugénie* (1767) and *Les deux amis* (1770), which attempted a simple type of prose drama unhampered by classical rules. His third play, *Le barbier de Séville ou La précaution inutile*, brought him more into the Parisian limelight. Originally designed as an *opéra comique*, it was rejected as such in 1772. Revised as a five-act comedy with songs, it was accepted for performance at the Théâtre Français. However, its appearance was delayed both by a scandal involving Beaumarchais and the Duc de Chaulnes that led to the playwright's imprisonment, and by an extended financial litigation involving the notorious judge Goëzman (later satirised as Don Gusman Brid'oison in *Le mariage de Figaro*). *Le barbier* was eventually performed on 23 February 1775 and was a failure. It was staged two days later remodelled into four acts and was a major success.

Le barbier was to be the first of three works by Beaumarchais on the life of Count Almaviva, a Spanish nobleman, and his wily servant, Figaro. It deals with an episode in the Count's youth. He is in love with Rosine, the ward of Doctor Bartholo. Bartholo intends to marry Rosine himself, but the Count has other ideas. The intrigue includes the Count dressing up as a drunken soldier, and then as a singing teacher (rather like Cléante in Molière's *Le malade imaginaire*). Finally, aided and abetted by Figaro, he succeeds in marrying Rosine under Bartholo's very nose.

Beaumarchais provided the first printed edition of *Le barbier* (1775) with an extended preface justifying the play against his critics. Here reference is made to a possible sixth act: Figaro, the illegitimate son of Marceline (Rosine's governess, who receives only a mention in

Le barbier), would turn out to have been fathered by Bartholo, who had renounced the child at birth and had made a mark on his head to ensure recognition should they ever meet. This sowed the seeds for a sequel to *Le barbier.* The result, *La folle journée ou Le mariage de Figaro* (possibly completed by 1778), was accepted by the Comédie-Française in 1781. However, rumours of its political content reached Louis XVI, who banned performances of the piece. There was a semi-private staging before the court in September 1783, although public performances were still forbidden. It reached the stage of the Théâtre Français only on 27 April 1784. By all accounts it was a spectacular success.

Le mariage continues the story of the Almaviva household. The Count has now been married for three years and his eye is roving to other women. Chief among these is Suzanne, the Countess's maid and Figaro's intended bride. Figaro and Suzanne's wedding is also under threat from another quarter: Marceline wishes to exploit a debt owed her by Figaro to marry him herself. Bartholo and the wily music master Bazile also reappear from *Le barbier,* while a new character, a young page called Chérubin (directed to be played by a young woman), adds further spice to the intrigue. Needless to say, all works out in Figaro's favour, with Bartholo and Marceline turning out to be Figaro's parents and the Count outwitted by his wife and servants.

The third play of the 'Figaro' trilogy, *L'autre Tartuffe ou La mère coupable*, was announced in the preface to *Le mariage.* It was first performed on 26 June 1792. Beaumarchais claimed that the play was a logical, indeed inevitable successor to *Le barbier* and *Le mariage*, although it scarcely reaches their heights. Indeed, it betrays a sense of resignation and fin-de-siècle gloom. The action is set in 1790, some twenty years after *Le mariage.* Almaviva, now plain 'Monsieur' after the events of 1789, lives with his wife in Paris. Figaro and Suzanne are still in the household, as is Major Bégearss, one of Almaviva's former soldiers (and another thinly veiled portrait of one of Beaumarchais's enemies). Rosine has had a child, Léon, by Chérubin, and Almaviva an illegitimate daughter, Florestine, who believes herself to be his ward. Léon and Florestine, unaware of their past, wish to marry, but Bégearss, the 'other Tartuffe' of the Molière-inspired title, conspires against them by playing on Rosine's guilt and Almaviva's jealousy. Figaro again saves the day and Bégearss is banished from the household.

Of the three 'Figaro' plays, *Le mariage* is perhaps the most effective.

Beaumarchais has clearly learnt many lessons from the *commedia dell'arte*, perhaps filtered through the plays of Carlo Goldoni: witness the derivation of his characters from *commedia dell'arte* stereotypes, the fast pacing of the action, and the physical comedy of characters hiding behind or in chairs, jumping out of windows, receiving blows or kisses by mistake, and making unexpected appearances in dressing-room doorways or out of garden pavilions. There is much pantomime slapstick throughout the play. But Beaumarchais also transcends the *commedia dell'arte* by turning his characters into individual human beings, by exploiting sophisticated dialogue and repartee, and by creating dramatic situations of a remarkable force. The preface to the first printed edition of 1785 suggests that Beaumarchais rightly felt proud of his work:

I have attempted what no man of letters has heretofore dared: a play that combines moralities of general effect and of detail spread on a sea of inalterable gaiety, a rather vivacious dialogue whose facility hides its workmanship, an effortlessly spun out intrigue where art conceals art and which knots and unravels itself ceaselessly through a crowd of comic situations, and piquant, varied tableaux which sustain without tiring the audience throughout the three-and-a-half-hour-long performance.[2]

The controversies surrounding *Le mariage* guaranteed Beaumarchais a *succès de scandale*, and pirated copies circulated quickly throughout Europe. Performances were planned for Vienna in February 1785, by the end of 1785 Johann Rautenstrauch had published a German translation (*Der närrische Tag*), and by the time Mozart's opera was performed there were several other German versions. The decision to turn the play into an opera, apparently made in early to mid 1785, was quick-witted as well as far-sighted. No doubt Mozart and da Ponte had to move quickly, mindful that other composers would be eager to follow the example of Paisiello's operatic version of *Le barbier*, first performed in St Petersburg in 1782 and in Vienna in 1783.

According to da Ponte, the idea of turning *Le mariage* into an *opera buffa* came from Mozart. The poet had been commissioned to write libretti for both Mozart and Vicente Martín y Soler:

As for the former, I quickly realised that the immensity of his genius demanded an extended, varied, sublime subject. Talking with him on this matter one day, he asked me if I could easily arrange as an opera the comedy by Beaumarchais entitled *Le nozze di Figaro*. The idea pleased me well, and I promised him to do it. But there was a very great difficulty to overcome. A few days earlier, the Emperor had forbidden the German theatre company to perform this comedy, which was written, he said, with too much licence for a well-mannered audience. So how could one offer it to him as an opera? Baron Wetzlar most generously offered to give me a very fair price for the words and to have the opera performed in London or in France if it were not possible in Vienna. But I refused his offers and decided to write the words and music in secret and to await a favourable opportunity to present it to the directors of the theatre or to the Emperor, which I courageously dared to do. Martín y Soler was the only one who knew the secret from me, and because of his admiration for Mozart, he liberally allowed that I should delay my writing [*Una cosa rara*] for him until I finished the drama of *Figaro*.[3]

When da Ponte finally revealed his plan to the Emperor Joseph II, the question of the play's political content did indeed arise. However, the librettist assured the Emperor that:

having written a *dramma per musica* and not a comedy, I have had to omit many scenes and shorten numerous others, and I have omitted and shortened anything that could offend the sensibility and decency of a spectacle at which His Sovereign Majesty presides. Furthermore, as for the music, as far as I can tell, it seems of wondrous beauty.[4]

The need to shorten the play is also mentioned in the preface to the printed edition of the libretto (1786). Here da Ponte offers some revealing insights into a librettist's art:

The duration prescribed as being usual for dramatic performances, a certain number of characters generally introduced into the same, and some other prudent considerations and exigencies imposed by morality, place and spectators, were the reasons why I did not make a translation of this excellent comedy, but rather an adaptation or, let us say, an extract.

To this end, I was obliged to reduce the sixteen characters of which it consists to eleven, two of which may be performed by a single person, and to omit, apart from an entire act, many a very charming scene and a number of good jests and sallies with which it is strewn, in place of which I had to substitute canzonettas, arias, choruses and other forms and words susceptible to music, things that can be supplied only by verse, but never by prose. In spite, however, of every effort, and of all the diligence and care taken by the composer and by myself to be brief, the opera will not be one of the shortest to have appeared on our stage, for which we hope sufficient excuse will be found in the variety of the threads from which the action of this play is woven, the vastness and grandeur of the same, the multiplicity of the musical numbers that had to be made in order not to leave the actors too long unemployed, to diminish the vexation and monotony of long recitatives, and to express with varied colours the various emotions that occur, but above all in our desire to offer as it were a new kind of spectacle to a public of so refined a taste and such just understanding.[5]

Da Ponte did indeed cut the sixteen characters of the play to eleven: the relatively minor parts of Double-Main, Gripe-Soleil, Pédrille, an usher, and a young shepherdess are all omitted. Fanchette of the play becomes Barbarina, and Don Gusman Brid'oison, Don Curzio. Two pairs of characters can be doubled, not just one as da Ponte says: Doctor Bartolo and Antonio (played in the first performance by Francesco Bussani), and Don Basilio and Don Curzio (played by Michael Kelly). Thus the opera can be performed with nine singers and a small chorus.

Da Ponte's mention of cuts suggested by 'prudent considerations and exigencies imposed by morality, place and spectators' presumably hints at the political comments in the play that were regarded as so inflammatory in Paris and Vienna. He omits a number of potentially dangerous passages, whether for fear of official disapproval or because he realised that much of this satire had a biographical and geographical significance that would have been lost on a Viennese audience; in 1788 the *Dramaturgische Blätter* of Frankfurt on Main commented that: 'The comedy by Beaumarchais, from which this operetta is taken, was written for Paris alone. The satire which is strewn about it everywhere was largely lost to us Germans.'[6] We lose Figaro's mockery of politics and his criticisms of the nobility ('And suppose I were better than my reputation? Are there many noblemen who could say as much?') in B:III.5 (trans. pp. 158–63).[7] The omission of the trial scene (B:III.12–15) avoids Beaumarchais's satire on the judiciary, which stemmed so much from personal experience. Marceline's comments on the misfortunes suffered by women at the hands of men (B:I.4 and III.16) and Bazile's on marriage (B:I.9) are also missing.[8] Perhaps most significant, however, is the transformation of Figaro's extended soliloquy in B:V.3 (see dP:IV.8). Da Ponte omits Figaro's tirade against the nobility and concentrates on another theme of the speech, the fickleness of women. To be sure, Figaro's pungent attack on his master takes up only a small part of Beaumarchais's scene, but it reveals the Figaro that has been handed down to history, the revolutionary before the Revolution:

> No, My Lord Count, you shan't have her, you shall not have her! Because you are a great nobleman you think you are a great genius. . .Nobility, fortune, rank, position! How proud they make a man feel! What have *you* done to deserve such advantages? Put yourself to the trouble of being born – nothing more! For the rest – a very ordinary man! Whereas I, lost among the obscure crowd, have had to deploy more knowledge, more calculation and skill merely to survive than has sufficed to rule all the provinces of Spain for a century! Yet you would measure yourself against me. . .
>
> (*Le mariage*, V.3, trans. p. 199)

But just how 'political' a play is *Le mariage*? There is no doubt that a noble Count gets his come-uppance at the hands of his servants. Moreover, through his dialogue Beaumarchais ensures that both Figaro and Suzanne appear as articulate as, and even more intelligent than, their master and mistress. It is indeed difficult to ignore the events of 1789 when reading Beaumarchais's play. Louis XVI said that 'this play will never be performed', another that it marked 'the end of the old order', and Napoleon claimed it to be 'the revolution in action'.[9] However, Beaumarchais's own career reveals no desire to overthrow the *ancien régime*, even if he was dissatisfied with much within it. He said of *Le mariage*: 'In the play. . .there is no attack on the classes, but only on the abuses of each class.'[10] Figaro 'intrigues against his lord only to guarantee that which he loves and to preserve what belongs to him'.[11] Moreover, 'no one wishes to perpetrate a deceit against the Count, but simply to prevent him from doing so against everyone', and although he is 'crossed in all his projects, Count Almaviva finds himself always humbled without ever being degraded'.[12] In this light, Figaro's comments in V.3 seem less an indictment of nobility at large. Of course, one must beware of taking Beaumarchais's comments at face value. Nevertheless, they suggest an alternative reading of the play that focusses less on pre-Revolution class warfare and more on its satire upon contemporary manners in the best comic tradition.

One might well say the same for the opera. Mozart certainly had grounds for resenting the nobility, and especially after his dismissal from Salzburg. Thus one critic has drawn a direct parallel between the sentiments expressed in *Figaro* and Mozart's earlier comments on the Archbishop of Salzburg's chief chamberlain, Count Georg Felix von Arco ('that arrogant jackass will certainly get a very palpable reply from me, even if he has to wait twenty years for it', and 'it is the heart that ennobles a man; and though I am no count, yet I have probably more honour in me than many a count').[13] Mozart may have enjoyed staging the misfortunes of his Count Almaviva. Moreover, his music does go some way to restoring what was omitted from the libretto: the servants adopt courtly dances as they challenge the Count (see Chapter 4), and their music (like Beaumarchais's dialogue) is often more sophisticated than one would expect for the lower classes. For Mozart, servants are entitled to 'feel' as much as their masters. But it is by no means clear that he intended *Figaro* to carry a more blatantly 'revolutionary' message, or even that the opera is concerned with anything more than the transgressions of an obscure nobleman in an obscure part of Europe on a particularly 'folle journée'.

Da Ponte claimed in his preface that the libretto was 'an adaptation or, let us say, an extract' of the play rather than a simple translation. No doubt he did so in part because of the need to distance himself from Beaumarchais. He also had to take into account the differing requirements of sung and spoken drama. It generally takes longer to sing something than to say it and music lacks the precision of words: Figaro's entire soliloquy in V.3 would have been difficult to work into an operatic context because of its length and multiplicity of themes. Therefore a librettist must provide clear-cut situations and strongly articulated characters with the utmost economy. However, da Ponte's claim for the difference between his libretto and the play must be treated with some caution: they are much more alike than we are led to expect. Indeed, it is clear that the opera owes much of its dramatic force, not to mention its verbal and physical comedy, to being so closely based on its fine model.

The scene-by-scene comparison of the play and libretto in Table 2 is revealing.[14] Although scenes are compressed (for example, B:II.3–9 in dP:II.3) little of substance is lost, and even da Ponte's claim to have cut out an entire act is unwarranted. He does remove the trial scene (B:III.12–15) and other 'politically' dangerous passages for reasons discussed above. Similarly, scenes associated with sub-plots missing from the opera (for example, B:II.23 and IV.10, concerning Bazile's attempts to marry Marceline) are omitted. However, the other deleted scenes are mostly minor and duplicate material presented elsewhere. Da Ponte adds some episodes to expand the roles of individual characters, notably IV.1 for Barbarina and, as we shall see, II.1 and III.8 for the Countess. He also adapts Beaumarchais's scheme to provide greater climaxes: for example, the omission of B:II.23–6 allows Act II to end with all the characters onstage, and it makes sense to finish Act III at B:IV.9, the wedding scene. On the whole, however, most of the play remains intact. Indeed, given that it is so tautly structured, da Ponte could do little else.

Not only does da Ponte follow Beaumarchais's general layout; he also matches closely the content of individual scenes in the play, often to the extent of providing a literal translation. Even when he needs to abbreviate and paraphrase particular speeches, he retains their substance. Thus da Ponte's process of adaptation is generally one of focussing the dialogue by means of omission and simplification where possible. A good example is provided by his treatment of B:III.9 (in the second part of dP:III.2), where Susanna arranges to

Table 2 *Le nozze di Figaro: scene-by-scene comparison of play and libretto*

da Ponte	Beaumarchais	da Ponte	Beaumarchais
Act I		*Act III*	
I.1 (1, 2)	I.1	x	III.1–3
I.2 (3)	I.2	III.1	III.4
x	I.3	x	III.5–8
I.3 (4)	I.4	III.2 (16)	III.9 (and see II.24)
I.4 (5)	I.5	III.3	III.10
I.5 (6)	I.6–7	III.4 (17)	III.11
I.6	I.8	x	III.12–15
I.7 (7)	I.9	III.5 (18)	III.16–18
I.8 (8, 9)	I.10	III.6	III.18–19
x	I.11	x	III.20
		x	IV.1–2
		III.7	x
		III.8 (19)	x
		III.9	IV.5 (part)
		III.10 (20)	IV.3
		III.11 (21)	IV.4
		III.12	IV.5
		III.13–14 (22)	IV.6–9
Act II		*Act IV*	
II.1 (10)	x	x	IV.10–13
II.2	II.1–2	IV.1 (23)	x
II.3 (11, 12)	II.3–9	IV.2	IV.14
II.4	II.10–11	IV.3	IV.15
II.5	II.12	IV.4 (24)	IV.16
II.6 (13)	II.13	IV.5	V.1
II.7 (14)	II.14–15	IV.6	V.2
II.8–12 (15)	II.16–22	IV.7 (25)	V.2
x	II.23–6	IV.8 (26)	V.3
		IV.9	V.4
		IV.10 (27)	V.5
		IV.11–12 (28)	V.6–10, 14, 16–19

meet the Count in the garden. The recitative prior to the duet 'Crudel! perchè finora' (No. 16) is an exact translation of Beaumarchais's dialogue, and da Ponte has little problem in fashioning the text of the duet itself from an exchange in the play. From here to the end of the scene, da Ponte begins to cut lines from the play: Susanna and the Count have agreed to meet and there is no need to prolong the action. As a result, he removes some of Beaumarchais's 'jests and sallies', as he said in his preface, but little is lost. This final section of Beaumarchais's scene (from the end of the exchange that became the duet, trans. pp. 164–5) is given below. Passages in italics are omitted from the libretto. The rest is translated almost *verbatim*.

COUNT: Why were you so obstinate this morning?
SUZANNE: *This morning* – with the page behind the chair?
COUNT: *She's quite right. I had forgotten. But why this persistent refusal* when Bazile, on my behalf. . .
SUZANNE: What need of a Bazile?
COUNT: She's right *again. But there's a certain Figaro to whom I fear you may have told things?*
SUZANNE: Why, of course! I tell him everything – except what he ought not to know.
COUNT: *Charming!* And you promise me? If you go back on your word, *let us be clear*, my dear: *no rendezvous no dowry – no dowry no marriage.*
SUZANNE [curtseying]: But no marriage also means no 'Droit de Seigneur', My Lord!
COUNT: *Where does she pick it all up? Upon my word I shall dote on her!* But your Mistress is waiting for the phial. . .
SUZANNE [laughing and handing it back]: I had to have some excuse to talk to you. . .
COUNT [trying to kiss her]: Delicious creature!
SUZANNE [evading him]: Someone is coming.
COUNT [aside]: She's mine. [Goes off.]
SUZANNE: I must go and tell Her Ladyship.

In the course of adapting the play, da Ponte had to find appropriate passages to be set as arias and ensembles. In Chapter 5 we shall see how he used certain poetic techniques to set such pieces off from the rest of his text. For the moment, it is worth exploring his reasons for treating particular episodes of the play in this way. It seems likely that the selection was made in collaboration with the composer. Certainly, da Ponte gauged Mozart's capabilities well: for example, his choice of ensemble scenes would scarcely have been appropriate for a composer who lacked the ability to present rapidly changing dramatic situations and sharply differentiated characters within a coherent musical framework. We shall return to this point in Chapter 6.

Sometimes da Ponte and Mozart appear to have been influenced by musical references in the play itself. *Le mariage*, unlike *Le barbier*, was conceived from the start as a spoken play. Nevertheless, music is required at five points: B:II.4, Chérubin, *romance*, 'Mon coursier hors d'haleine' (to be sung to the melody of 'Malbroug s'en va-t-en guerre', i.e. 'For he's a jolly good fellow!'); B:II.23, Figaro, *séguedille*, 'Je préfère à richesse'; B:IV.9, a march, fandango, and a duet for two girls, 'Jeune épouse, chantez les bienfaits et la gloire'; B:IV.10, Bazile, *vaudeville*, 'Cœurs sensibles, cœurs fidèles'; and B:V.19, all, *vaudeville*, 'Triple dot, femme superbe'. In the libretto, Chérubin's *romance* is replaced by 'Voi che sapete' (No. 11, dP:II.3), B:IV.9 becomes the finale to Act III (with the duet translated word-for-word as 'Amanti costanti'), and the final *vaudeville* is matched by the final chorus. Furthermore, the aria 'Venite, inginocchiatevi' (No. 12, dP:II.3), sung as Susanna dresses Cherubino, stems from a moment in B:II.6 when Suzanne sings a snatch of the popular song 'Tournez-vous donc envers ici'; and the 'letter'-duet for the Countess and Susanna, 'Che soave zeffiretto' (No. 20, dP:III.10), echoes another popular song to which reference is made at the same point in the play (B:IV.3, 'Qu'il fera beau, ce soir, sous les grands marronniers').

For the other arias and ensembles, da Ponte and Mozart were left to choose speeches or episodes in the play that would be suitable for musical treatment. The choice was not entirely free; nor was it always dictated by purely dramatic considerations. Da Ponte's reference in his preface to 'the multiplicity of the musical numbers that had to be made in order not to leave the actors too long unemployed, to diminish the vexation and monotony of long recitatives, and to express with varied colours the various emotions that occur' offers some indication of the constraints on the librettist and composer. They had to bear in mind the balance of the opera as a whole, the need for variety in the scoring and emotional content of successive items, and the expectations of an audience familiar with the conventions of *opera buffa*. If nothing else, they also had to meet the requirements of the singers in the cast according to their rank. Da Ponte gave a revealing account of the first rehearsals of Martín y Soler's *Una cosa rara* (1786), for which he had written the libretto:

> Scarcely were the parts distributed than all hell seemed to break loose. One [singer] had too many recitatives, another not enough; for one, the aria was too low, for another, too high; some did not enter into the ensembles, others had to sing in too many; one was sacrificed to the first lady, another to the first, second, third and fourth man. The fire spread everywhere.[15]

Ensembles and arias had to be apportioned correctly and every singer needed at least one aria. This may well explain the presence of Marcellina's and Basilio's Act IV arias, which seem less than appropriate dramatically and are often omitted in modern performances (but see below, p. 65).

In the case of the ensembles, the opera adapts sections of the play which were suited to extended musical treatment by virtue of their pace, their importance to the overall intrigue, or their possibilities for comic characterisation. Da Ponte was also helped by the organisation of the play, for Beaumarchais documents the fluctuating fortunes of his characters by a series of mostly self-contained episodes, each of which builds to successive climaxes. The ensemble texts follow their parallel episodes in the play very closely. The Act I trio, 'Cosa sento! tosto andate' (No. 7, dP:I.7, see B:I.9) is a good example. The text is often an exact translation of Beaumarchais. Da Ponte adds some interjections to allow the characters to follow each other in an orderly sequence. Presumably this is for musical reasons: all the characters need to take part in the various sections of the ensemble and their regular alternation allows the composer to build up balanced musical structures. The librettist also removes some of the dialogue and abbreviates individual speeches, no doubt bearing in mind the different speeds of sung and spoken delivery. But these omissions scarcely affect the scene. Indeed, most involve phrases that are redundant in terms of the action but are used by Beaumarchais to pace the events on the stage. In the opera, this pacing is to be provided instead by the music.

The episodic construction of the play also helped da Ponte organise the finales of the operas. The Act III finale (No. 22, dP:III.13–14) follows B:IV.6–9 closely. The same is true of the larger sectional finales of Acts II and IV. Convention decreed that such large-scale finales should be organised in specific dramatic and musical ways, as da Ponte himself was well aware:

[A] *finale*, which has to be closely connected with the rest of the opera, is a sort of little comedy in itself and requires a fresh plot and a special interest of its own. This is the great occasion for showing off the genius of the composer, the ability of the singers, and the most effective 'situation' of the drama. Recitative is excluded from it; everything is sung, and every style of singing must find a place in it – *adagio, allegro, andante, amabile, armonioso, strepitoso, arcistrepitoso, strepitosissimo*, and with this the said finale generally ends. This in the musicians' slang is called the *chiusa* or *stretta* – I suppose because it gives not one twinge but a hundred to the unhappy brain of the poet who has to write the words. In this finale it is a dogma of theatrical theology that all the singers should appear on the stage, even if there were three hundred of them, by ones, by twos, by threes, by sixes, by tens, by sixties, to sing solos, duets, trios, sextets, sessantets; and if the plot of the play does not allow of it, the poet must find some way of making the plot allow of it, in defiance of his judgement, of his reason, or of all the Aristotles on earth; and if he then finds his play going badly, so much the worse for him![16]

Le mariage contains scenes organised precisely in this manner, with the characters appearing one by one in close succession and with the action building up to a dramatic climax. In turning B:II.16–22 into the finale of Act II (No. 15, dP:II.8–12), da Ponte could solve the problem of the large-scale finale simply by following the play.

Although all the ensembles in *Figaro* are modelled closely on Beaumarchais, the arias raise different issues. Some of da Ponte's aria texts are translations of particular speeches in the play, as with Cherubino's 'Non so più cosa son, cosa faccio':

Beaumarchais, I.7:

I no longer know what I am. But for some time I have felt an agitation in my breast. My heart quivers at the very sight of a woman. The words 'love' and 'pleasure' make it throb and confuse it. In fact, the need to say to someone 'I love you' has become so pressing for me that I say it to myself as I run through the park, to your mistress, to you, to the trees, to the clouds, to the breeze which carries them off with my fleeting words.[17]

da Ponte, No. 6, I.5:

I no longer know what I am, what I do;
now I burn, now I freeze.
Every woman makes me blush,
every woman makes me tremble.

At the mere words 'love' and 'delight'
my breast heaves and pounds,
and there forces me to speak of love
a desire which I cannot explain.

I speak of love when I am awake,
I speak of love when I am asleep,
to the stream, to the shade, to the mountains,
to the flowers, to the grass, to the fountains,
to the echo, to the air, to the breezes
which bear away the sound of my fleeting words. . .

And if I have no one to hear me,
I speak of love to myself.

This is near enough a word-for-word translation, although da Ponte reorders the last section of Chérubin's speech to bring it to a more subtle climax. Similarly, Figaro's 'Non più andrai farfallone amoroso' (No. 9, I.8) is scarcely altered from Figaro's equivalent speech in B:I.10 (trans. p. 126). However, such examples are not common, and more frequently da Ponte must rely on his own initiative to elaborate upon a character's reaction to a particular dramatic situation: Figaro's 'Se vuol ballare' (No. 3, I.2, see B:I.2),[18] the Count's 'Vedrò mentre io sospiro' (No. 17, III.4, see B:III.11) and Figaro's 'Aprite un po' quegl'occhi' (No. 26, IV.8, see B:V.3) are good examples.

The arias may be an essential part of the opera, whether for characterisation, pacing, or simply because of convention, but they begin to take the opera away from the play. Here da Ponte ceases to be an essentially neutral intermediary, simply translating one language into another, or the conventions of one genre into those of another. Instead, he must interpose his own view of the characters. There are inevitable repercussions. For example, although the texts of Figaro's 'Se vuol ballare' or the Count's 'Vedrò mentre io sospiro' are logical expansions of particular situations in the play, they offer a reading of the characters that may well go beyond Beaumarchais's intentions. Indeed, the mere fact of solitary introspection on a single theme fundamentally alters the tone of the play. Beaumarchais only rarely gives his characters time to reflect on their particular situation. The play's 'folle journée' passes quickly, with little regard for its effect on them. In the opera, however, the introspection of the arias slows down the action and alters the characters. Far from being carried along by events, they are required to articulate emotions and motives scarcely acknowledged in the play. The libretto must delve more deeply into the characters than Beaumarchais might have wished. Of course, Mozart's music will delve deeper still.

Da Ponte and Mozart's treatment of the Countess illustrates the point most clearly. In the opera, she is first seen in a solo scene at the beginning of Act II: in the play, she enters rather innocuously in I.10. Moreover, her two arias, 'Porgi amor qualche ristoro' (No. 10, II.1) and 'Dove sono i bei momenti' (No. 19, III.8) have no parallel in *Le mariage*. All this forms part of a seemingly deliberate policy of giving the Countess a new emphasis and thereby making her the focal point of the events of the 'folle journée'. Any victim of a heartless husband who can bear her travails with the dignity of 'Porgi amor qualche ristoro' and 'Dove sono i bei momenti' deserves prime place in our attentions. This is even more the case in performances that cast the Countess as a mature woman instead of the young wife at most in her early twenties of the play. She becomes a noble heroine almost in the manner of a character from *opera seria.*

This change to the Countess is emphasised by da Ponte's treatment of her relationship with Cherubino. In the play, she is obviously attracted to the page. In B:I.10, she bids him an over-fond farewell that raises the Count's suspicions, as he remarks in B:II.16. The Countess 'dreams' during Suzanne's references to Chérubin in B:II.1, she preens herself before the page's arrival in B:II.3, she reacts emotionally to the sentiments of Chérubin's *romance* (in the libretto, she merely praises his singing), and the ribbon with which Chérubin had bandaged his wounded arm (see B:II.6–9) comes to represent her feelings for him:

> It's quite audacious – my little scheme. [*Turning round.*] Oh, my ribbon, my dear little ribbon! I had forgotten you! [*She rolls it up.*] I won't part with you, you shall remind me of the incident when the poor child – Ah, My Lord the Count! What have you done? And what am I doing now? [*Enter Suzanne. The Countess slips the ribbon into her bosom.*]
>
> (*Le mariage*, II.25, trans. p. 156)

The ribbon reappears in subsequent acts – note the references to it in B:IV.3 – until the Countess signifies her reconciliation with her husband by casting it aside in B:V.19. The Count's suspicions of Chérubin are not without foundation, as the third play of the trilogy, *La mère coupable*, is to prove.

Beaumarchais had good reasons for making the Countess fall prey to the charms of Chérubin. For example, it is dramatically important (both in the play and in the opera) to have the Count jealous (for whatever reason) not only of Figaro but also of the page. Moreover, Beaumarchais claimed in his preface that he thereby showed the Countess to her best advantage:

> the author opposes this insensitive husband with the most virtuous of women in taste and morals. Abandoned by a husband whom she loves too much, when does she come into your view? At the critical moment when her concern for a likeable child, her god-son, can become a dangerous affection if she allows her pressing resentment [against the Count] too much sway. . . What pleases us in the Countess is to see her fighting honestly against a growing passion which she condemns and against her legitimate resentment. The efforts which she makes to regain her faithless husband place the two hard-won sacrifices to her affection and her anger in the best light. It takes no thought to applaud her triumph. She is a model of virtue, an example of her sex. . .[19]

He also equivocated about the precise nature of the Countess's attraction for the page – is he a substitute son or a potential lover? – and the ambiguity is heightened still further by having the boy played by a young woman. This equivocal relationship remains in the opera, and indeed it was a kind of relationship that Richard Strauss and Hugo von Hofmannsthal were to explore so thoroughly in *Der Rosenkavalier.* But it is significant that da Ponte seems to have removed as many hints as he could of the Countess's feelings for Chérubin in his libretto, and it is by no means certain that they should be restored by way of emphatic stage business, as is the current fashion. One can see why he should have done so: the redefined Countess is best seen to be unwavering in her love for the Count. However, it produces a potential imbalance. In the play, Beaumarchais presents complex characters whom flaws render all the more human. Figaro and Suzanne are quick-witted servants guaranteed to maintain the upper hand, but they both lose control at various stages in the proceedings and come to mistrust each other, albeit briefly. The Count is magnanimous with his subjects but unfaithful to his wife. The Countess bears her suffering with dignity but is attracted to Chérubin. The characters all have their strengths and weaknesses and thus stand on an equal footing.

In the opera, the Countess lacks her 'human' flaw and so remains apart. Moreover, she changes and develops as the day progresses. In the play, the characters are scarcely altered by the events of the 'folle journée', and none seems to emerge the better for them. This is not the case in the opera. Here the Countess moves on from the despair and inaction of her first scene in Act II to dominate the intrigue. As we shall see in Chapter 7, her second aria, 'Dove sono i bei momenti', marks a crucial point in this transition. The climax comes with her final forgiveness of the Count in the Act IV finale. For the Countess of the opera, the 'folle journée' is a day of intense personal exploration and renewed self-understanding.

At times, Figaro's wedding seems only a sub-plot of *Le nozze di Figaro.* Figaro is a curious hero: he can be remarkably slow-witted, his scheming in Acts I and II is somewhat preposterous, and by the end of the opera he has lost all control of events to Susanna and the Countess. Moreover, the wedding is more or less assured by the Act III sextet, when the Count's chief ally against Figaro, Marcellina, is removed from the running. The rest of Acts III and IV is concerned less with Figaro and Susanna than with the Countess and her attempts to recover the love of her husband. The simple explanation is that da Ponte and Mozart had to re-focus the play when forced to omit the more overtly political comments from Figaro's speeches and thus water down the character. But perhaps they saw the deeper significance of Beaumarchais's comedy: the playwright himself said of his work that 'the major interest centres on the Countess'.[20] Whatever the case, if there is a 'message' in the opera, it seems less the equality of man than the redeeming power of a woman's love.

In the play, Beaumarchais was careful to keep things on a comic plane. The fast pace, the witty repartee, the general lack of emotional introspection, the equal status of the characters, the essential superficiality of the plot, all tend towards a comedy of manners *par excellence.* In the opera, the pace cannot be sustained, the repartee must be cut, and one character stands out from the rest and undergoes a fundamental change. At times, da Ponte and Mozart match Beaumarchais's tone, wit and pace perfectly. Elsewhere, they hint at dramatic and emotional depths which Beaumarchais was careful to avoid but which Mozart avidly explored.

4 *Synopsis*

Dramatis personae

Count Almaviva	A Spanish lord	Baritone
Countess Almaviva	His wife	Soprano
Susanna	The Countess's maid and engaged to be married to	Soprano
Figaro	The Count's servant	Bass
Cherubino	A page	Soprano
Marcellina	A governess	Soprano
Doctor Bartolo	A doctor from Seville	Bass
Don Basilio	A music master	Tenor
Don Curzio	A judge	Tenor
Barbarina	The daughter of	Soprano
Antonio	The Count's gardener and Susanna's uncle	Bass

Chorus of peasants and girls

It is the morning of Figaro and Susanna's wedding in Count Almaviva's castle. The bustling overture (Presto, D major) sets the pace of the 'folle journée'. Unlike the overtures to *Die Entführung aus dem Serail*, *Don Giovanni*, *Così fan tutte* and *Die Zauberflöte*, it does not present thematic material used elsewhere in the opera, but its bright key and fast quaver runs are clearly appropriate to what follows. Mozart originally planned a slow middle section ($\frac{6}{8}$, D minor; compare the overture to *Die Entführung*), but he changed his mind.[1] Indeed, he even omits the Development section that one would expect in a sonata-form movement: instead there is just a sixteen-bar dominant pedal leading straight back to the Recapitulation. The curtain opens to reveal Figaro and Susanna in a half-furnished room with a chair in the centre.

Act I

Scene 1 No. 1 DUET (Allegro. G major. Figaro: 'Cinque, dieci, venti, trenta')[2] Figaro is measuring the room that the Count has designated their bedchamber, and Susanna is trying on her bridal hat. The key of the duet, G major, is the subdominant of the overture's D major and thus gives the feeling of relaxing into a pre-established situation. Moreover, the running semiquavers in the accompaniment suggest that the action began before the curtain rose. Figaro calls out his measurements with a rather plodding line that suggests a stolid character concerned only with life's practicalities. Susanna's melody, its stepwise movement and long-breathed phrases contrasting with Figaro's disjointed leaps, is much more appealing. Musically, she has the upper hand, a point that is emphasised when Figaro adopts her melody ('Sì, mio core, or è più bello', 'Yes, my dear, now it's more beautiful') as he is forced to stop measuring and admire her hat.[3] (Recitative) Susanna asks what Figaro is measuring: he replies that he wants to see whether the bed that the Count will give them for their wedding will fit in here. Susanna protests: she does not want to live here. But Figaro argues that the room is ideal. **No. 2 DUET** (Allegro. B flat major. Figaro: 'Se a caso madama') When the Countess rings for Susanna ('ding-ding', imitated in the orchestra), she can be there in two steps; and when the Count rings for Figaro ('don-don'), he can be there in a trice. But what happens, says Susanna (with a significant shift to the minor), if the Count sends Figaro away on an errand: 'ding-ding', he appears at the door! Figaro, his jealousy aroused, seeks an explanation. (Recitative) According to Susanna, the Count is tired of chasing women outside the castle and wants to try his luck with her. Basilio, Susanna's singing teacher, has been acting as the Count's go-between, and the Count has promised her a dowry should she allow him the *droit de seigneur*, even though this custom has been officially abolished. The Countess's bell rings, and Figaro and Susanna take their farewell. Their two duets have sown the seeds of the plot with remarkable efficiency: two arias would scarcely have performed the task as well, and recitative would have meant losing the depth of characterisation provided by Mozart's music.

Scene 2 Figaro, left alone, now understands the reason for the Count wanting to take him and Susanna on his new appointment as ambassador to London, with Figaro as a courier and Susanna as. . .private attaché. This is the first solo scene and aria of the opera, but it is less a moment of contemplation, as one might expect from the arias of *opera seria*, than a declaration of intent. He will have none of the Count's plans. **No. 3 CAVATINA** (Allegretto–Presto–Tempo primo–Presto. F major. 'Se vuol ballare') If the Count wishes to dance, Figaro will call the tune. His challenge is issued in the guise of a stately minuet: this is the first of several instances where servants adopt ostensibly courtly dances through which to challenge their master.[4] As Figaro says in Act I scene 8, 'Eccoci in danza!' ('Here we are in the dance!'). The pizzicato strings in the accompaniment imitate the 'chitarrino' ('little guitar') that Figaro will play, and the horns suggest the idea of a hunt and also mock the potential cuckold with 'horns' growing from his head (see the reference in B:I.1). Figaro leaves in fury.

Scene 3 (Recitative) Marcellina and Bartolo enter, discussing a contract. They plan to disrupt the wedding, even at this late stage. Bartolo had been the guardian of Rosina (the Countess) before she eloped with the Count, and Marcellina her governess (see Beaumarchais's *Le barbier de Séville*). Marcellina now wants to marry Figaro and will take advantage of certain 'obligations' owed her: Figaro signed a contract promising to marry her if a debt were not paid back by a certain date and that date has now arrived. She will also encourage Susanna to continue refusing the Count so that he will take Marcellina's part. Bartolo approves: he will gain his own revenge by giving the hand of his old servant to someone who had helped the Count prevent him marrying his ward. **No. 4 ARIA** (Allegro. D major. 'La vendetta, oh la vendetta!') Bartolo proclaims the sweetness of vengeance to the sound of trumpets and drums. His bombastic aria is rendered all the more fatuous by its contrast with the intense inner rage of 'Se vuol ballare' (and see below, pp. 113–14). Bartolo leaves.

Scene 4 (Recitative) Susanna enters carrying a bonnet, a ribbon and a dress. Marcellina pretends not to see the maid and insults her out loud: 'and he wishes to marry that fine pearl'. But one cannot expect anything else from Figaro, who will do anything for money, even, she hints, money paid by the Count for seducing Susanna. As for Susanna's modest appearance. . .**No. 5 DUET** (Allegro. A major. Marcellina: 'Via resti servita') Both start to leave and meet at the door. Their polite curtseys scarcely veil their antagonism and they exchange insults, 'dancing' verbally as well as physically. But Susanna has the upper hand: Marcellina's dress, her position and above all, she crows, her age ('l'età') make her ridiculous. Marcellina, defeated, gives way and leaves in a huff.

Scene 5 (Recitative) Susanna continues to hurl insults at the 'vecchia pedante' and places the dress on the chair. Cherubino rushes in. Yesterday the Count found him in Barbarina's room and now he is to be dismissed from the castle. Only the intercession of the Countess can save him. He will never see Susanna again! But Susanna knows that he is really sighing for the Countess. Cherubino scarcely denies it: how fortunate Susanna is to see her at every time of day, to dress and undress her. . .He steals the ribbon carried by Susanna – it belongs to the Countess – and offers in return a canzonet, which is to be read to the Countess, to Susanna, to Barbarina, to Marcellina, to all the women in the castle. 'Poor Cherubino', says Susanna, 'are you mad?' **No. 6 ARIA** (Allegro vivace. E flat major. 'Non so più cosa son, cosa faccio') Cherubino scarcely knows what has come over him: all he can think of is love. The breathless vocal line and the murmuring accompaniment capture perfectly the pains of the love-sick youth. He starts to leave but sees the Count coming and hides behind the chair.

Scene 6 (Recitative) The Count enters and notices Susanna's agitation. She asks him to leave: what if they were to be found together? But he sits on the chair, tries to take her hand and pursues his amorous advances, mentioning the imminent trip to London. He will do whatever she asks if only she will meet him in the garden at dusk. Basilio is heard offstage: he is looking for the Count. The Count instructs Susanna not to let anyone enter and moves to hide behind the chair. She tries to stop him and then places herself between the Count and Cherubino, who creeps round to the front of the chair. She covers the page with the dress. **Scene 7** Basilio enters to ask if Susanna has seen the Count, who is wanted by Figaro. They start to argue and the Count watches to see how Basilio will take his part. The music master encourages Susanna to yield to the Count: surely he is a better match than the page. She protests at his innuendoes, but Basilio knows too much. Was not Cherubino outside her room this morning, and was the canzonet for her or the Countess? After all, the page so obviously dotes on the Countess that if the Count were to find out. . .Susanna accuses Basilio of spreading lies, but he claims that he is only reporting what everyone is saying. 'What everyone is saying?' cries the Count, rushing from his hiding-place. Basilio is intrigued at the turn of events; Susanna is in despair. The situation provokes the kind of piece that Mozart delighted in writing, an action-ensemble where both music and movement reflect the twists and turns of the action. **No. 7 TRIO** (Allegro assai. B flat major. Count: 'Cosa sento! tosto andate') This trio will be analysed in detail in Chapter 6. The Count furiously orders Cherubino to be thrown out of the castle, Basilio apologises for his untimely entry and Susanna 'faints'. They carry her to the chair (where Cherubino is hiding) and assure her of their good intentions. She swiftly 'recovers', Basilio apologises for what he said about Cherubino – it was only his 'suspicion' – but the Count says that the page must go (and he will spend much of the opera trying to make him do so). This is not the first time that Cherubino has been caught out. Only yesterday, the Count went to Barbarina's room, knocked on the door, and became suspicious when Barbarina took some time to answer. Finding her in some disarray, he searched the room. Gently lifting the table-cloth – and here he demonstrates by lifting up the dress on the chair – he found. . .the page! Once again, Cherubino is uncovered: as we shall see, in each act of the opera the page manages to be discovered in the wrong place at the wrong time. The characters' surprise is matched perfectly by their short phrases and the soft accompaniment. Then the Count draws the obvious conclusion, Basilio rejoices in the confirmation that 'Così fan tutte le belle' ('all women are like that'), and Susanna laments the turn of events. (Recitative) The Count orders Figaro to be summoned to witness the scene. Susanna says he must indeed hear everything, which makes the Count pause. She describes how Cherubino had come to seek the Countess's intercession, had taken fright at the approach of the Count and had hidden first behind the chair, then in it. The Count realises that Cherubino has heard everything. Well, Cherubino replies, he did his best not to listen.

Scene 8 No. 8 CHORUS (Allegro. G major. 'Giovani liete') A group of peasants, duly 'orchestrated' by Figaro, enter to sing the Count's praises in a country-bumpkin $\frac{6}{8}$ metre.[5] Figaro follows carrying a white dress. (Recitative) He wants the wedding to take place as soon as possible so that he and Susanna may be the first to benefit from the Count's renunciation of the *droit de seigneur*. The Count can do little else but agree in front of his subjects, although he delays the ceremony, claiming that the proper pageantry must be prepared. Meanwhile, he mutters, he will seek out Marcellina. **No. 8a CHORUS** (Allegro. G major. 'Giovani liete') The peasants repeat their praise and leave. (Recitative) 'Long live the Count!' Figaro asks why Cherubino is not applauding and learns of his dismissal. He and Susanna plead on behalf of the page: he is so young ('Not as young as you think', retorts the Count). Cherubino admits his guilt and promises not to utter a word about what went on in Susanna's room when he was behind the chair. The Count takes the hint and reconsiders: he will make Cherubino an officer in his regiment. He tells the page to embrace Susanna for one last time, Figaro shakes 'capitano' Cherubino's hand, whispering that he wants to speak with him before he leaves. **No. 9 ARIA** (Allegro vivace. C major. 'Non più andrai farfallone amoroso') Figaro paints a vivid picture of army-life for Cherubino's benefit, with plenty of stage business to match, and all leave to the sound of a march.

Act II

The Countess's boudoir: a magnificent chamber with an alcove, a door stage right, a dressing-room door stage left, a door at the rear leading to Susanna's room, and a window to one side. We see the Countess alone.

Scene 1 No. 10 CAVATINA (Larghetto. E flat major. 'Porgi amor qualche ristoro') The Countess begs for release from her grief: either let her husband return to her or let her die. This is an addition to the play, and the aria, with its long orchestral introduction, takes us into a world far removed from the bustle of Act I, a world of private introspection that contrasts with the 'public' march at the end of 'Non più andrai farfallone amoroso' (No. 9). It is a short piece, a mere 51 bars of which the voice sings for only 29. Thus the Countess can remain onstage (a longer aria might have required a conventional exit) and the act can get underway. But the compression of 'Porgi amor qualche ristoro' serves only to emphasise its intensity. We shall see in Chapter 7 how the aria has both emotional and musical implications for the rest of the opera.
Scene 2 (Recitative) Susanna enters and finishes recounting the events in her room earlier that morning (Act I scenes 6–7). It is clear to the Countess that her husband no longer loves her, and that his jealousy is simply the result of male pride. Only Figaro can save them. Figaro enters humming confidently and summarises the situation: the Count wants to seduce Susanna by reviving the *droit de seigneur*; he will take them to London, with Susanna as 'private counsellor'; because she refuses his advances, he is threatening to protect Marcellina; that is all there is to it. He now announces his plan. First, he has given an 'anonymous' letter to Basilio revealing that the Countess will meet a lover at the ball that evening. The Count will be so jealous that he will forget Figaro and Susanna's wedding until it is too late, and he will not be able to refuse it in front

of the Countess. Second, Susanna will promise to meet the Count in the garden at dusk and Cherubino will go dressed up in her place. The Countess will surprise them together and the Count will be trapped. At the moment the coast is clear because the Count has gone off hunting. Figaro leaves to send Cherubino to them so that his costume can be prepared. Then the Count really will dance to Figaro's tune.

Scene 3 The Countess is upset that Cherubino overheard the Count in Susanna's room and wonders why the page did not come direct to her for help. She asks where the canzonet is and Susanna suggests that Cherubino be made to sing it. The page enters and laments having to leave the Countess. **No. 11 ARIETTA** (Andante. B flat major. 'Voi che sapete') He sings his delightful canzonet to Susanna's guitar accompaniment (provided by pizzicato strings in the orchestra).[6] (Recitative) The Countess praises Cherubino's singing, while Susanna turns to the more serious matter of dressing him up for the evening's masquerade. He and Susanna are the same height, so all should go well. She takes off his coat. The Countess is worried that they might be discovered, but according to Susanna they are doing nothing wrong. To be safe, however, Susanna locks the door. The Countess sends Susanna out for a bonnet to cover Cherubino's hair and catches sight of the page's commission, which he has just received from Basilio. She remarks on the unseemly haste and notices that it is not sealed. Susanna returns and, singing, dresses Cherubino as a girl. **No. 12 ARIA** (Allegretto. G major. 'Venite, inginocchiatevi') He cuts a fine figure: small wonder all the girls love him. For the audience, there is the extra joke of a girl dressed as a boy being dressed as a girl. (Recitative) While adjusting Cherubino's costume the Countess discovers the ribbon stolen from Susanna (see Act I scene 5) tied to his arm. It has blood on it as a result of Cherubino having stumbled and scratched himself. Susanna remarks on the whiteness of his skin, and the Countess sends her for some sticking-plaster. She is loath to lose the ribbon because of its colour. Susanna returns with the plaster and is sent off again for another ribbon to bandage the arm. She leaves through the door at the rear of the stage. Cherubino claims that he would rather have the first ribbon: it is said that when a ribbon binds the hair or touches the skin of someone. . .(loved, Cherubino means to say, but the Countess interrupts him), it has healing properties. The Countess dismisses such foolishness and Cherubino bursts into tears. If only he could die, then perhaps his lips would dare. . .The Countess hushes him and wipes his eyes. Someone knocks at the door. **Scene 4** The Count is heard asking why the door is locked. Cherubino and the Countess are thrown into disarray: for the second time in the opera, Cherubino is in the wrong place at the wrong time. The Countess says through the door that she is alone – but who is she talking to, asks the Count – and the page hides in the dressing-room stage left. The Countess opens the door in panic.

Scene 5 The Count enters in his hunting outfit. He is suspicious, for the Countess rarely locks her door. She explains that Susanna was trying on some dresses and that the maid has just gone to her room. The Count pulls out the letter written 'anonymously' by Figaro (see Act II scene 2) and a noise is heard from the dressing-room: Cherubino has knocked over a table and chair. The Count asks what the noise was; the Countess pretends to have heard nothing and then says that it must have been Susanna. But, asks the Count, did she not go to her room? Her room, the dressing-room, the Countess cannot remember. But if it is Susanna, why is the Countess so disturbed? She tries to turn the tables on her husband: surely only he is disturbed by Susanna. **Scene 6** Susanna enters through the door of her room unseen by the Count (who is standing by the dressing-room door) and watches the scene from the alcove. Once again, the situation provokes an action-ensemble. **No. 13 TRIO** (Allegro spiritoso. C major. Count: 'Susanna or via sortite') The Count orders Susanna to come out, but the Countess says that she cannot: she is trying on a dress which the Countess intends to give her as a wedding present. Meanwhile, Susanna comments from a distance. The Count returns to his opening music: well at least she can speak. The Countess orders her to stay silent. The Count advises his wife to be careful – the chromaticism and sliding modulations in the accompaniment emphasise the point – and the situation is in deadlock. (Recitative) The Countess still refuses to open the door and the Count threatens to break it down. His call for assistance is hushed by the Countess: does he want to create a public scandal? He decides to go and get tools to do it himself. To make sure that everything stays as it is, he locks Susanna's door and asks the Countess to accompany him. They leave together: Susanna will have to wait until they return. The Count locks the door behind him.

Scene 7 No. 14 DUET (Allegro assai. G major. Susanna: 'Aprite, presto aprite') Susanna rushes from the alcove and tells Cherubino to open the door of the dressing-room from the inside. They try to find a means of escape, but all the other doors are locked. The rapid orchestral figures and the breathless vocal lines mirror their panic. The only way out is through the window overlooking the garden. Susanna is frightened of the drop, but Cherubino will risk anything to save the Countess's honour. He kisses Susanna and jumps. (Recitative) Susanna cries out but is relieved to see the page running away safe and sound. She enters the dressing-room to await the Count.

Scene 8 The Count and Countess return, with the Count carrying tools. The Countess, at her wits' end, confesses that Cherubino is in the dressing-room. The Count is furious. **No. 15 FINALE** There now follows one of Mozart's most glorious achievements in *Figaro*, an extended ensemble that lasts over twenty minutes, far longer than any of his symphonic movements. It is a fine illustration of Mozart's ability to cope with rapidly changing dramatic situations, sudden reversals and conflicts or resolutions, while developing a musical argument that retains its coherence and structural integrity. There are eight sections contrasted in tempo and metre, although as we shall see in Chapter 7, they are linked by a clearly conceived tonal plan. **No. 15.1** (Allegro. E flat major. Count: 'Esci omai, garzon malnato') The Count orders the page to come out of the dressing-room, while the Countess, giving him the key, protests that his presence there is entirely innocent, even if he is only half-dressed. The Count refuses to listen, curses her infidelity (in a ferocious F minor), threatens to kill the page, and opens the door. **Scene 9 No. 15.2** (Molto andante. B flat major. Susanna: 'Signore, cos'è quel stupore?') Susanna stands coyly on the threshold and the orchestra plays an elegantly pointed minuet: now it is Susanna's turn to teach the Count how to dance. Both he and Countess are amazed – all motion in the music seems to be suspended – and Susanna has glorious triplet figures that soar above the texture as she savours her triumph. As when Cherubino was discovered in the chair in the Act I trio, Mozart finds just the right musical means to depict the silence that accompanies surprise. The Count goes into the room to make sure that it is empty. **No. 15.3** (Allegro. B flat major. Countess: 'Susanna, son morta') The musical action resumes as the orchestra initiates a succession of typically *buffo* accompanimental clichés. The Countess is half-dead with fright and Susanna explains that Cherubino escaped through the window. The Count returns: the room is indeed empty. Susanna and the Countess, who is gradually recovering, mock him, and the Countess throws the Count's accusations back in his face. Even his appeal to the 'Rosina' of old fails

('Crudele, più quella non sono', 'Cruel one, I am no longer she', says the Countess). The Count, mystified, seeks an explanation and discovers that the women were only playing a joke to test him. He asks about the letter and the Countess explains that Figaro gave it to Basilio. But now it is time to forgive and forget. The Count asks for pardon (he will do so again before the end of the day), the Countess gradually softens – after all, women always give way to men in the end – and the section ends in sublime homophony.

Scene 10 No. 15.4 (Allegro. G major. Figaro: 'Signori, di fuori') Figaro makes another entrance to brazen things out. The musicians are ready (we can hear them practising offstage via the flourishes in the orchestra) and it is time for the wedding ceremony to begin. But the Count first wants to get a few things clear. **No. 15.5** (Andante. C major. Count: 'Conoscete, signor Figaro') He asks about the letter. Figaro denies all knowledge of it, despite the promptings of Susanna and the Countess. He does so again in terms of an ostensibly noble dance, the gavotte. The Count accuses Figaro of lying, he denies it, and Susanna and the Countess attempt to bring the comedy to an end. What better, says Figaro, than a happy ending in the best theatrical tradition: a wedding. A firm pedal in the bass turns the gavotte into a musette, a dance with pastoral overtones, that 'grounds' the music and gives it a new emotional depth. The Countess, Susanna and Figaro urge the Count to proceed. He, on the other hand, awaits Marcellina.

Scene 11 No. 15.6 (Allegro molto. F major. Antonio: 'Ah! signor, signor') Just as everything seems resolved, Antonio rushes in carrying a broken pot of carnations. The orchestra picks up a furious pace. People are always throwing things out of windows, says the gardener, but now it has gone too far – a man! The Count's suspicions are aroused once more, while Susanna and the Countess urge Figaro to think quickly. It was the page, whispers Susanna to Figaro, but he had already seen him. Figaro accuses Antonio of being drunk, but the Count wants to get the story straight: yes, a man definitely jumped out of the window into the garden. Figaro finally claims that it was he. But Antonio thought it was someone smaller, like the page. Figaro bluffs: one always crouches when jumping, and anyway Cherubino has gone off to Seville on horseback. Well, says Antonio, it cannot have been Cherubino, because no horse jumped out of the window! The Count is exasperated, 'Finiam questo ballo!', 'Let's finish this dance!', and Figaro explains: he was waiting in Susanna's room, heard the Count's angry voice, took fright because of the

letter, jumped out of the window, and. . .hurt his foot. **No. 15.7** (Andante. B flat major. Antonio: 'Vostre dunque saran queste carte') The pace slows again as the orchestra takes up a menacing three-quaver pattern that repeats obsessively while meandering through a wide range of keys. In that case, says Antonio, these papers which he found in the garden must be Figaro's. The Count seizes them and Figaro is trapped. The Count asks what they are, Figaro plays for time by rummaging through his pockets, and Antonio is dismissed. The Countess catches sight of the papers – the page's commission – and Susanna manages to pass the information on to Figaro. Figaro 'remembers' that the page gave him his commission. The Count asks why. Once again the Countess prompts Susanna, and she Figaro: it needed an official seal. Figaro savours his triumph (matched by a marvellous modulation onto the dominant in the orchestra as the tonality finally becomes clear). The Count gives up in exasperation, and Susanna and the Countess say that if they can get out of this, they can get out of anything.
Scene 12 No. 15.8 (Allegro assai– Più allegro–Prestissimo. E flat major. Marcellina, Bartolo, Basilio: 'Voi signor, che giusto siete') We now build up to the climax of the finale. Marcellina, Bartolo and Basilio enter, much to the Count's relief. Marcellina explains about the marriage contract, and Bartolo and Basilio take their turn to support her claim. The Countess, Susanna and Figaro protest, only to be silenced by the Count. According to him, the contract must be examined and due action taken. The Countess, Susanna and Figaro despair at the turn of events; the Count, Marcellina, Bartolo and Basilio rejoice; and the finale ends with brass fanfares and string flourishes.

Act III

A large hall prepared for the wedding celebration. Act I began with Figaro and Susanna, and Act II with the Countess. Now it is the turn of the Count.

Scene 1 (Recitative) The Count, alone, ponders on the situation: an anonymous letter, the maid in the room, the Countess distraught, a man leaping out of the window, someone else claiming that it was he. He scarcely knows what to think. But can he really mistrust the Countess? Surely she respects both herself and his honour too much. But what price *his* honour now? **Scene 2** The Countess and Susanna

enter unseen by the Count, who continues his ruminations and announces that he has sent Basilio to Seville to see if Cherubino has arrived. The Countess orders Susanna to tell the Count that she will meet him in the garden. Susanna is worried about Figaro finding out, but he is not to be told and anyway the Countess will go in her place. Susanna is still frightened, but, says the Countess, this is the only way to ensure her mistress's happiness. The Countess leaves. The Count, still talking to himself, fears that Susanna has told Figaro everything: if so, he will make his servant marry Marcellina. Susanna interrupts. She says that she has come for a flask of smelling salts: the Countess has had one of her 'turns'. He gives her the flask: she can keep it. Oh no, she says, 'turns' are not for the like of a mere serving wench. Even if she is about to lose her lover on the point of marrying him? But Susanna says that she will pay Marcellina with the dowry that the Count has promised her. What dowry? Surely that depends on certain things. Of course, says Susanna. Is it not her duty to obey her master in everything? **No. 16 DUET** (Andante. A minor–A major. Count: 'Crudel! perchè finora') Why did she not say so sooner, exclaims the Count with a plangent minor-key melody. Susanna replies confidently in the major: a woman always takes time to say yes. They agree to meet in the garden, and as the music moves firmly to a luxuriant A major the Count rejoices and Susanna asks all who understand love to forgive her lie. (Recitative) Why did Susanna treat him so harshly this morning? Of course, the page was there. And why did she refuse Basilio? But such affairs have no need of a Basilio. True, says the Count, but now it is time to take the flask back to the Countess. Susanna admits that this was only a pretext to see him. He moves to embrace her but she withdraws: someone is coming. 'She is mine', proclaims the Count.
Scene 3 Figaro enters and meets Susanna, who says that their case is already won, and without a lawyer. They leave together. **Scene 4 No. 17 ACCOMPANIED RECITATIVE** (Maestoso, etc., 'Hai già vinta la causa! cosa sento!') 'You have won your case!' The Count has overheard them and realises the trap. He declares that he will get his revenge and punish them for this trick. But what if Figaro manages to pay Marcellina. . .With what? And there is always Antonio, whose pride will not allow his niece to marry someone who does not even know his parents. The Count will work on Antonio's pride: after all, one must stoop to anything when it comes to intrigue. His accompanied recitative (with orchestra rather than just harpsichord) fulfils a function typical of *opera seria*: a 'noble' character is alone onstage to

explore a moment of particular dramatic and emotional significance. **ARIA** (Allegro maestoso–Allegro assai. D major. 'Vedrò mentre io sospiro') The Count's anger explodes: he will not be outwitted by a mere servant. We may have felt some sympathy with the Count at the beginning of this act, and in his duet with Susanna there seem to be grounds for believing that he really does love her. Lest we become too involved with him, however, Mozart now paints a terrifying picture of blind fury (and see below, pp. 113–15). What was more than glimpsed in Act II now becomes a frightening reality. Moreover, by being raised to new musical and dramatic heights, the Count has that much further to fall in the next scene.

Scene 5 (Recitative) Don Curzio, Marcellina, Figaro and Bartolo enter. The case has been tried and Don Curzio announces his verdict: Figaro must either pay Marcellina or marry her. Marcellina breathes a sigh of relief and Figaro despairs. The Count agrees with the verdict, no doubt with a private gloat, and Bartolo rejoices. Figaro refuses to marry Marcellina without the consent of his 'noble' parents. They have yet to be found, even though he has been searching for them for ten years. Figaro recounts how he was stolen by gypsies as a child; moreover, his nobility is proved by the precious jewels and clothes which the thieves found on his person, and in particular by a mark on his right arm. Marcellina cries out: it is he, Raffaello. Who? Bartolo announces that Marcellina is Figaro's mother, and Marcellina that Bartolo is his father. **No. 18 SEXTET** (Andante. F major. Marcellina: 'Riconosci in questo amplesso') The moment of reconciliation has come. Marcellina, Bartolo and Figaro rejoice; the Count and Don Curzio are amazed. Clearly Figaro cannot marry his own mother. The music moves to the dominant. Susanna enters with money to pay Figaro's debt and sees him embracing Marcellina. She assumes the worst and boxes his ears. However, as the music resolves back to F major Marcellina explains everything to Susanna. Susanna, Figaro, Marcellina and Bartolo are ecstatic – they now have some of the most glorious music in the opera – while the Count and Don Curzio are furious and leave. **Scene 6** (Recitative) Marcellina and Bartolo are reconciled and will marry today, making it a double wedding. She gives Figaro the contract as a wedding present, Susanna gives him the money with which she had planned to pay the debt, and Bartolo hands over a purse. Susanna decides to tell the Countess and Antonio, and all leave rejoicing. The Count can whistle for all they care. **Scene 7** Barbarina takes Cherubino to her house. He is worried that the Count will catch him out yet again, but Barba-

rina tells the page to trust her: she will dress him up as a girl and they and their friends will go to present flowers to the Countess.
Scene 8 No. 19 ACCOMPANIED RECITATIVE (Andante, etc., 'E Susanna non vien! Sono ansiosa') Now it is the Countess's turn for an accompanied recitative. Alone, she wonders why Susanna has not yet come with news of the assignation with the Count. She fears that the endeavour is too bold, but there seems little harm in her exchanging clothes with Susanna. See how her husband's cruelty forces her to resort to such measures. **ARIA** (Andante–Allegro. C major. 'Dove sono i bei momenti') In the opening slow section, the Countess laments the passing of happier days, but as the setting moves to its faster conclusion, she finds resolve in the thought that her constancy will change his heart. Again, we shall be exploring the emotional and musical implications of this aria in Chapter 7. However, at last the Countess has decided to take firm control of events – 'I take full responsibility for everything' she says in her next scene with Susanna – and her new self-possession will undoubtedly bring its reward. She leaves.
Scene 9 (Recitative) The Count and Antonio enter, and the gardener tells him that Cherubino is still in the castle, offering his hat as proof. The page is being dressed up as a girl in Barbarina's room. They go off to find him. **Scene 10** Susanna tells the Countess of the events of the trial and the discovery of Figaro's real parents. The Count, she says, was furious. The Countess asks about the assignation and decides to write a letter fixing a place for the meeting. **No. 20 DUET** (Allegretto. B flat major. Countess: 'Che soave zeffiretto') The Countess asserts her new-found control by dictating to Susanna a letter to the Count: they will meet by the pine trees in the woods. This marvellous duet became one of the most popular pieces in the opera. Significantly, it is in $\frac{6}{8}$ metre, but not the rustic $\frac{6}{8}$ of the peasant choruses (Nos. 8, 21). Here we have a more sophisticated $\frac{6}{8}$ writing with longer phrases and a more subtle melodic construction (see also Susanna's 'Deh vieni non tardar, oh gioia bella', No. 27, and the duet 'Pace, pace, mio dolce tesoro' for Figaro and Susanna in the Act IV finale, No. 28). In all these examples, a lower-class musical *topos* is refined as the servants themselves transcend their class to achieve their own kind of nobility. (Recitative) The Countess and Susanna decide to seal the letter with a pin, which the Count will return as a sign of acceptance. Susanna says that this seal is even more bizarre than that of the page's commission. Hearing someone coming, she hides the letter.

Scene 11 No. 21 CHORUS (Grazioso. G major. 'Ricevete, oh padroncina') Barbarina enters with a chorus of girls, including Cherubino in disguise. They are bringing flowers to the Countess and sing her praises. (Recitative) The Countess is charmed, especially by one of the girls who, according to Barbarina, is a cousin who arrived yesterday for the wedding. The Countess receives a bouquet from the 'cousin' and kisses her. Does she not remind Susanna of someone, asks the Countess. Certainly. . .**Scene 12** The Count and Antonio enter, with the gardener carrying Cherubino's hat. He creeps up behind the mysterious 'cousin', takes off her bonnet and replaces it with the hat. Cherubino stands before them: again he is in the wrong place at the wrong time. The Count questions the Countess, who is equally surprised and angry. She admits that she and Susanna were dressing him in a similar fashion that morning. The Count threatens to punish Cherubino's disobedience, but before the whole company Barbarina reminds the Count of all the promises he made while kissing her: 'If you love me', he would say, 'I will give you all that you ask.' So she says that if she may marry Cherubino, she will love the Count just as she loves her little kitten. Antonio remarks that his daughter has obviously learnt her lessons well, while the Count can only wonder at his devilish bad luck.

Scene 13 Figaro enters. If the girls are detained much longer, the festivities and dancing will never begin. But, asks the Count, how can Figaro dance with an injured foot? Figaro proclaims himself cured, trying out a little dance. The Countess senses danger, but Susanna trusts Figaro to retrieve the situation. The Count and Antonio lead Figaro on about the events of earlier in the day – did Figaro jump out of the window, has Cherubino gone to Seville, did the page give Figaro the commission? Figaro confirms it all only to be confronted by the page, who, says the Count, has admitted jumping into the garden. 'Well', says Figaro, 'if I jumped, so could he.' **No. 22 FINALE No. 22.1** (Marcia. C major. Figaro: 'Ecco la marcia, andiamo') A march is heard in the distance and Figaro orders everyone to their places. Once again he is 'orchestrating' events, and as at the end of Act I, he does so to the sound of a march. He takes Susanna's arm. The Countess, still anxious, urges the Count to receive the two wedding couples. The Count sits down reluctantly, meditating revenge.

Scene 14 The wedding procession enters, with young girls carrying bridal hats with white feathers, veils, gloves and bouquets. Bartolo leads Susanna to the Count, and Figaro leads Marcellina to the

Countess. The two women kneel. **No. 22.2** (Allegretto. C major. Two girls: 'Amanti costanti') Two girls, and then the chorus, sing in praise of the Count for his magnanimity in renouncing the *droit de seigneur.* **No. 22.3** (Andante. A minor) The company begin to dance a fandango, for which Mozart borrowed a melody from Gluck's ballet *Don Juan* (Vienna, 1761), although it seems to have had still earlier Spanish origins.[7] Its minor mode and irregular phrases cast a curious shadow over events onstage. While kneeling before the Count, Susanna manages to pass him the letter. He hides it in his jacket as Susanna rises and goes to dance with Figaro. The Count moves aside to read the letter and pricks his finger on the pin. He complains that women stick pins everywhere and drops it on the ground before realising its significance. He searches for the pin and hides it in his sleeve. Figaro, seeing the whole episode, remarks gleefully to Susanna on the foolishness of the Count's receiving a love-letter. **No. 22.4** (Maestoso. Count: 'Andate, amici, e sia per questa sera') In solemn recitative, the Count orders the wedding festivities to be prepared for the evening, with music, fireworks, dancing and a banquet. Everyone will see how he treats those whom he favours. **No. 22.5** (Allegretto. C major. Chorus: 'Amanti costanti') The chorus repeats its praise of the magnanimous Count.

Act IV

A garden-clearing in the evening; one pavilion to the left, another to the right.[8] The 'folle journée' is nearing its end. We move from the castle into a garden, from daylight to twilight, and into a world ruled by Cherubino-Amore. The pastoral dances of the earlier acts (for example, the musette-gavotte in the Act II finale and the $\frac{6}{8}$ pastorale of 'Che soave zeffiretto', No. 20) reach their fruition here, and much of the music of Act IV has pastoral overtones. This pastoral world is a neutral space where characters of different social stations can meet, exchange roles and coexist as equals.[9] Moreover, the darkness creates a world of error and delusions that will be dispelled only by the enlightenment of the final scene.

Scene 1 No. 23 CAVATINA (Andante. F minor. 'L'ho perduta, me meschina') Barbarina enters carrying a lantern and searching the ground. She has lost something: it is not yet clear what. This short aria was a late addition to the opera: apparently Mozart needed to be sure that the young Anna Gottlieb (later the first Pamina) would be able to cope with a solo piece. However, it establishes perfectly the curiously bitter-sweet tone of the last act.

Scene 2 (Recitative) Figaro enters with Marcellina and questions Barbarina. She reveals that she has dropped the pin which the Count gave her to deliver to Susanna. Although she has been sworn to secrecy, Figaro wheedles the story out of her and establishes that it is indeed the pin which sealed the letter passed to the Count at the dance. He dismisses the matter until Barbarina leaves. **Scene 3** Left alone with Marcellina, Figaro is desolate. She urges caution, for Figaro cannot be sure what game Susanna is playing. He resolves to go to the rendezvous to see for himself and leaves in a rage, threatening revenge on behalf of all husbands.

Scene 4 Marcellina decides to warn Susanna and to take her side in the face of male injustice. **No. 24 ARIA** (Tempo di Menuetto–Allegro. G major. 'Il capro e la capretta') Why can humans not follow the example of the animals and live amicably with those of the opposite sex? Marcellina's aria is often omitted in modern performances because it is deemed redundant to the action. However, it does seem necessary to reinforce a character that has shifted awkwardly from being an enemy of Figaro and Susanna to being an ally.[10] The aria also emphasises the increasing importance of the women in the cast as the opera moves towards its conclusion. Marcellina leaves. **Scene 5** (Recitative) Barbarina enters. She is to meet Cherubino in the left pavilion, and has brought an orange, a pear and a bun, even if they did cost her a kiss from the servants. But she loves Cherubino and hopes that he will repay it. She hears someone coming and hides in the pavilion.

Scene 6 Figaro enters and notices Barbarina. Then Bartolo, Basilio and followers appear. They ask what is happening, but Basilio has already guessed: the Count and Susanna have got together without his help. Figaro tells them to lie in wait for his signal. All leave except Bartolo and Basilio. **Scene 7** Basilio explains the situation to Bartolo: Susanna pleases the Count, and she has given him an appointment of which Figaro disapproves. Bartolo asks whether Figaro must grin and bear it. Of course, says Basilio: it is dangerous to play games with one's masters, for they always win. **No. 25 ARIA** (Andante–Tempo di Menuetto–Allegro. B flat major. 'In quegl'anni, in cui val poco') Basilio recounts that in his youth he was as impetuous as Figaro, but with age he has learnt that it is always better to wear an ass's skin and to play the fool. Again, this aria is often omitted, although it is a fine piece that allows us to explore Basilio's character more fully. Basilio and Bartolo leave.

Scene 8 No. 26 ACCOMPANIED RECITATIVE (Andante. 'Tutto è disposto: l'ora') It is significant that Figaro now has an accompanied recitative to match that of the Count in Act III, even though he is not a 'noble' character (see above, pp. 60–1). As with Susanna's accompanied recitative later in this act (compare the Countess in Act III), we have another example of how Mozart allows the servants to rise to the musical level of their masters. Figaro is alone, the trap is set, and in the darkness he is to learn the true role of a husband. At the very moment of the wedding ceremony the Count read the letter and Figaro watched unknowingly. Susanna, Susanna, what torment she causes. It is madness to love any woman. **ARIA** (Moderato. E flat major. 'Aprite un po' quegl'occhi') Figaro upbraids the fickleness of women. The aria is a skilful evocation of jealousy – note the restive accompaniment and the uneven phrases in the vocal line – and at the end prominent horn fanfares again mock the potential cuckold ('il resto nol dico, già ognuno lo sa', 'I'll not talk about the rest: everyone knows it already'). He moves aside.

Scene 9 (Recitative) The Countess and Susanna, each wearing the other's clothes, enter with Marcellina. This is where Marcellina has said that Figaro would be, and there indeed he is. So, says Susanna, one is listening and the other is about to seek her out. Let the show commence. Marcellina hides in the left pavilion. **Scene 10** The Countess withdraws and Susanna decides to take the air. Figaro cannot see her, but he hears her voice and is furious. She decides to punish him for doubting her. **No. 27 ACCOMPANIED RECITATIVE** (Allegro vivace assai. 'Giunse alfin il momento') The moment has arrived and all cares must be banished, for love is in the air. **ARIA** (Andante. F major. 'Deh vieni non tardar, oh gioia bella') Let not the moment of joy delay any longer. Susanna's invocation, in a significant $\frac{6}{8}$ with a wonderfully phrased vocal line and given a pastoral air by pizzicato strings and prominent wind writing, provides a wonderful moment of repose between the fury of 'Aprite un po' quegl'occhi' and the Act IV finale. But its studied ambiguity is lost on Figaro.

Scene 11 (Recitative) Figaro has assumed that Susanna's aria was sung for the Count, and he curses her infidelity. Cherubino enters singing.[11] He has come to meet Barbarina but catches sight of the Countess, who he thinks, of course, is Susanna. **No. 28 FINALE** There follows a large-scale finale in seven sections. Dance rhythms are again prominent: indeed, the Count is quite literally led a dance, first a gavotte (No. 28.1) and then a contredanse (No. 28.2, compare

'Se a caso madama', No. 2). The contredanse is traditionally a peasant dance - see the example in the Act I finale of *Don Giovanni* - and it points up the ridicule of the Count's plebeian antics in his efforts to seduce 'Susanna'. **No. 28.1** (Andante. D major. Cherubino: 'Pian pianin le andrò più presso') The page decides to approach 'Susanna' and begins to woo her. She repulses him as Figaro, the Count and Susanna watch from a distance. Cherubino insists on kissing her; after all, the Count will get no less when he arrives. The Count moves forward and receives the kiss himself. Cherubino flees into the left pavilion. Figaro comes forward to see more clearly and finds himself at the receiving end of a blow from the Count intended for Cherubino. He retires to lick his wounds. **No. 28.2** (Con un poco più di moto. G major. Count: 'Partito è alfin l'audace') The Count approaches 'Susanna'. Figaro watches furiously, and he and Susanna comment separately on the scene. The Count offers 'Susanna' the dowry and a ring, and attempts to lead her into the left pavilion. In the dark? Well, he does not want to read in there! Figaro enters to disturb the couple, the Count leaves, and 'Susanna' moves into the right pavilion. **No. 28.3** (Larghetto. E flat major. Figaro: 'Tutto è tranquillo e placido') All is calm, but Figaro, a new Vulcan, will set the trap for his Venus and her Mars. **No. 28.4** (Allegro di molto. E flat major. Susanna 'Eh Figaro! tacete!') Susanna enters and adopts the manner of the Countess. Figaro explains the situation to her and then recognises Susanna's voice. He decides to turn the tables, kneels at her feet and pours out his passion for the 'Countess', singing a gloriously burlesque minuet with exaggerated end-accents ('Eccomi a vostri pie*di*, ho pieno il cor di fuo*co*. . .'). Susanna hits him furiously. **No. 28.5** (Andante. B flat major. Figaro: 'Pace, pace, mio dolce tesoro') Figaro explains to Susanna that he recognised her from the outset, and their sensuous melody in a sophisticated $\frac{6}{8}$ and with prominent parallel thirds signifies their reconciliation. The Count enters: he cannot find 'Susanna' anywhere. Susanna explains to Figaro that the Countess is dressed up as her and they decide to bring things to a conclusion. Figaro once again makes love to the 'Countess' in an extra-loud voice. They move towards the left pavilion as the Count fumes at his apparently faithless wife.

Scene 12 No. 28.6 (Allegro assai–Andante. G major. Count: 'Gente, gente! all'armi, all'armi!') The Count shouts for assistance, seizing Figaro by the arm. Susanna runs into the left pavilion. Antonio, Basilio and servants enter.[12] Their lighted torches illuminate the scene. The Count publicly accuses Figaro of seducing his wife.

Basilio and Antonio are surprised, and Figaro enjoys the general confusion. The Count grabs hold of whoever is in the pavilion and pulls. First Cherubino (again!) appears, then Barbarina, Marcellina and the 'Countess'. This is pure pantomime, but it is time for the slapstick comedy apparent throughout this finale to give way to something much more serious. The 'Countess' (i.e. Susanna) kneels before the Count and pleads forgiveness. He refuses. Figaro pleads; again the Count refuses. All plead; once more a refusal. The real Countess then comes out of the right pavilion – perhaps *she* can obtain the Count's forgiveness? The Count, Basilio and Antonio stammer their amazement and the pace suddenly slows as the Count kneels and asks forgiveness for himself. He had done so once before, in the Act II finale, but here the music raises the action to a new level: with the light has come true enlightenment. The Countess pardons him in a magical moment of translucent serenity. Everyone joins in her wish that all will end happily in a solemn hymn of rejoicing. Then a falling idea in the orchestra relaxes us into the final chorus. **No. 28.7** (Allegro assai. D major. All: 'Questo giorno di tormenti') The day of troubles and madness will finish in joy and contentment.

There is little doubt that the final order of pieces in *Figaro* was reached only in the course of the opera's composition, and that Mozart and da Ponte abbreviated and rearranged their original scheme. This seems especially to have been the case in Acts III and IV.[13] Full consideration of these changes lies outside the scope of this study, but some apparent alterations merit brief discussion. For example, at the end of Act III scene 7, the 1786 edition of the libretto contains the text of an arietta for Cherubino (see Plate 2):

Se così brami, teco verrò; so che tu m'ami, fidar mi vo.	If you so desire, I shall come with you; I know that you love me, I wish to trust [you].
Purchè il bel ciglio riveggia ancor, nessun periglio mi fa timor.	Providing that her fair brow I may see again, no danger makes me afraid.

The metre and rhyme-scheme are similar to 'Voi che sapete' (No. 11). The first stanza is addressed to Barbarina, and the second, marked 'a parte' ('aside'), refers to the Countess. This aria was apparently excised at a late stage, perhaps because of the effect such a static piece would have on the dramatic progression of the act.

Plate 1 *Orphea Taschenbuch* (1827), an engraving of the scene in the finale to Act IV

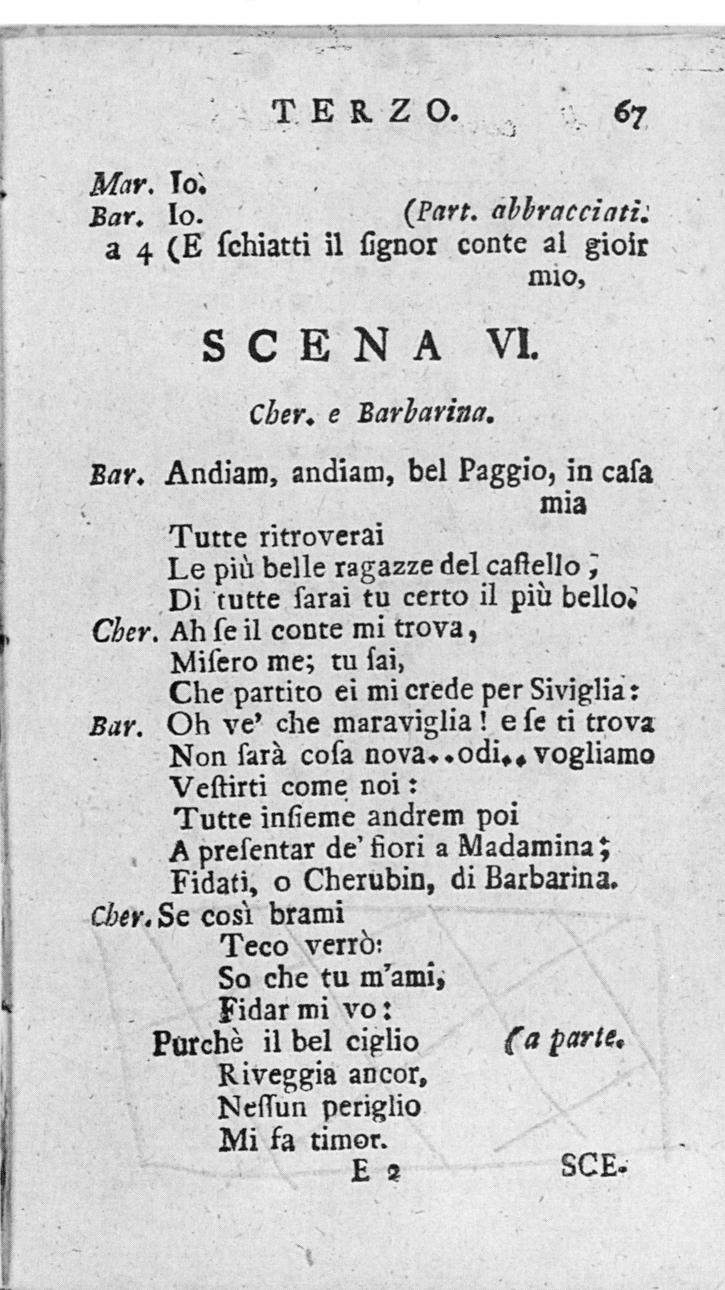

TERZO. 67

Mar. Io.
Bar. Io. (*Part. abbracciati.*
a 4 (E ſchiatti il ſignor conte al gioir mio,

SCENA VI.

Cher. e Barbarina.

Bar. Andiam, andiam, bel Paggio, in caſa mia
Tutte ritroverai
Le più belle ragazze del caſtello;
Di tutte ſarai tu certo il più bello.
Cher. Ah ſe il conte mi trova,
Miſero me; tu ſai,
Che partito ei mi crede per Siviglia:
Bar. Oh ve' che maraviglia! e ſe ti trova
Non ſarà coſa nova..odi.. vogliamo
Veſtirti come noi:
Tutte inſieme andrem poi
A preſentar de' fiori a Madamina;
Fidati, o Cherubin, di Barbarina.
Cher. Se così brami
Teco verrò:
So che tu m'ami,
Fidar mi vo:
Purchè il bel ciglio (*a parte.*
Riveggia ancor,
Neſſun periglio
Mi fa timor.
E 2 SCE-

Plate 2 *Le nozze di Figaro*, libretto (1786), p. 67, showing the excised arietta for Cherubino in Act III scene 6 (i.e. 7)

Similarly, Act IV scene 10 – Susanna's accompanied recitative and aria – seems to have caused the composer and librettist some problems. Susanna's accompanied recitative 'Giunse alfin il momento' was originally somewhat longer and more clumsily worded:[14]

Giunse il momento alfine	At last the moment comes
che godrò senz'affanno	which I shall enjoy without anxiety
in braccio a l'idol mio	in the arms of my beloved.
Timide cure, partite dal mio petto,	Timid cares, leave my breast,
a turbar non venite il mio diletto.	do not come to disturb my delight.
Oh come in questo istante	O, how in this instant
tutto ad amor risponde;	everything responds to love;
l'aura che tra le fronde	the breeze which among the leaves
dolce sospira, il cielo	sweetly sighs, the sky,
che del placido velo della notte	which with the peaceful veil of the night
copre l'amato amante e i furti miei,	covers my dear beloved and my own deceits,
e nel suo grato orrore	and in its welcome darkness
a trasporti di gioia invita il core.	invites the heart to transports of joy.

This led to a 'Rondò' for which we have the following, perhaps partial, text:

Non tardar, amato bene,	Do not delay, my dear beloved,
vieni, vola al seno mio,	come, fly to my breast,
a finir le lunghe pene,	to end these long torments,
a dar tregua a' miei sospir.	to give respite to my sighs.
Giusto ciel! perchè mai tardi,	Just heavens! why do you delay,
è sì lento il tuo desir?	is your desire so slow?
Crederò che tu non ardi	I shall believe that you do not burn
se mi fai così languir.	if you make me languish thus.

The texts are not as ambiguous as in the final versions: the recitative refers to 'l'idol mio' and 'l'amato amante', and the aria is addressed to Susanna's 'amato bene' rather than 'gioia bella'. Sketches for the music of the recitative and rondò survive. The latter is in E flat major and begins with the two-upbeat 'gavotte' pattern that appears in other such arias by Mozart. The sketch for the rondò covers only the first slower section (in ABA form): presumably there would have been a faster second section to a third strophe of the text. Again, one can only speculate on whether the change to 'Deh vieni non tardar, oh gioia bella' (in F major) was made for dramatic or musical reasons, or because of the demands of the singers. An extended rondò might have been appropriate for Susanna dressed as the Countess, but it would perhaps have caused problems of pacing in an act that already suffers from an excess of arias. Moreover, the elegant simplicity of 'Deh vieni non tardar, oh gioia bella', with its beautifully managed erotic tinges, inevitably seems better suited to the character and situation. However, 'Deh vieni non tardar, oh gioia bella' was not composed without difficulty, as sketches for the vocal line and alterations in the autograph score reveal.[15]

There are a number of problems in defining an accurate musical text of the opera. The score in the old complete edition of Mozart's works (L. von Köchel and others (eds.), *W. A. Mozarts Werke* (Leipzig, Breitkopf & Härtel, 1877–83), series V, vol. 17 (1879)) can no longer be regarded as definitive. Performers should consult the edition by Finscher in the *Neue Mozart-Ausgabe*, or at second best, the miniature score edited by Gerber. Both make significant corrections to the 1879 edition, whether in terms of wrong notes, tempo indications or articulation markings. Only two particular problems can be discussed here, relating to passages in 'Susanna or via sortite' (No. 13) and 'Aprite, presto aprite' (No. 14).[16] In No. 13, two scalic ascents, the first to *g″* (bars 51–3) and the second to *c‴* (bars 115–17, repeated in 130–2), are variously given to the Countess (by Gerber and Finscher) and to Susanna (in Dent's vocal score, following the 1879 edition). The choice of one or the other also necessitates some rearrangement of the two soprano lines in the bars immediately preceding each run. Mozart himself changed his mind – the runs were given first to the Countess and then to Susanna – perhaps after working on the trio with Luisa Laschi (the first Countess) and Nancy Storace (the first Susanna): indeed there are several cases in the opera where Mozart seems to have switched their parts. Producers will have to decide whether to return to Mozart's original conception or to accept the changes he apparently made in rehearsal: in terms of the drama, one can argue in favour of either solution. In No. 14, bars 13–16, 28–9 and 37–40 are often omitted in performance (and are not present in Dent's vocal score, following the 1879 edition). These cuts are indicated in the autograph, but it is not clear whether the markings are by Mozart and on balance they seem unjustified.

Finally, there is the question of the ordering of Act III. Robert

Moberly and Christopher Raeburn have identified a number of problems in the action here.[17] First, the trial scene must be deemed to take place within scene 4, the Count's accompanied recitative and aria (No. 17). This is a short space of time and one might even expect the Count to be in court. Second, scene 7 reveals that Cherubino is to be dressed as a girl, and by scene 9 Antonio has already discovered that plot and seen Cherubino in his disguise. Third, one would expect Susanna to inform the Countess of the result of her meeting the Count in scene 2 immediately after scene 3 (in the play she actually announces her intention of doing so, see the extract given on p. 41 above), but in scene 8 the Countess remarks that Susanna has not yet been to see her. Nor is it clear when, and from where, Susanna gets the money to pay Figaro's debt (in the play, she says that the money came from the Countess). Fourth, at the end of scene 6, Susanna resolves to tell the Countess of the discovery of Figaro's parents in scene 5, but she does so only in scene 10, after the Countess's 'Dove sono i bei momenti' (No. 19). Fifth, it is rather unkind to the singer to have the Countess sing 'Dove sono i bei momenti' and 'Che soave zeffiretto' (No. 20) one after the other.

To counter these problems, Moberly and Raeburn suggest that Mozart and da Ponte first planned to have the Count's aria and the reconciliation scene (Don Curzio: 'È decisa la lite. . .') separated by the short recitative scene between Barbarina and Cherubino and then the Countess's accompanied recitative and aria. Thus the original order was scenes 4, 7, 8, 5, 6, 9, 10. However, at the end of scene 6 Bartolo leaves, and at the beginning of scene 9 Antonio enters. At the first performance, Bartolo and Antonio were played by the same singer, Francesco Bussani. Therefore Mozart and da Ponte had to make a late change to the order of scenes in the act to allow time for Bussani to change his costume. But given that Bartolo and Antonio are now normally played by two singers, Moberly and Raeburn see no reason why producers should not revert to the 'original' order.

Their hypothetical scheme would remove most of the difficulties listed above. Admittedly, the source of the money is still unclear, but Susanna has time to see the Countess after 'Dove sono i bei momenti' and before her entry in the middle of the sextet. Another benefit is that the key scheme of this part of the act will move more straightforwardly through a circle of fifths: 'Dove sono i bei momenti' in C major, 'Riconosci in questo amplesso' in F major, and 'Che soave zeffiretto' in B flat major. However, Alan Tyson has noted that the layout of the autograph score precludes the possibility of there having been a late change in the order due to particular problems in casting.[18] This seriously undermines the case for reorganising the present Act III, however attractive it may seem.

5 *Verse and music in Le nozze di Figaro*

Leopold Mozart had been wary of his son's plans for *Le mariage de Figaro*:

I know the piece; it is a very tiresome play and the translation from the French will certainly have to be altered very freely if it is to be effective as an opera. God grant that the text may be a success. I have no doubt about the music. But there will be a lot of running about and discussions before he gets the libretto so adjusted as to suit his purposes exactly.[1]

As we have seen, the play was not altered quite as freely as Mozart's father feared. Much of the play remains intact, and it is clear that the dramatic strength of *Le nozze di Figaro* is due in no small part to the taut construction of its model. In fact, although da Ponte had a fine sense of what would work on the operatic stage, he was probably better at adapting pre-existing works than writing new ones. His first stage efforts (in 1779) included translations of a German tragedy, a French tragedy (J. F. de la Harpe's *Le comte de Warwick*), and portions of Philippe Quinault's *Atys*. Many of his libretti for Vienna were also adaptations, including *Il burbero di buon cuore* (1786, after Carlo Goldoni's *Le bourru bienfaisant*), *Una cosa rara o sia Bellezza ed onestà* (1786, after Luis Vélez de Guevara's *La luna della sierra*), *Gli equivoci* (1786, from Shakespeare's *The Comedy of Errors*), and *Il dissoluto punito o sia il Don Giovanni* (1787, after Giovanni Bertati's libretto *Il convitato di pietra*).[2] The fact that da Ponte was more gifted at adaptation may partly explain why *Figaro* seems to falter in the later acts as the libretto deviates increasingly from the play, whether to compress the action, to have an appropriate number of arias, or to accommodate the changes made to the characters.

No doubt there was 'a lot of running about and discussions' between da Ponte and Mozart before the final text of the libretto was prepared. No details of these discussions survive, but presumably they did more than cover the treatment of the plot. Mozart would also have been concerned with how da Ponte cast his verse: convention decreed that a librettist should employ different types of verse at various points in a libretto depending on whether the text was for a recitative, aria or ensemble. Recitative texts are normally in free-rhyming seven- and eleven-syllable lines, while texts for arias and ensembles have more regular metrical and rhyming structures, with a wider choice of line-lengths and some measure of strophic organisation. Thus the librettist's use of verse, whether or not pre-arranged with the composer, will influence the musical structure of the opera and even the fine detail of the setting. As we shall see, da Ponte's carefully crafted text makes skilful use of poetic procedures that have clear musical implications. An examination of these procedures reveals a remarkable interaction between verse and music throughout *Figaro*. It also suggests an approach to opera that may have considerable potential for future analytical enquiry.

It may be useful to review some basic principles of Italian versification. The quality of Italian verse is dictated by line-length (number of syllables) and accentuation. A line of verse may be one of three types according to the position of the main accent. The *verso piano*, the most common, has its main accent on the penultimate syllable, producing a feminine (trochaic) ending to the line:

Vedrò mentre io so*spi*ro

The *verso tronco* has its main accent on the last syllable, producing a masculine (iambic) ending to the line:

ei posseder dov*rà*?

The *verso sdrucciolo* has its main accent on the antepenultimate syllable, producing a dactylic ending to the line:

e forse ancor per *ri*dere

In counting up the syllables of a line, it is necessary to take into account elisions and diphthongs. Diphthongs may be counted as one or two syllables depending on their context. Thus 'Ve/drò/ men/tre io/ so/spi/ro' is a seven-syllable line, with an elision between 'mentre io' and the diphthong 'io' counted as one syllable.

The immediate benefits of paying close attention to the verse structure of da Ponte's libretto are best demonstrated by analysing his handling of one scene. In Act I scene 2, Figaro is left alone onstage to muse over Susanna's revelation that the Count's intentions towards her are less than honourable. His speech divides into a recitative and an aria (called a 'cavatina' in the score): in the former,

Figaro thinks through the problem; in the latter, he resolves upon a course of action:

Bravo, signor padrone! Ora incomincio
a capir il mistero. . . e a veder schietto
tutto il vostro progetto. A Londra, è vero?
Voi ministro, io corriero, e la Susanna. . .
secreta ambasciatrice.
Non sarà, non sarà: Figaro il dice.

Bravo, my lord and master! Now I begin
to understand the mystery. . . and to see clearly
your whole scheme. To London, is it?
You as minister, I as courier, and Susanna. . .
private attaché.
It shall not be, it shall not be: Figaro says so.

Se vuol ballare,
signor Contino,
il chitarrino
le suonerò.

If you wish to dance,
my dear little Count,
the guitar
will I play for you.

Se vuol venire
nella mia scuola,
la capriola
le insegnerò.

If you wish to come
to my school,
the capriole
will I teach you.

Saprò. . . ma piano,
meglio ogni arcano
dissimulando
scoprir potrò.

I'll know. . . but soft,
better every secret
by dissembling
can I discover.

L'arte schermendo,
l'arte adoprando,
di qua pungendo,
di là scherzando,
tutte le macchine
rovescierò.

Acting by stealth,
acting openly,
thrusting here,
teasing there,
all your plans
will I overthrow.

(Se vuol ballare,
signor Contino,
il chitarrino
le suonerò.)

(If you wish to dance,
my dear little Count,
the guitar
will I play for you.)

For the recitative, da Ponte provides appropriately weighty eleven-syllable lines: the one seven-syllable line ('secreta ambasciatrice') is carefully placed, with an ironic hesitation, to underline Susanna's 'position' in London. However, given Figaro's anger, one would not expect him to speak in elegant verse. Thus da Ponte exploits enjambment in the first lines of the speech, and internal rhymes ('mistero. . .

vero. . .corriero', 'schietto. . .progetto') mark caesuras and break up the text into fragmentary phrases. The elisions between these phrases are in effect ignored, precisely as occurs in Mozart's setting. The aria consists of five-syllable *versi piani*, with rhymed *versi tronchi* to mark off the strophic divisions. The structure of the text matches its content, where fury is first contained and then released. The first three quatrains suggest a regular strophic pattern only to have this pattern destroyed by the succeeding sestet, which also delays the arrival of the *verso tronco*. The rhyme-scheme established in the first two quatrains (*ABBC*) is altered in the third (rhyming *AABC*) and gives way to alternating rhymes in the sestet. Similarly, in terms of the syntax, the two-line groupings of the first two quatrains are avoided in the third (where the strophe divides into one plus three lines) and are replaced by one-line groupings in the sestet. By manipulating metre, rhyme and syntax, da Ponte drives forward to the last line of the sestet, 'rovescierò'. This *verso tronco*, one word instead of two as in the other *versi tronchi*, is rendered all the more forceful by the immediately preceding *verso sdrucciolo*, 'tutte le *mac*chine'. All these poetic devices emphasise the cumulative fury of Figaro's ejaculations.

There is a close relationship between the text of 'Se vuol ballare' and Mozart's music. The accentuation of da Ponte's five-syllable lines (1 2 3 4̀ 5) strongly suggests the minuet pattern adopted by Mozart. Divisions in the musical structure correspond to the strophic divisions of the text, and the *versi tronchi* become significant cadence points for the composer (the iambic endings of *versi tronchi* are more suited to cadences from weak to strong beats than the trochaic endings of *versi piani*). Furthermore, Mozart responds to the contrasts in content and structure of the sestet by changing tempo and metre. However, there are some aspects of Mozart's setting that do not seem attributable to da Ponte, including Figaro's assertive 'sì' in the first and second strophes, and the pointed repetitions of individual words ('Saprò', 'piano') in the third. Nor is it clear who decided to end the aria with a sardonic repeat of the text and music of the first strophe before the final burst of fury in the orchestral postlude.

This discussion has established some useful lines of enquiry upon which any further analysis of the libretto can be based. The free-rhyming seven- and eleven-syllable lines that constitute recitative verse admit a flexibility that befits its dramatic and musical function. However, although recitative texts are relatively unstructured, da

Ponte often carefully exploits line-length and rhyme for comic effect. A fine example occurs in Act I scene 7 after the trio 'Cosa sento! tosto andate' (No. 7), where the Count questions Cherubino discovered hiding in Susanna's chair:

Count:	Ma s'io stesso m'assisi quando in camera entrai!	But if I sat there myself when I came into the room!
Cherubino:	Ed allora di dietro io mi celai.	And then I hid myself behind it.
Count:	E quando io là mi posi?	And when I moved there?
Cherubino:	Allor io pian mi volsi e qui m'ascosi.	Then I softly crept round and hid here.
Count:	Oh ciel! dunque ha sentito[3] quello ch'io ti dicea!	Heavens! Then he has heard what I said to you!
Cherubino:	Feci per non sentir quanto potea.	I did as much as I could not to hear.

Here da Ponte's witty rhymes are complemented by the careful juxtaposition of seven- and eleven-syllable lines, with short lines for the Count's exclamations and long lines for the replies of the precocious page. Similarly, single lines of verse are often subdivided between one or more characters to point up fast-moving dialogue, the comic effect of which can again be enhanced by rhyme, as in this extract from Act III scene 5:

Marcellina:	Una spatola impressa al braccio destro. . .?	A spatula on your right arm. . .?
Figaro:	E a voi chi 'l disse?	And who told you that?
Marcellina:	Oddio, è egli. . .	Oh Lord, it is he. . .
Figaro:	È ver, son io.	It's true, I am me.
Don Curzio:	Chi?	Who?
Count:	Chi?	Who?
Bartolo:	Chi?	Who?
Marcellina:	Raffaello.	Raffaello.
Bartolo:	E i ladri ti rapir. . .?	And robbers kidnapped you. . .?
Figaro:	Presso un castello.	Near a castle.
Bartolo:	Ecco tua madre.	Behold your mother.
Figaro:	Balia?	Nurse?
Bartolo:	No, tua madre.	No, your mother.
Count; *Don Curzio*:	Sua madre!	His mother!

Figaro:	Cosa sento!	What do I hear!
Marcellina:	Ecco tuo padre.	Behold your father.

This careful use of poetic techniques becomes even more important in the arias and ensembles, where the metre and rhyme-scheme of da Ponte's texts often have quite specific musical implications. Different line-lengths can be exploited for dramatic or rhetorical effect: note the gushing ten-syllable lines of the first part of Cherubino's 'Non so più cosa son, cosa faccio' (No. 6) as the page blurts out his adolescent cravings, or the frequent *versi sdruccioli* in the middle section of Bartolo's 'La vendetta, oh la vendetta!' (No. 4) to point up the doctor's blustering invective. These various line-lengths also limit the melodic patterns available to the composer, as we have seen with the five-syllable lines of 'Se vuol ballare', and it seems possible that Mozart may sometimes have requested lines of a particular length to match a musical idea.[4] The regular masculine endings, which are often rhymed, have a bearing on the structure of both the text and the music: witness their importance for the cadences. They may also have some significance in terms of characterisation. In 'Aprite un po' quegl'occhi' (No. 26), the masculine rhyme changes from the soft '-on' through '-ar' to the harsh '-à' to match Figaro's increasing anger as the aria progresses. On the other hand, Susanna's 'Deh vieni non tardar, oh gioia bella' (No. 27) is exceptional in being entirely without *versi tronchi*. Here the flowing *versi piani*, in luxurious eleven-syllable rhyming couplets, give the text a rhapsodic quality that was to be matched by the music.

Da Ponte's aria texts range from single stanzas (Nos. 10, 23) through regular strophic groupings (Nos. 11, 19, 24) to more complex structures. Many of the larger-scale arias are variants of the format already seen in 'Se vuol ballare'. Two quatrains, each with similar metre and rhyme-scheme, lead to a section (often employing a contrasted line-length and rhyming couplets or alternating rhymes) ranging from six to seventeen lines. This middle section ends with a *verso tronco* and may be followed by a final envoi (often a couplet or quatrain) with the same line-length and masculine rhyme as the middle section. A good example is provided by Cherubino's 'Non so più cosa son, cosa faccio' (No. 6, compare Nos. 4, 9, 12, 17, 25, 26; a translation is given on p. 44):

> Non so più cosa son, cosa faccio,
> or di fuoco, ora sono di ghiaccio,
> ogni donna cangiar di colore,
> ogni donna mi fa palpitar.

Solo ai nomi d'amor di diletto,
mi si turba, mi s'altera il petto,
e a parlare mi sforza d'amore
un desio ch'io non posso spiegar.

Parlo d'amor vegliando,
parlo d'amor sognando,
all'acque, all'ombre, ai monti,
ai fiori, all'erbe, ai fonti,
all'eco, all'aria, ai venti,
che il suon de' vani accenti
portano via con se. . .

E se non ho chi m'oda,
parlo d'amor con me.

This format is well suited to the lively exhortation or vengeance aria, where the quatrains set the scene and the middle section contains quick-fire comments or accusations, leading to a climax in the envoi.

Mozart clearly responds to the formal and stylistic implications of these aria patterns, just as we have seen in 'Se vuol ballare'. 'Dove sono i bei momenti' (No. 19) and 'Il capro e la capretta' (No. 24) each have three quatrains, and in both cases the third quatrain is set to a faster tempo. A close correlation between verse and music is equally apparent in the larger-scale arias structured as 'Non so più cosa son, cosa faccio'. All these arias (Nos. 4, 6, 9, 12, 17, 25, 26) begin with two quatrains. In each case, the end of the first quatrain (often the first *verso tronco*) marks a significant point in the musical structure, with a firm cadence in the tonic (Nos. 6, 9, 12, 25, 26) or on the dominant (Nos. 4, 17). With the second quatrain comes a new section in the dominant or, in the case of Nos. 4 and 17, on the dominant of the dominant. This similarity between No. 4 (Bartolo's 'La vendetta, oh la vendetta!') and No. 17 (the Count's 'Vedrò mentre io sospiro') is striking given that they are both 'revenge' arias (and see below, pp. 113–15). Since the middle sections of all these arias are often contrasted in content and line-length, Mozart normally changes his style of delivery accordingly, sometimes moving into more declamatory 'patter'. The *verso tronco* at the end of the middle section is generally emphasised by a firm cadence, leaving the setting of the envoi to act as a coda. If reference is made to the opening musical material in this coda, the music designed for the line-length of the first quatrain must often be adapted to the new line-length of the middle section and envoi (Ex. 4).

Only rarely does Mozart deviate significantly from the structural implications of da Ponte's aria texts, and when he does so it is

Ex. 4 'La vendetta, oh la vendetta!' (No. 4)

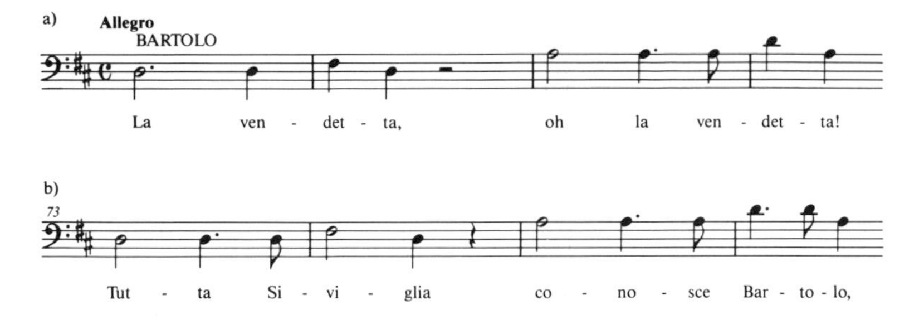

presumably for a reason. In Figaro's 'Non più andrai farfallone amoroso' (No. 9), Mozart repeats and reorders parts of the text to produce an extended rondo with a long coda: perhaps he wanted an emphatic conclusion to Act I.[5] In Cherubino's 'Voi che sapete' (No. 11), the text consists of seven four-line stanzas (plus a repeat of the first) with a regular rhyme-scheme. This simple structure matches that of the song's equivalent in the play, 'Mon coursier hors d'haleine', and it is clearly appropriate for a set-piece canzonet. One would expect Mozart's setting to be strophic, with the same music repeated for each stanza. Instead, it is through-composed: the page is more artful (or just confused?) than the naïve text suggests.[6] Nevertheless, the organisation of the text clearly influences the musical structure (with successive strophes beginning in bars 9, 21, 29, 37, 45, 52, 56, 62).

Da Ponte's ensemble texts emphasise still further the importance for the composer of regular line-lengths, carefully managed rhyme-schemes and recurring masculine endings. Giving each character lines of the same length encourages balanced phrase structures and allows these lines to be presented simultaneously when necessary, the presence or absence of rhyme can indicate agreement or disagreement, and the masculine endings, which again are often rhymed, serve a structural function.

Perhaps the simplest example is the duet 'Crudel! perchè finora' (No. 16):

Count:	Crudel! perchè finora farmi languir così?	Cruel one, why have you so far caused me to languish?
Susanna:	Signor, la donna ognora tempo ha di dir di sì	My lord, a woman always takes time to say yes.
Count:	Dunque in giardin verrai?	Then you will come to the garden?

Susanna:	Se piace a voi, verrò.	If it pleases you, I will come.
Count:	E non mi mancherai?	And you will not fail me?
Susanna:	No, non vi mancherò.	No, I will not fail you.
Count:	Mi sento dal contento	At this delight I feel
	pieno di gioia il cor.	my heart full of joy.
Susanna:	Scusatemi se mento,	Forgive me if I lie,
	voi che intendete amor.	you who understand love.

The text (in seven-syllable lines) consists of three quatrains, each with its own masculine rhyme ('-ì', '-ò', '-or'). This matches the three stages of the action: interrogation, arrangement of assignation, and reaction. The line-endings help to characterise the comments of the protagonists. For example, in the second quatrain, where the Count and Susanna have alternate lines, the feminine endings of the Count's questions are firmly answered by Susanna's masculine '-ò' endings. Furthermore, the insinuating '-ai' rhymes well match the Count's intentions and are complemented by the suave melodic lines of Mozart's setting. However, at least one feature of this setting does not seem attributable to da Ponte. Mozart indulges in a delicious 'yes–no' game as Susanna muddles her answers to the Count. This lies outside the metrical scheme of the verse and thus is probably Mozart's invention. There are other examples in the opera of phrases which, for the same reason, may have been additions by Mozart: we have already noted the assertive 'sì' in 'Se vuol ballare' (No. 3), and see also 'Riconosci in questo amplesso' (No. 18, the 'figlio amato!'/ 'parenti amati!' interchange between Marcellina, Bartolo and Figaro) and the finales to Acts II and IV (Nos. 15, 28).

The procedures adopted in No. 16 are flexible enough to be worked on a larger scale, as for example in the Act I trio 'Cosa sento! tosto andate' (No. 7). Here the text consists of eight-syllable lines. Each of the three characters has an opening couplet in which to establish a position. Thereafter the verse falls into loosely organised two-, three- and four-line strophes each set off by rhymed *versi tronchi* ('e scacciate il seduttor', 'perdonate, o mio signor'. . .'ma da me sorpreso ancor'). Lines are sometimes subdivided between the characters in the manner already seen in the recitatives. At the point where the Count narrates his earlier discovery of Cherubino in Barbarina's room ('. . .Da tua cugina'), da Ponte uses *versi piani* alone, delaying the arrival of a *verso tronco* for some ten lines (until 'or capisco come va'). This enhances the suspense of the Count's narration and sets it apart. Mozart acts accordingly and treats these lines in a manner approaching accompanied recitative. Once Cherubino has been discovered in the chair, the masculine rhyme changes ('or capisco come va', 'giusti dei, che mai sarà', 'non c'è alcuna novità') as each character has a concluding couplet to express a reaction to the situation.

The change of masculine rhyme here is significant. In da Ponte's ensemble texts, such changes frequently occur at significant points in the action. So, too, do changes of line-length. The Act III sextet, 'Riconosci in questo amplesso' (No. 18), is a good example of how such shifts can relate to the prevailing dramatic situation:

(1)	Reconciliation of Marcellina, Bartolo and Figaro	8-syllable lines; masculine rhyme '-ir'
(2)	Susanna's entrance and anger	8-syllable lines; masculine rhyme '-à'
(3)	Explanation to Susanna and universal reaction	6-syllable lines; masculine rhyme '-à'

As we shall see, in the finales a change of line-length generally prompts Mozart to move into a new musical section with a change of tempo and/or metre. It would be intriguing if da Ponte similarly intended the Act III sextet to be in two musical sections. If so, Mozart overruled him, taking advantage of the dramatic parallels between the first and third sections (in the first, Marcellina explains the situation to Figaro, and in the third to Susanna) to create a single movement in sonata form (see Chapter 6). As a result, some of the musical material of the first section must be adapted to the new line-length of the third (compare Marcellina's melody and accompaniment in bars 1–5 with 74–80).

Of the three finales in *Figaro*, the one to Act III (No. 22) is unusual: the verse is in free-rhyming seven- and eleven-syllable lines, and only the duet and chorus 'Amanti costanti' has a regular metre and rhyme. It would appear that da Ponte intended the bulk of his text to be set as recitative, and that it was Mozart's decision to deliver this verse above the march and fandango suggested by the play. Recitative over a march has a precedent in *Idomeneo* (Electra's 'Odo da lunge armonioso suono' in Act II scene 5, No. 14), and recitative over a dance anticipates the first finale of *Don Giovanni*.[7] In the Act III finale of *Figaro*, Mozart transforms what seems to be a recitative–chorus–recitative scene in the libretto into a continuous musical whole.

For the finales to Acts II and IV (Nos. 15, 28), da Ponte provided texts more like those of the other ensembles. In Chapter 3 (pp. 43–4) we saw da Ponte's views on the dramatic problems posed by such finales and how Beaumarchais provided ready-made solutions. However, sectional finales also created difficulties in terms of versification, for the text had to be cast in a manner flexible enough to respond to changing dramatic situations while retaining some measure of structural integrity. The various sections of da Ponte's finales, as well as being marked out by the action and the number of characters onstage, are also distinguished by contrasts in metre and masculine rhyme. In moving from one musical section to another, Mozart was influenced by a change in verse structure as much as by dramatic considerations.[8]

The Act II finale is a fine example of da Ponte's technique (Table 3). The text is no less tautly conceived than Mozart's music. It falls into sections distinguished by line-length and/or masculine rhyme, and in those sections which have more than one masculine rhyme, the change marks a new direction in the action. Whether coincidentally or not, the final section also has the same line-length and masculine rhyme as the first. However, Mozart once again appears to override da Ponte in particular instances. For example, neither the verse nor the number of characters onstage justify the new start in sections 3 and 7. Here, Mozart seems to be reacting on his own initiative to changes in the dramatic situation.

It should now be apparent that da Ponte's verse shows a skilled hand and has clear musical implications. Some of these implications were followed by Mozart, and others were not. Whatever the case, an analysis of this verse illuminates, if not explains, a number of compositional decisions made by the composer. Two further points must be made. First, most of the techniques used by da Ponte in his libretto were the stock-in-trade of the eighteenth-century librettist. All the devices discussed here have clear precedents in the *opera buffa* libretti of Carlo Goldoni, and indeed many go back to the *opera seria* libretti of Metastasio and beyond. Second, as I have already suggested, it is quite possible that some of the examples of musical implications in da Ponte's verse are in fact attributable to the composer himself. The surviving correspondence concerning *Idomeneo* and *Die Entführung aus dem Serail* makes it clear that Mozart often harassed his librettists with detailed specifications (see above, p. 7), even, significantly enough, to the extent of requesting certain line-lengths and rhymes at particular points in the work.[9] Da Ponte also complained of similar, and in his view unreasonable, demands made upon him by some composers with whom he worked.[10] We have little information on the genesis of *Figaro*: one can only assume that Mozart's treatment of da Ponte was little different from that meted out to his earlier collaborators.

Table 3 *'Esci omai, garzon malnato' (Act II finale, No. 15)*

Section	Characters	Time signature	Tempo mark	Key	Line-length	Masculine rhyme
1	Count, Countess	C	Allegro	E flat major	8	-ar
2	Count, Countess, Susanna	$\frac{3}{8}$	Molto andante	B flat major	6	-à
3	Count, Countess, Susanna	C	Allegro	B flat major	6	-à -ar -à
4	Count, Countess, Susanna, Figaro	$\frac{3}{8}$	Allegro	G major	6	-ir
5	Count, Countess, Susanna, Figaro	$\frac{2}{4}$	Andante	C major	8	-ò -ir
6	Count, Countess, Susanna, Figaro, Antonio	C	Allegro molto	F major	10	-ù -ì -à -è
7	Count, Countess, Susanna, Figaro, Antonio	$\frac{6}{8}$	Andante	B flat major	10	-è
8	Count, Countess, Susanna, Figaro, Marcellina, Bartolo, Basilio	C	Allegro assai–Più allegro–Prestissimo	E flat major	8	-ar

But my aim has not been to stake a claim for da Ponte's originality in handling the libretto of *Figaro*. Nor do I assert his precedence over Mozart in determining the opera's musico-dramatic structure. Instead, I have sought to illustrate the benefits of an approach to opera that pays close attention to all aspects of the libretto. Much recent operatic criticism has tended to devalue the role of the librettist, emphasising instead the primacy of the composer. This stance has a long historical tradition, from Mozart's own comment 'in an opera the poetry must be altogether the obedient daughter of the music' (1781) to Joseph Kerman's claim that 'in opera, the dramatist is the composer' (1956).[11] Even da Ponte complained that 'in comic operas, the words are generally reckoned only as the frame of a beautiful picture which supports the canvas'.[12] Nevertheless, a librettist has a clearly defined task and, in a given period, particular techniques with which to fulfil that task. To ignore his contribution to an opera is to ignore the crucial interaction of word and music that distinguishes the best *dramme per musica*.

6 *Opera buffa and the Classical style: the Act I trio*

The fast-moving action of Beaumarchais's play made it an ideal source for a comic opera, and we have seen da Ponte's efforts to adapt his model to the needs of his composer. But all these efforts would have been to no avail were Mozart's musical style unable to cope with the demands of comedy. For example, a style best suited to the slow-moving presentation of rigorously ordered emotional states, as we find in Baroque *opera seria*, would scarcely have been right for *Le nozze di Figaro.* What are the characteristics of the Classical style, in particular Mozart's version of the Classical style, that made it so appropriate for *opera buffa*?[1]

It seems no coincidence that both the Classical style and *opera buffa* have their roots in Italy, and particularly Naples, in the first half of the eighteenth century. Just as the history of eighteenth-century *opera buffa* begins in Naples, so can we find stylistic features in the work of at least one Neapolitan composer, Domenico Scarlatti (1685–1757), that prefigure the Classical style adopted subsequently by other Italians and which eventually spread north to reach its peak in the works of the Viennese masters of the high Classical period. These features include a move away from the complex harmonic and contrapuntal textures of much Baroque music towards a simpler, melody-dominated style with clear-cut, regular phrase structures, more straightforward harmonies, and lighter textures. C. P. E. Bach (1714–88) deplored this shift in significant terms: 'I believe. . .that the present love for the comic accounts for this more than does anything else.'[2]

Charles Burney explained that these changes in style were the result of 'simplifying and polishing melody, and calling the attention of the audience chiefly to the voice-part, by disintangling it from fugue, complication and laboured contrivance'.[3] The Classical style, at least in its early stages, is essentially conceived in terms of melody and subordinate accompaniment. Melodies are made up of balanced but varied rhythms – unlike the repetitive rhythmic patterns of much Baroque music – and strongly articulated phrases that each drive melodically, rhythmically and harmonically towards a goal, the cadence. These regular phrases become building-blocks in the construction of large-scale musical structures. The style also allows for the presentation of strongly contrasted musical, and therefore emotional, ideas in close succession, in contrast to the Baroque technique where a movement generally adheres to a single emotional affect by elaborating upon a single musical idea.

The early Classical style appears much simpler than that of the high Baroque. It is also prone to cliché. But this need not be a weakness. The clichés of the Classical style facilitate a familiarity with its musical processes that can be turned to the composer's advantage. In a musical style with a high level of predictability, the unpredictable becomes much more musically and emotionally effective. Mozart was to become a master at playing musical games, leading us to expect one thing only to do something else. Moreover, the simplicity of the style brings into the foreground the tensions that exist within it. Classical harmony is generally more straightforward than that of the Baroque: it relies more on simple primary chords and stock cadential patterns. However, these primary chords, and the hierarchy of relationships that by convention exist between them, create tensions that require resolution. The unstable dominant chord needs to resolve to the stable tonic chord, as in the simple perfect (V–I) cadence. By extension, a phrase based on dominant harmony will be resolved by a phrase based on tonic harmony, and so on through themes to larger formal units. Tonality becomes a potent means of generating musical structure.

The creation and resolution of tensions by means of tonal relationships is a basic element of eighteenth-century musical syntax. It is also the essence of sonata form – or perhaps better, the sonata principle – on which a majority of Classical movements are based. Briefly stated, this principle relies on the fact that the juxtaposition of one firmly established key with another generates a structural tension that can only be resolved by a return to the first. Of course, Baroque composers were well aware of the need for tonal balance, but in the Baroque style keys are not primarily established as dissonant poles that create tension and demand resolution. In the Classical style, however, this is precisely how composers articulated their musical argument.

Movements constructed according to the sonata principle are

usually divided into three broad sections: the Exposition, Development and Recapitulation. The Exposition establishes a large-scale dissonance by allocating distinct formal units to two different keys, normally the tonic and dominant in a major-key movement (for example, C major and G major), and tonic and relative major in a minor-key movement (for example, C minor and E flat major). These units may or may not be distinguished by contrasted thematic material in the form of first and second subjects, and the tonal polarities will be emphasised more or less strongly depending on the scale of the movement. The Development prolongs the tonal dissonance of the Exposition by itself exploring tonally unstable areas, often, but not necessarily, with some development of the thematic ideas presented earlier. The Recapitulation resolves the tonal dissonance of the Exposition, first by beginning firmly in the tonic, and second and most important, by matching the dominant (or relative major) material of the Exposition with equivalent material in the tonic. The dominant (or relative major) is thus subjugated to the tonic, and the movement can now end with or without an extended flourish of cadential tonic harmony in a coda.

This explanation of the sonata principle as essentially a tonal process rather than a thematic mould emphasises the fact that its procedures are extremely adaptable and can operate even in contexts where an overt adherence to a clear formal outline is not readily apparent. We are accustomed to analysing nearly all first, many last and some slow movements of Classical instrumental works in terms of 'sonata form'. However, the sonata principle governs nearly all Classical instrumental and vocal forms. Furthermore, this exploitation of tonal conflict is an overtly dramatic procedure.

The opening of Mozart's Piano Quartet in G minor, K478, composed in October 1785 when he was also at work on *Figaro*, is an excellent illustration of the above points on the Classical style. It also reveals a musical conception that might well be described as 'dramatic', 'operatic' or even, as we shall see, 'comic'. The first sixteen bars (Ex. 5) present five terse, well-characterised musical ideas (marked A, B, C, x, D) in dramatic succession. The stark unison statements of bars 1–2 and 5–6 (A, A′) contrast with the smoother line and chordal accompaniment of the piano phrases in bars 2–4 and 6–8 (B, B′). The silences emphasise the disjunct phrases. In bar 9, the string instruments take the lead with a more lyrical idea (C) that is repeated in 11, while the piano adds interjections (x, derived from B). In bar 13, we return to stark unisons (based on x) and a forceful

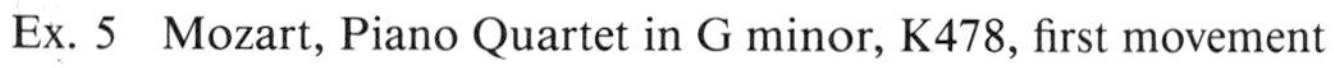

Ex. 5 Mozart, Piano Quartet in G minor, K478, first movement

cadence on the dominant. This cadence is the focal point of the sixteen-bar period, and motion towards it is emphasised by the increasing compression of the phrases (four-bar groupings in 1–4, 5–8; two-bar groupings in 9–10, 11–12; and then one-bar patterns in 13–15). Thus although the separate musical events in the sixteen-bar period are sharply individuated, their succession works towards a clearly defined goal. However, this dominant cadence is itself unstable, creating a new set of expectations. We are left guessing what will happen on the first beat of bar 17.

Although the basic texture is one of melody and accompaniment, the inner parts are rich in interest. In bars 9–12, the four instruments each have material of a distinct character: the lyrical phrase in the violin, the vibrant chordal pattern in the viola, the sustained G in the 'cello, and the almost vocal interjections of the piano. As every player of Mozart's chamber music knows, each line in his textures has a shape and elegance that make it an individual entity while also being part of the whole. Such is the contrapuntal richness of Mozart's musical thought. Early Classical composers may have banished counterpoint, Burney's 'fugue, complication and laboured contrivance', for the sake of elegant melody and clear-cut harmony, but with Haydn and Mozart counterpoint is reintegrated into the musical design. This becomes even more apparent later in the first movement of K478. In Ex. 6, one idea is treated imitatively between the violin and viola, another between the upper and lower staves of the piano, and the 'cello has an independent line. Yet the contrapuntal writing remains bound by the Classical norms of regular phrase structures (two-bar patterns) and simple harmonic progressions (tonic–dominant, tonic–dominant).

This reintegration of counterpoint might be said to mark the appearance of the 'high' Classical style. Mozart may have learnt lessons both from Haydn and from his discovery of the music of J. S. Bach and Handel under the influence of Baron Gottfried van Swieten in 1782. Whatever the case, contrapuntal skill was crucial for Mozart as an opera composer. In an operatic ensemble, characters must sing together even if they hold very different views of the events taking place onstage. Only by combining individuated lines in a contrapuntal complex can disparate reactions be portrayed effectively. In Ex. 6, five 'characters' present three contrasted musical ideas. Four of the 'characters' are joined in pairs (violin/viola, upper/lower stave of the piano), while the fifth ('cello) is kept distinct. Compare this with Ex. 7, an extract from the Act III sextet in

Ex. 6

Ex. 7 *Le nozze di Figaro*, 'Riconosci in questo amplesso' (No. 18)

Figaro. Here, too, there are five characters, two pairs and one alone. Marcellina and Bartolo are united in having found their long-lost son, while the Count and Don Curzio are both amazed at the turn of events. The allied characters each have related material, while the pairs are musically contrasted. Figaro is kept apart. Not only does the setting preserve the individuality of the characters; it also emphasises their interaction. But again this is a regular (four-bar) phrase, and the harmony is simple (dominant–tonic over a dominant pedal). It is a remarkable musical technique.

The quoted passages from K478 might well be described as 'dramatic' in juxtaposing sharply contrasted musical events (as in Ex. 5), or 'operatic' in combining distinctive musical 'characters' in a single texture (as in Ex. 6). They might also be described as 'comic' both in terms of their pacing – in Ex. 5 much happens within only sixteen bars – and of the way in which Mozart plays on our expectations (what will happen in bar 17?). All these features are prominently exploited in *Figaro.* But there is another sense in which the musical processes involved in Ex. 5 might be termed 'comic'. The opening unison statement (A), on the tonic, is 'interrupted' by the contrasted idea for the piano alone (B), cadencing on the dominant. This pattern of proposition–interruption is then repeated (A′, B′), moving from the dominant to the tonic. In bar 9, a synthesis of the two preceding ideas (C) is achieved. The first note of the violin in bar 9 continues the rising line initiated by A and A′ (*g*′, *a*′, *b*♭′), while the piano interjections (x) develop a motif from B and B′. Thus Mozart ensures a smooth transition between the successive events A, B, C, and later D. However, C also fuses the textural characteristics of A and B: all the instruments play, as A, but they do so in harmony, not unison, as B. This effect of synthesis is reinforced by the flowing quavers in the viola, which contrast with the preceding rhythmic disjointedness, and by the firm tonic pedal in the 'cello. Nevertheless, by bar 13, the texture has thinned out to bare unisons once more, leading to another interruption, the dominant cadence (D). These sixteen bars establish a process (proposition–interruption–synthesis–interruption) that operates throughout the movement. It is also a process that works on several levels. For example, bars 1–16 could themselves be seen as a 'proposition' that will be 'interrupted' by whatever happens in bar 17. On the highest level, of course, the process underpins the sonata principle: the first key area is the 'proposition' that is 'interrupted' by the second key area, and this interruption is resolved by the 'synthesis' of the Recapitulation.

In Chapter 3 we saw that Beaumarchais's play is organised as a series of episodes producing a chain of small-scale crescendos leading to successive climaxes. The comic rhythm is consistently created as follows: a balanced situation is presented (proposition), something occurs to upset the balance, causing disruption (interruption), and the characters react and strike a new balance (synthesis). However, this new balance is often only temporary and is soon disrupted by a new event, whereupon the cycle continues. A good example is provided by B:II.16–22, which became the Act II finale, where the entry of each new character destroys a previously established balance. This chain reaction works on the large scale as well as the small. Thus it governs the whole structure of the play (Figaro and Susanna wish to be married, the Count disrupts the situation by seeking to seduce Susanna, the Count is defeated and all the characters are duly reconciled), as well as the action in individual scenes. On the smallest scale, it is also one mechanism of the joke. There are clear parallels with the features noted in K478. The Classical style was ideally suited to *opera buffa* not only because of its pacing, contrasts, contrapuntal possibilities and musical 'jokes', but also because it involved processes that are fundamentally comic.

To see how Mozart exploits the Classical style in an operatic context, it is best to analyse one typical section of *Figaro* in depth. The Act I trio, 'Cosa sento! tosto andate' (No. 7), is a fine example of the dramatic ensembles which commentators rightly note as a hallmark of the opera. Without a secure technique of ensemble writing, Mozart would have been unable to present the rapid succession of events in Beaumarchais's play. However, ensembles are not easy to write. They pose at least three specific problems for the composer: first, he must establish sharply differentiated characters as efficiently and as quickly as possible; second, he must construct a musical argument that is flexible enough to cope with rapidly changing dramatic situations; third, this musical argument must retain at least some degree of structural coherence. How are these problems solved in the Act I trio?

Mozart makes full use of the clear-cut phrase structures and dramatic contrasts inherent in the Classical style to depict his characters. The trio begins abruptly as the Count suddenly appears from behind the chair. The preceding recitative does not end with the usual cadence in the continuo (see below, p. 106). Instead, a cadence (V–I in B flat major) is supplied by the orchestra as it bursts in *fortissimo* with furious semiquavers and emphatic chords. The Count begins with a forceful rising line built up of fragmentary phrases that emphasise his rage (Ex. 8). In contrast, Basilio has an unctuous descending line, with chromatic harmonies, as he fawns on his master. Susanna appears (genuinely?) frightened, with a fluttering

Ex. 8 'Cosa sento! tosto andate' (No. 7)

melody that is again fragmentary and which also seems to get stuck on one note, *c''*. These contrasted periods capture the emotional states of the three protagonists. They are also progressively compressed (twelve bars for the Count, eight for Basilio, four for Susanna), which drives the setting forward. Throughout the rest of the trio, Mozart reveals the same ability to create vocal lines that capture the essence of a character at any given moment, despite the complexity and pace of the action. Moreover, he does so even when the characters sing together. In Ex. 9, from the end of the trio, Susanna's dotted rhythms suggest agitation, the Count's stentorian tonic–dominant leaps emphasise his pompous judgement of the maid, while Basilio crows out what he sees to be the moral of the episode, with a musical idea that returns in the overture to the opera that takes his maxim one stage further, *Così fan tutte*.

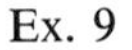
Ex. 9

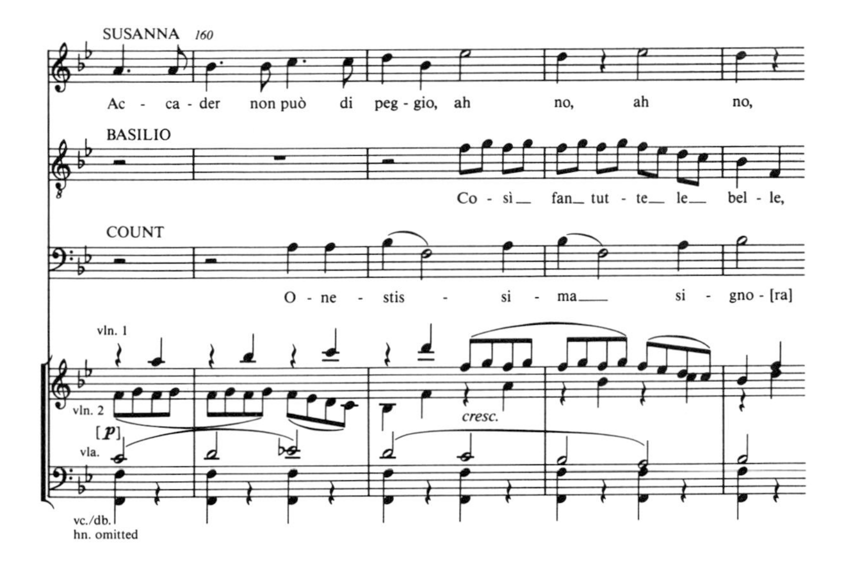

Mozart's skill in musical characterisation is equalled by his ability to match the dramatic pacing of the trio in musical terms. The action of the trio reveals precisely the comic rhythm described above. It consists of a series of episodes that each shift from points of relative stability (the Count expresses anger, the Count and Basilio reassure Susanna, the Count narrates events in Barbarina's room the day before) to relative instability (Susanna 'faints', she hysterically orders the Count and Basilio to leave, Cherubino is discovered in the chair). These shifts are mirrored both by the orchestral accompaniment and by Mozart's use of tonality. Although the accompanimental patterns often seem repetitive and essentially neutral, they have a kinetic energy that maintains the momentum – note the predominant quaver motion – and they also underline the events onstage in supportive and sometimes revealing ways. One delightful example is the manner in which the orchestra mimics the discovery of Cherubino in the chair by reversing the Count's previous descending line just after the recitative interlude (see bar 139). Similarly, at the point where the Count and Basilio lead the 'fainting' Susanna to the chair, the orchestra takes Susanna's opening idea, turns it from the minor into the major, and makes it much more poised (see bar 57). Even if Susanna was genuinely frightened at the beginning of the trio, she has now recovered control of herself and of the situation, as her expedient recovery reveals.

Points of dramatic stability are matched by areas of tonal stability (B flat major, F major, E flat major and various returns to B flat major), while dramatic instability is reinforced by tonal instability, whether by way of sudden modulations or, more frequently, dominant pedals (V/F, V/g, etc.). Sudden modulations are important: in particular, a move to G minor, the relative minor of B flat major, consistently matches disruptions in the dramatic action (see bars 16, 66, 112, 127), as indeed occurs throughout the opera. Even more significant is Mozart's use of the dominant pedal, a lengthy insistence on the dominant note, usually in the bass. Such pedals are generally reinforced by an elaboration of dominant harmony in the inner parts, often with rapid chord changes, chromaticism and minor inflections. In the Classical style, the dominant pedal is a standard means of generating harmonic tension because of its need to resolve to the tonic, and it is particularly suited to the presentation of unstable dramatic situations (Ex. 10).[4] Dominant pedals take up almost one-third of the trio.

There is no doubt that Mozart provides an appropriate musical response to matters of both characterisation and pacing in the trio.

Ex. 10

But the third of our problems remains. At the same time as supporting the forward-moving drama as situations develop and characters change, Mozart must also have care for the overall structure and balance of the trio. There is a potential conflict here that affects any operatic composer: if he veers too much in favour of dramatic momentum, the setting may lack coherence; if he concentrates instead on the musical structure, then he may not cope effectively with the ebb and flow of the action. It is a difficult balance to strike, and one that highlights the fact that the relationship between music and drama is not entirely free of tensions.

In the Classical style, structural coherence is normally achieved by thematic consistency (whether involving direct repetition or motivic variation) and tonal symmetry. Both, of course, are inherent within the sonata principle. Straightforward thematic repetition does occur in the trio. The Count's initial ascending line (Ex. 8) returns twice in a more compressed form (bars 101, 147, now in regular four-bar phrases) as his fury repeatedly breaks out. Basilio's opening idea (bar 16) appears four times in all. At its second and fourth appearances (bars 85, 175), Basilio transfers his excuses to a dismissal of his report on Cherubino as mere 'suspicion' on his part. At the third appearance (bar 129), the line (extended to five rather than four two-bar units) is given to the Count during his drawn-out narration of his earlier discovery of Cherubino, perhaps a hint that the Count is now descending to Basilio's level of intrigue. Repetition also occurs in the accompaniment. Bars 57–9 hark back to 23–5; the figuration in bar 60 recurs in 92, 103, 107–21, 149, etc. to 213–19; the pattern in bars 98–100 derives from 66; and the descending scales in the orchestral coda (bars 201–13) are perhaps related to the descending scales prominent earlier in the setting (see bars 26, 38, 48, 52). There are also motivic relationships between various musical ideas that appear on the surface to be quite dissimilar. Thirds are particularly prominent. The *f′–d′* of Basilio's opening idea (bar 16) refers back to the *f–d* of the Count's first statement (Ex. 8, bars 4–5) and the falling thirds in his cadence in bars 13–15. Rising or falling thirds recur throughout the vocal parts of the trio and also permeate the accompaniment.

The Count's opening *f–d* also has other implications. After this falling third, the Count begins a rising line from *d* to *b♭*. However, the implication of the *f–d* is that it will be followed by another falling third, *d–B♭*, to complete the triad. The Count's rising *d–b♭* is only a temporary solution. Indeed, the search for a strong *B♭* and for a falling motion from any D to any B flat dominates the trio. In the first sixteen bars, the Count's line ostentatiously avoids the low *B♭*. When Basilio enters, his *f′–d′* is indeed followed by *d′–b♭*, although the harmony renders the progression weak. Successive leaps from D down to B flat (in whatever octave) are also weakened harmonically. The Count succeeds in gaining a *B♭* in bars 101 and 105, but only on weak beats of the bar. He repeats his original *f–d* at the beginning of the recitative section (bars 121–2), but once again he fails to go to *B♭*. Only from bar 147 onwards, as the trio reaches its conclusion, does the Count have a *B♭* on a strong beat of the bar, and even the *B♭* in bar 147 is marked *pianissimo.* Moreover, is it mere coincidence that D to B flat appears in various octaves in the final orchestral cadence?

This search for *B♭* is as much a tonal problem as a melodic one, for it is rooted in the need for a complete tonic triad. Indeed, tonality serves a structural as much as a dramatic function in the trio according to the requirements of the sonata principle. The key of B flat major is strongly established in the first fifteen bars, emphasised by the Count's 'closed' phrase and strong cadence (the continuation of Ex. 8). We then move through a pedal (V/F, see Ex. 10) to a new area of tonal stability, the dominant key, F major (bar 43, Basilio and the Count's 'Ah già svien la poverina'), which is affirmed by a cadence (bars 56–7). The tonal conflict between tonic and dominant is now established. Susanna's shift to an unstable V of G minor (bar 66, 'Che insolenza, andate fuor') leads to a lengthy section in E flat major (bar 70, Basilio and the Count's 'Siamo quì per aiutarvi(-ti)' to the melody of bar 43), that ultimately moves onto another dominant pedal, V/B♭, in bars 92–100 (Susanna's 'È un'insidia, una perfidia'). The E flat major episode is curious. E flat major is the subdominant of B flat major and gives an impression of tonal relaxation. This is dramatically appropriate, for the Count and Basilio are attempting to defuse the situation after Susanna's 'faint'. However, if the E flat major section is not to sound out of place, it must also have a part to play in the overall musical structure. An examination of the large-scale bass progression from bars 1–100 reveals its musical, as opposed to dramatic, role in an ascending scale from the I in bar 5 to the V in bar 92 (Ex. 11).[5]

It does not seem contrived to view bars 1–100 of the trio as a sonata-form Exposition and Development. The Exposition contains two strongly established key areas based on the tonic (B flat major) and the dominant (F major), each articulated by well-structured thematic ideas, a 'first subject' group and a 'second subject'. The

Ex. 11

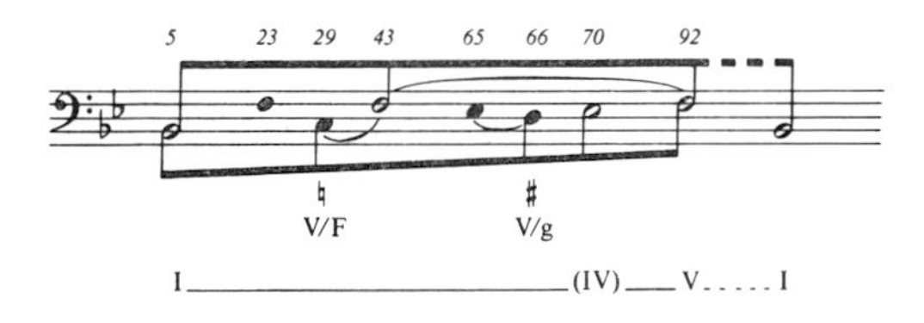

Development begins just before Susanna's shift to V of G minor and contains a lengthy subdominant episode. Even the dominant pedal that begins in bar 92 has its place in the scheme. In sonata-form movements, dominant pedals frequently appear in the bridge passage of the Exposition, preparing for the second key area (often a pedal on V/V), and in the retransition at the end of the Development, preparing for the Recapitulation (a pedal on V). The V/F pedal in bars 29–42 of the trio (including a diversion to D flat major) is clearly one such bridge passage. Similarly, the V/B♭ pedal which arrives in bar 92 signals that the retransition has begun. This is standard procedure in the Classical style. We are prepared for a return to B flat major in bar 101, where there is also a varied recapitulation of the Count's opening thematic idea (to 'Parta, parta il damerino').

Bar 101 has all the appearances of beginning a straightforward recapitulation: after all, the Count's decision to dismiss Cherubino could easily mark the conclusion of the action. But Mozart now plays a joke on our expectations. Another diversion through G minor leads to another V/B♭ pedal (bars 115–21) which indicates yet another retransition. The tonic returns in bar 122, as does the Count's *f–d*. But this is an unexpected recitative which again moves via G minor to the dominant as Cherubino is discovered in the chair. The V/B♭ pedal in bar 138 marks the beginning of a third retransition. Only with the return of B flat major in bar 147 (at the Count's 'Onestissima signora') does the Recapitulation proper begin. In retrospect, the return of B flat major in bar 101 seems a favourite trick of Classical composers, the false recapitulation. In addition to the dramatic reversals in the trio, Mozart also plays a game of musical reversals. It is a game that relies on our understanding of Classical procedures.

A Recapitulation must balance the Exposition in terms of length, match its thematic presentation at least to a significant degree, and resolve the preceding tonal conflict by emphasising the tonic. If the dominant key was emphasised by new thematic material in the Exposition, that material, or at least a good part of it, should now return in the tonic. This is precisely what occurs here. The Recapitulation, excluding the coda, is more or less the same length as the Exposition (57 bars compared with 54); the main thematic ideas return (the Count's rising line and Basilio's descending line are repeated, and Susanna's agitated quavers find their reflection in Basilio's crowing 'Così fan tutte le belle', see Ex. 9); and much of the 'second subject' material is restated in the tonic (compare bars 168–75 and its repeat for emphasis in 191–201 with 47–57). However, the order of presentation is altered and Basilio's line comes only after the first restatement of the 'second subject', which is accordingly foreshortened. The fact that Basilio separates two statements of the 'second subject' allows for a more extended repetition of this material, thereby emphasising the tonic. It also makes the return of his line all the more surprising – we suspect at first that Mozart has left it out of the reckoning – and underlines its significance.

The tonal stability of this Recapitulation is justified dramatically: the situation may not be resolved but the characters are at the point of acknowledging their various reactions to the events of the ensemble. Similarly, the return to the home key, B flat major, emphasises the fact that despite all these events things have hardly changed – the trio scarcely advances the action of the opera – and that we are in effect back where we started in terms of the overall plot. However, to what extent is the repetition of thematic material in the Recapitulation related to the drama, necessary though it may be in terms of the musical structure? This highlights the problem of musical repetition for the composer of dramatic music. The sonata principle has considerable dramatic potential, but in order to employ it on the stage, the composer must be able to justify the reiteration of previously heard material. Musical repetition is possible in the static set-pieces of the Baroque *opera seria* (witness the da capo aria), where it does little damage to the slow-moving drama. In *opera buffa*, however, the comic pace requires that the characters look forwards, not backwards, and therefore that straightforward repetition be avoided.

One solution is to establish dramatic parallels between the opening and closing sections of the movement, even if the actual situation has changed. A straightforward example is provided by the trio in Act II, 'Susanna or via sortite' (No. 13). Here the action falls into two parts: in the first ('Susanna or via sortite'), the Count orders Susanna to leave the dressing-room, the Countess forbids her to do so, Susanna (hiding upstage) reacts; in the second ('Dunque parlate almeno'), the Count orders Susanna at least to make herself heard, the Countess forbids her to do so, and Susanna reacts. These parallel sections form respectively the Exposition and Recapitulation of an abridged sonata-form movement (with a short dominant pedal substituting for a Development). The same occurs in the Act III sextet, 'Riconosci in questo amplesso' (No. 18), which is again in abridged sonata form. At the beginning of the Exposition, Marcellina and Bartolo are reconciled with Figaro; at the beginning of the Recapitulation, they are reconciled with Susanna. In this sextet, there are also further parallels between the Exposition and Recapitulation – compare the Count's and Don Curzio's reactions in the former with Susanna's in the latter – while the tensions between Susanna and Figaro in the dominant area of the Exposition are resolved in the tonic area of the Recapitulation.

Similarly, in 'Cosa sento! tosto andate' there are dramatic parallels to be reinforced by the thematic repetitions. The Exposition, false recapitulation and Recapitulation proper each begin with the Count's ascending line: first, he orders Basilio to search out Cherubino ('Cosa sento! tosto andate, e scacciate il seduttor'); second, he orders the youth to be dismissed from the castle ('Parta, parta il damerino'); and third, he accuses Susanna ('Onestissima signora, or capisco come va'). The repetition of the 'second subject', which was first presented when the Count and Basilio were commenting on Susanna's 'faint', is less obviously motivated by the action, although Susanna remains under stress and the material is still concerned with the effect of the situation upon her. But the return of Basilio's cringing opening line (to the words from the middle section, 'Ah, del paggio quel ch'ho detto/era solo un mio sospetto', 'Ah, what I said about the page was only my suspicion') is much more problematic. Although it may be necessary for musical balance, it finds no obvious justification in the action; nor is it indicated in da Ponte's libretto.

Mozart devises a glorious solution. Basilio's line may be unnecessary in terms of the drama, but its return is wonderfully ironic. It is clear that what Basilio said about the page is more than just 'my suspicion' – Cherubino now stands before them – but the music master can drive the point home 'con malignità', 'with malice', as Mozart's score is marked. Irony is exploited to make a virtue out of a musical necessity. The effect is further emphasised by displacing Basilio's entry and therefore drawing our attention to it. This is marvellous comedy.

'Cosa sento! tosto andate' raises a number of important issues concerning Mozart's handling of characterisation and dramatic pacing, not to mention his use of the sonata principle in an operatic context. We have also seen how he exploits the Classical style to achieve true comedy through music. It may seem perverse to have devoted so much space to a piece that runs for less than five minutes in performance. Analysis, alas, always appears heavy-handed in its attempts to explain what both composer and listener take for granted. But if we are to participate in Mozart's game, we must first learn his rules.

7 *Music and drama in Le nozze di Figaro*

In our discussion of 'Cosa sento! tosto andate' (No. 7), we saw how Mozart uses specific musical techniques to pace the action, to depict the emotional states of his characters, and to provide structural coherence. It is worth taking some time to explore how Mozart responds to these three concerns - pacing, characterisation and coherence - in the opera as a whole.

There seems little doubt that Mozart and da Ponte were anxious to maintain the dramatic momentum throughout *Le nozze di Figaro*. The overture establishes a fast pace for the 'folle journée' and its impetus carries forward into the first act. We move straight into the action with two duets for Figaro and Susanna, and indeed Act I passes remarkably quickly, with only brief moments of repose. Of the nine numbers in Act I, eight are marked to be played 'Allegro' or faster (and the exception, Figaro's 'Se vuol ballare', No. 3, has two 'Presto' sections). Only at the beginning of Act II does the pace slow (No. 10 is marked 'Larghetto'; No. 11, 'Andante'; and No. 12, 'Allegretto'). As we have seen, the brake applied by the Countess's 'Porgi amor qualche ristoro' (No. 10) is important for the character, and even if the following 128 bars of recitative, which are needed to clarify the plot, seem to lose momentum, the trio 'Susanna or via sortite' (No. 13) and most especially the magnificent Act II finale (No. 15) restore the pace. Similarly, if the first part of Act IV, with its four full-scale arias for Marcellina, Basilio, Figaro and Susanna, seems to flag, the momentum is regained in the Act IV finale as the opera drives towards its conclusion.

Mozart's and da Ponte's achievement in maintaining the pace in *Figaro* is all the more remarkable given that a 'number' opera is prone both to lulls in the action and to segmentation as a result of shifting between recitatives, arias and ensembles. Da Ponte did his best to avoid such lulls by creating the opportunity for action-ensembles and even action-arias that make much play of stage business (witness Figaro's 'Non più andrai farfallone amoroso', No. 9, and Susanna's 'Venite, inginocchiatevi', No. 12, both of which are effectively duets with a silent partner, Cherubino). Even those arias that halt the action (such as Figaro's 'Se vuol ballare', No. 3, the Count's 'Vedrò mentre io sospiro', No. 17, or the Countess's 'Dove sono i bei momenti', No. 19) are emotionally dynamic in terms of the changes wrought in the characters as the setting progresses. Similarly, Mozart uses a number of specific techniques to maintain the momentum and counter the dangers of segmentation. For example, he generally avoids long orchestral introductions. Only seven pieces in the opera have introductions eight or more bars long: Nos. 1, 8, 10, 11, 21, 23 and 24. Nos. 1, 10 and 23 are each at the beginning of an act, where an introduction is needed to establish a scene, to cover a change of set, or simply to quieten down the audience; while Nos. 8, 11, 21 and 24 are all set pieces - two choruses and two arias - that suspend the action anyway. On the other hand, in no fewer than thirteen pieces, the voice enters in the first or second bar, often with little more than a preliminary chord (as in Nos. 6, 9, 15, 18, 26) or even on the first beat (Nos. 3, 4, 19). Mozart wastes little time in getting down to business.

These abbreviated introductions emphasise the flow of the drama from the preceding recitative and minimise a potentially awkward stylistic divide. Similarly, there are other ways of connecting a recitative with its succeeding aria or ensemble, either by avoiding the clear cadence required by convention at the end of a recitative (as before Nos. 2, 6, 19, 20), or by eliding this cadence so that it is completed by the first chord of the succeeding number (see the start of Nos. 13, 16, 17, 18). Tonal relationships can also be used to foster continuity, particularly when the tonic chord at the end of the recitative becomes a dominant to the succeeding number (see Nos. 2, 3, 6, 8, 9, 12, 15, 25, 26). Three other examples deserve closer examination. The recitative before 'Cosa sento! tosto andate' (No. 7) ends in F without the expected cadence, and an extended V–I cadence in B flat is provided by the first five bars of the trio, resolving over the Count's entry (see Ex. 8). In 'Via resti servita' (No. 5), the preceding recitative ends with the V of a V–I cadence in E, the duet begins in I of E, but this I turns out to be V of A, the key of the duet. Similarly, in the finale to Act III (No. 22), the preceding recitative ends on the V of a V–I cadence in G, the march begins in G, supplying the I, but this G is actually V of C. No. 5 has a parallel in *Idomeneo* (compare No. 22 Arbace's 'Se colà ne' fati è scritto'), as does the remarkable opening of No. 22 (compare No. 14, the march with Electra's recitative 'Odo da lunge armonioso suono'). In both march examples, beginning on the dominant gives the impression that the music has begun before we actually hear it as the band appears from the distance.

The autonomy of the arias and ensembles of *Figaro* is undermined not just by their relationship to their surroundings but also by their scale. With the obvious exception of the three finales, these pieces are generally compressed in terms of their formal structure and musical argument. For example, three of the fourteen arias are shorter cavatinas, and even in the more extended solo numbers, Mozart does not write full-scale sonata-form movements as in most of the arias of *Idomeneo*, still less the typical tripartite da capo arias of *opera seria*. Indeed, it is remarkable how Mozart can exploit the tonal contrasts and resolutions inherent in the sonata principle without adhering to the standard sectional divisions and regular repetitions of sonata form: 'Venite, inginocchiatevi' (No. 12) repays close study in this context. Similarly, even the larger ensembles are frequently in abridged sonata form, with a short passage of dominant preparation replacing a more extended Development section: see 'Susanna or via sortite' (No. 13) and 'Riconosci in questo amplesso' (No. 18).

Mozart's musical argument is often based on the tersest thematic material. Similarly, his modulations are invariably swift and economical. We saw in Chapter 5 that in the arias he nearly always reaches the dominant by the beginning of the second stanza of the text. He does so directly, often within a bar, saving the usual preparation for the new key (a move to V/V) for later in the tonal exposition. Thematic compression and tonal directness are also apparent in even the most complex dramatic and musical situations. For example, the third section of the Act II finale (No. 15.3, bars 167–327) presents an elaborate chain of events: the Countess reacts to the appearance of Susanna from the dressing-room, Susanna explains how Cherubino escaped, the Count is dumbfounded and begs forgiveness, the Countess refuses and stands on her dignity, the Count enlists the help of Susanna, Susanna points up a moral, the Countess finally relents, and all become temporarily reconciled. Yet the vocal lines in this 161-bar-long section are built upon only five short rhythmic/melodic ideas. In part, these rhythmic repetitions are the result of the regular metre of the verse (in six-syllable lines), illustrating once again the importance of the poetic structure of the text. However, they also create a taut musical coherence. Similarly, there are only four main ideas in the accompaniment, while the whole musical argument is constructed according to a clearly conceived tonal scheme.[1] Even when the vocal lines lapse into mere declamatory patter, as in the sixth section of this same finale (the episode of the page's commission, bars 605–96), the accompaniment presents an ever-repeating pattern that gives the section a cohesion governed, again, by a large-scale tonal process that matches the ebb and flow of the action.

Related to this formal and thematic compression is the fact that Mozart often avoids literal textual and/or musical repetition. Because of the concentration of Mozart's music and the length of da Ponte's texts, there is little redundant text repetition, with a word or words repeated simply as fodder for the development of a musical argument. Consequently, when it does occur, text repetition makes a strong rhetorical effect, as with the humorous bickering between Susanna and Marcellina in 'Via resti servita' (No. 5). Similarly, Mozart elaborates his musical argument by a process of continuous development, where extensive literal musical repetition at any stage of the proceedings is often avoided. Therefore, such repetition is often comic, as with the delightful 'sua madre'/'suo padre' passage of 'Riconosci in questo amplesso' (No. 18). Moreover, when Mozart states a musical antecedent phrase not just twice, which is a Classical norm, but three times before its consequent appears, it is done to deliberate effect. 'Se a caso madama' (No. 2) makes great play of this device to mimic Figaro's slow-wittedness at catching on to the designs of the Count. It can also be seen on an even larger scale both in the opening of 'Cinque, dieci, venti, trenta' (No. 1, where bars 1–18, 18–36 and 36–44 are statements of substantially the same material) as Figaro persists in pacing out the room, and at the entrance of Marcellina, Bartolo and Basilio in the Act II finale (No. 15.8, bars 729ff, although here the repetitions are in different keys).

Da Ponte's and Mozart's evident concern for dramatic momentum means that of the seven major characters in the opera, only three – Bartolo, Cherubino and the Countess – are introduced by arias that allow time to establish a particular stance. On the other hand, Figaro, Susanna, the Count and Marcellina are each introduced by ensembles. One wonders what effect this has on characterisation, for in general da Ponte and Mozart seem to give us little opportunity to come to know their characters before the comic imbroglio begins.

Of course, history and convention are on the opera's side. An audience familiar with *Le barbier de Séville* will be forewarned of the characters of Figaro and the Count and of their rather ambivalent servant–master relationship. Susanna, the pert, cunning, yet virtuous maid, and Marcellina, the frustrated spinster, both belong among the conventional characters of the *commedia dell'arte* or mid-eighteenth-century *opera buffa*. For that matter, Figaro, the rebellious servant, and the Count, the lecherous nobleman, are also stereotypes. Thus all four need only brief introductions. Only the Countess, who is drastically changed from the Rosine of *Le barbier* ('più quella non sono', 'I am no longer she', says the Countess in the Act II finale), and who is to become the focal point of the opera, requires the more extensive presentation provided by 'Porgi amor qualche ristoro' (No. 10).

The fact that the main characters are not securely grounded in a fixed presentation may even work to da Ponte and Mozart's advantage, for it throws the emphasis on the development of these characters through the opera. What Figaro, Susanna, the Count and Marcellina are is largely clear from past history and convention: it is what they become in the course of the 'folle journée' that matters. It is significant that their major arias come late in the opera, after the action of the ensembles has taken its effect. Moreover, the initial presentation of characters within ensembles emphasises that their interaction is of paramount importance. Thus Susanna appears in all six duets of the opera as she is shown in relation to Figaro, Marcellina, Cherubino, the Count and the Countess. Moreover, she is at least equal to, if not the better of, her partners in these duets, not to mention most of her other ensembles, and this is reflected as much in Mozart's music as in the dramatic action.

This question of interaction deserves further exploration, for it illustrates one of the most distinctive contributions of Mozart's music to the drama of *Figaro*. In Chapter 4, we saw how the music of 'Cinque, dieci, venti, trenta' (No. 1) establishes not only the differences between Figaro and Susanna but also their relationship, with Susanna the dominant partner. In the larger ensembles, too, Mozart is concerned no less with relationships between the characters than with their individuality. According to the dramatic situation, the characters form and re-form musical alliances with shared or related material to map out the shifting events onstage. At the beginning of the Act III sextet, 'Riconosci in questo amplesso' (No. 18), Marcellina, Bartolo and Figaro are set against the Count and Don Curzio (see Ex. 7). Susanna enters and in her fury at seeing Figaro embracing Marcellina she joins her master and the judge; she adopts their dotted rhythms and triadic lines in bars 54–72 and even sings in imitation with the Count for a time. This alliance, although unexpected, is justified by their anger at the turn of events. However, once things are explained she moves to take her rightful place beside Figaro and his parents, leaving the Count and Don Curzio musically apart from the rejoicing (see bars 101–36). This technique is even more extensive in the Act II finale (No. 15). For example, in its second and third sections (bars 126–327, from Susanna's appearance in the dressing-room doorway to just before the entrance of Figaro), the three characters onstage – the Count, Countess and Susanna – group and re-group according to the situation. At first, the Count and Countess have similar material – they are both astonished to see the maid – and Susanna stands apart both dramatically and musically (see bars 146–55); then the Countess and Susanna form a musical alliance against the Count as they both admonish him (bars 191–5); and for a brief moment, Susanna is even paired with the Count as she pleads on his behalf (bars 241–53). All possible combinations of the three characters have been exploited. So the process continues through the finale, until by the end the music of Figaro, Susanna and the Countess, is pitted against that of Marcellina, Bartolo, Basilio and the Count.

The Countess stands apart from Figaro, Susanna and the Count, not only in terms of the drama, as we saw in Chapter 3, but also in terms of the music. They are introduced by action-ensembles; she, on the other hand, first appears onstage alone singing a contemplative aria. 'Porgi amor qualche ristoro' (No. 10) takes us into a private world far removed from the bustle of Act I. Its vocal line is a potent expression of yearning and hopelessness; witness the rich appoggiaturas and the sudden changes of melodic direction. The rise to the Countess's highest note, an *a*♭″ held on a pause, for 'o mi lascia almen morir' ('or let me at least die', Ex. 12) also has far-reaching implications. It is followed by a repeat of the single quatrain of the text to a vocal line that is melodically and rhythmically unstable: the natural accentuation of the melody is misplaced by a semiquaver. There is no repetition of the opening musical material to provide a balanced setting. Most significantly, the *a*♭″, a seventh above a dominant chord, requires a resolution to a strong *g*″. This *a*♭″ does not resolve in the vocal line – of the two later appearances of *g*″, the first (bar 42) lasts only a semiquaver, and the second (bar 45) is harmonically weak by being over a second-inversion chord – and a *g*″ is stated only briefly in the orchestral postlude. In both formal and harmonic terms, the cavatina closes on a question-mark that emphasises both

Ex. 12 'Porgi amor qualche ristoro' (No. 10)

the uncertainty of the Countess's present position and the need for some manner of resolution, be it emotional or musical, on the part of the character.[2]

For much of the rest of Act II, the Countess's situation scarcely improves. By 'Susanna or via sortite' (No. 13) she has resorted to lying to her husband and is accused, correctly, though for the wrong reasons, of harbouring a man in her boudoir; and in the Act II finale, she is threatened with her husband's curse and exile from the castle. However, she manages to turn the tables on the Count. Her recovery after Susanna has appeared in the dressing-room doorway is perhaps a turning-point in the character. But there is a crucial point here. As the Count pleads forgiveness, he calls the Countess by her old name, Rosina, appealing to their first love. Her reply, 'più quella non sono' ('I am no longer she'), is revealing. Of course she is no longer Rosina, and the Count would do well to take the point. But the remark also has something to say about the Countess: perhaps it is time for her to be more like the Rosina of old and less inclined to adopt the passive role of the betrayed wife.

In fact, the rest of the opera is concerned precisely with the Countess taking a more active role in the proceedings. She may have a noblewoman's qualms about consorting with her servant, Susanna, to dupe the Count into submission, but she finally becomes involved in a convoluted scheme of clothes-swapping and play-acting to win back her husband. Thus she decides for better or for worse to play the same tricks that might have been adopted by a younger Rosina. The change is both dramatically and musically felt in her second aria, 'Dove sono i bei momenti' (No. 19). Now the Countess's nostalgia for times past is framed within a balanced musical framework (ABA) that contrasts with the formal imbalance of ‘Porgi amor qualche ristoro’: things now seem in a clearer perspective. Moreover, the aria is concluded by a faster coda that marks a crucial change in the character. The silent pause in bar 77, just before the coda, is pregnant with significance: from here on, the Countess decides to take control in the hope that her constancy, whatever it may lead her to do, will bring its reward. This coda is a remarkable musical representation of renewed optimism. Moreover, now that the Countess has resolved her emotional situation, so does her vocal line resolve the musical tensions left hanging from ‘Porgi amor qualche ristoro’. There an $a\flat''$ never entirely achieved its required resolution to g''. Here this note, already the implicit goal of the first bars of the aria, comes to glorious fruition in a line that soars from a'' through $a\flat''$ to the long awaited g'' (Ex. 13). The triumphant phrase is immediately repeated to bring the point home (see bars 109–17, and note the g'' in bars 122 and 127).

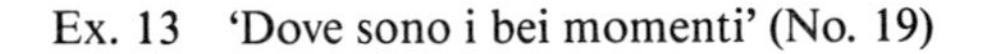
Ex. 13 ‘Dove sono i bei momenti’ (No. 19)

With this g'', now a more stable fifth of a C major triad rather than the third of an E flat triad, the Countess’s emotional maturity is established. She is now in control of herself and of the situation. Significantly, she can say to Susanna ‘tutto io prendo su me stessa’ (‘I myself take responsibility for everything’). Now the Countess leads Susanna, not vice versa, and the ‘letter’-duet, ‘Che soave zeffiretto’ (No. 20), cements this re-formed relationship. Indeed, she does take responsibility for everything that happens in the rest of the ‘folle journée’ and eventually receives her just reward, reconciliation with her husband. Moreover, this reconciliation is crowned by precisely the same *g″* that was so lacking in 'Porgi amor qualche ristoro' and so portentous in 'Dove sono i bei momenti'. Now it is the even more stable root of a G major triad (Ex. 14).

Ex. 14 Finale to Act IV (No. 28), voices only

Although the Countess stands apart from the other characters by being developed primarily through arias rather than ensembles, this is not to deny the importance of the other arias in the opera. *Figaro* may be noted for its large number of ensembles, but even so, one half of the musical numbers in the opera (14 out of 28) are for solo voice. *Don Giovanni* has slightly more arias (15 out of 26 numbers), and *Così fan tutte*, much more an ensemble opera, has significantly fewer (12 out of 31 numbers). Most of these arias have clear associations with operatic convention. 'Rage' arias (Figaro's 'Aprite un po' quegl'occhi', No. 26), 'love' arias (Cherubino's 'Non so più cosa son, cosa faccio', No. 6), 'martial' arias (Figaro's 'Non più andrai farfallone amoroso', No. 9), 'revenge' arias (Bartolo's 'La vendetta, oh la vendetta!', No. 4, and the Count's 'Vedrò mentre io sospiro', No. 17), 'pastoral' arias (Susanna's 'Deh vieni non tardar, oh gioia bella', No. 27), and arias which point up a moral (Marcellina's 'Il capro e la capretta', No. 24, and Basilio's 'In quegl'anni, in cui val poco', No. 25), are all clichés of eighteenth-century opera. Mozart's audience would have expected nothing less.

The arias in *Figaro* are fine examples of how Mozart can capture a character with the most economical musical means, whether by way of the vocal line or the orchestral accompaniment. Even in the case of pieces which involve similar emotions, Mozart succeeds in differentiating between them according to differences between the characters. A comparison of Bartolo's 'La vendetta, oh la vendetta!' (No. 4) and the Count's 'Vedrò mentre io sospiro' (No. 17) makes the point clear. Both are 'revenge' arias, both are in D major, the key normally associated with such arias in eighteenth-century opera, and both have the same scoring, with prominent horns, trumpets and drums. Here the similarities cease. As we saw in Chapter 2 (p. 27), Bartolo's aria is a masterful parody of the standard 'revenge' clichés. The vocal line moves in stops and starts, ties itself in knots and frequently gets 'stuck' on a single note as Bartolo's rage prevents him from piecing together a coherent musical thought. Silences, pauses and abrupt shifts of direction abound, and at times the melody repeats itself to the point of obsession (see bars 30–56). Antecedent phrases fail to receive an adequate consequent, or else the appropriate consequent is delayed to the extent that there is no longer any connection with what has gone before (see bars 51–3, a consequent of sorts to bars 15–17, and note the consequent to bars 1–4 in 77–80). Mozart indulges in over-literal word-play (note the descending line to Bartolo's lowest note in the aria on 'è bassezza, è ognor viltà', 'is low and cowardly', in bars 20–3), and the accompaniment repeatedly pokes fun at the character (see bars 30ff, where the *forte* chords belie the 'astuzia', 'cunning', and 'giudizio', 'judgement', that Bartolo claims will defeat Figaro). Then in the middle section Bartolo is reduced to typical *buffo* patter. He blusters through to the end, with the orchestra's running semiquavers and stormy cadential chords emphasising his rather fatuous stance. Bartolo's aria, like Bartolo himself, is a *buffo* pastiche of a *buffo* convention.

The Count presents a very different case. He, too, is furious and wishes to gain revenge on Figaro, but his anger results from a threat to his very being, his dignity, honour and his rights as lord of the manor. The orchestra still provides appropriate flourishes, and the vocal line is again repetitive and moves in circles. However, there is a greater use of *piano* wind writing, and Mozart employs tortuous chromaticism with strong minor inflections. This is no superficial ranting. Moreover, the vocal line has a far clearer sense of direction than Bartolo's, with more strongly emphasised goals and fully-formed phrases (see bar 66ff). The Count is more able to articulate his feelings and thus control them to his advantage. The effect is felt increasingly as the setting progresses. The musical 'point' of the aria, as it were, is for the Count to complete an octave scale from *d–d′* and the reverse. In the first section, his phrases often outline sevenths from *e–d′*, but always conspicuously avoid the *d* or reach it only by leap rather than by step. Only in the faster second section does the possibility of completing the scale, whether rising or descending, turn into a probability, and only towards the end does the Count triumphantly proclaim the complete descending scale, filling the structural gap left by his previous material and allowing the piece to conclude (Ex. 15, and note also bars 98–106).[3] The Count has done more

Ex. 15 'Vedrò mentre io sospiro' (No. 17)

than bluster, and the articulation and eventual control of his deep-seated fury have both emotional and musical consequences. From now he is a man to be feared. Moreover, once again there are implications that reach to the end of the opera. In the aria, phrases are constructed on incomplete sevenths rather than complete octaves, and *d′* is an important goal. In the finale to Act IV, when the Count is forced to beg the Countess's forgiveness, we once again find a phrase outlining a seventh, this time *d–c′*, with the Count's goal, *d′*, supplied an octave higher by his forgiving wife (Ex. 16).

Ex. 16 Finale to Act IV (No. 28)

The fact that Mozart might be said to establish musical processes in a given piece that are resolved only later in the opera, as seems to be the case in the music for the Count and the Countess, raises the question of whether *Figaro* can be viewed as a musically coherent whole. It is debatable whether one can or should seek out signs of large-scale unity in a 'number' opera: attempts to do so often seem little more than analytical wishful thinking. Nevertheless, there are parallels between the various sections of the opera that deserve further exploration. For example, Acts I and III each begin with a duet (Nos. 1, 16) and end with a march (Nos. 9, 22); Acts II and IV each begin with a cavatina (Nos. 10, 23); each of the first three acts has a major ensemble at its centre (Nos. 7, 13, 18); and in each of these acts Figaro makes a dramatic entrance at or just after a section in G major (the two choruses, Nos. 8, 21, and in the Act II finale, No. 15.4, bar 328). Mozart also seems to link certain instruments consistently with certain characters. Figaro is often partnered by the bassoon, a prominent instrument throughout the opera, and Susanna by the oboe (see No. 1). Thus in the Act II finale (No. 15.5), when Figaro's thoughts turn to expediting his marriage with Susanna, oboes and bassoons in octaves are prominent (see bars 445–9). Similarly, clarinets are associated with Cherubino: they stand out in his two arias (Nos. 6, 11) and even seem to refer to the page when he is absent but in the minds of the characters (for example, in No. 7 and the first half of No. 15). It is also curious that clarinets should be so prominent in the Countess's 'Porgi amor qualche ristoro' (No. 10). Does Mozart use them just for their mellow tone, or is this a hint of the relationship between the Countess and Cherubino that was expunged from the play?

Similarly, certain motivic ideas seem to recur throughout the opera. In 'Cinque, dieci, venti, trenta' (No. 1), Susanna has a cadential phrase that returns in the orchestral cadence of 'Via resti servita' (No. 5) and forms the basis for her melodic line in 'Deh vieni non tardar, oh gioia bella' (No. 27), where, in a typical Classical pun, it acts as both a beginning and an ending (Ex. 17).[4] The descending three-note groupings that form the basis of the melody of Cherubino's 'Non so più cosa son, cosa faccio' (No. 6) recur in material later associated with Cherubino (Ex. 18; see also the melodic outlines of Nos. 21, 23, and compare No. 11, bars 17–20, with No. 9, bars 1–5). Frits Noske notes the extent to which pieces in Act IV, and particularly the finale, seem to quote from material heard earlier to match the conflicts and resolutions in the dramatic action (for example, note the similarities between 'Aprite un po' quegl'occhi', No. 26, and 'Se vuol ballare', No. 3, and between Barbarina's 'L'ho perduta, me meschina', No. 23, and Susanna's line in 'Cosa sento! tosto andate', No. 7, bars 23–7; the way in which Figaro adopts the

Ex. 17 (a) 'Cinque, dieci, venti, trenta' (No. 1); (b) 'Via resti servita' (No. 5); (c) 'Deh vieni non tardar, oh gioia bella' (No. 27)

Ex. 18 (a) 'Non so più cosa son, cosa faccio' (No. 6); (b) 'Cosa sento! tosto andate' (No. 7); (c) 'Venite, inginocchiatevi' (No. 12); (d) Finale to Act II (No. 15)

triadic outlines of Susanna's melodies as he first plays at seducing the 'Countess', see No. 28, bars 189–92; and the echo of 'Amanti costanti' in the Act III finale in the final chorus of the opera, No. 28, bars 456–60).[5] Other thematic relationships may exist between Marcellina's themes in 'Riconosci in questo amplesso' and 'Via resti servita' (compare No. 18, bars 74–6, with No. 5, bars 4–6), the Act IV finale and 'Aprite un po' quegl'occhi' (compare No. 28, bars 47–50, with the orchestral accompaniment in No. 26), and this finale and 'Cinque, dieci, venti, trenta' (compare No. 28, bars 10–12, and No. 1, bars 9–11). Finally, Siegmund Levarie notes that the outline of the overture's main theme, a fifth plus a step (D–A–B–A) forms the basis for other melodic material in the opera: a transposition of this pattern can even be discerned at the Countess's final forgiveness of the Count (see Ex. 16).

Critics seeking to demonstrate unity in *Figaro* also focus on Mozart's use of tonality. Keys seem to recur in association with characters or situations: for example, 'sharp' keys for Marcellina, Bartolo and the Count; F major for Figaro's 'Se vuol ballare' and Susanna's 'Deh vieni non tardar, oh gioia bella', as well as the Act III sextet, which clears the way for their wedding. G minor, Mozart's 'tragic' key, is often used for moments of danger or tension, and as one would expect in the eighteenth century, other choices of key seem influenced by conventional associations with particular emotional affects. Similarly, the whole opera may well be governed by coherently conceived tonal progressions. In Chapter 6 we saw the importance of tonal processes in the Act I trio, and there is no doubt that they also work on a larger scale. For example, the Act II finale (No. 15) is so constructed that the keys of its eight sections move through a clearly conceived arch (see Table 3). The first three sections exhibit a straightforward tonic–dominant relationship (E flat major, B flat major), and the abrupt jump from B flat major to G major is appropriate given the unexpected arrival of Figaro. Thereafter, the finale moves through a circle of fifths back to its starting point, E flat major. The return is emphasised by motivic similarities between the two E flat major sections (compare bars 697–713 with 1–13). This provides tonal coherence and also suggests that by the end of the finale things are more or less back where they were at the beginning, with Figaro and Susanna's wedding no nearer fruition. Moreover, the two B flat major episodes are dramatically parallel: in the first, Susanna outwits the Count, and in the second, Figaro does so. The whole finale is a masterpiece of tonal planning that creates a firm structure through no less than 940 bars of music and despite all the twists and turns of the action. Moreover, its key scheme has broader resonances. The E flat major of the finale is the same as the key of the Countess's 'Porgi amor qualche ristoro' (No. 10); thus the whole of Act II might be said to elaborate the Neapolitan (flat supertonic) area of the opera's main key, D major. It is a distant relationship that emphasises just how far we have gone since the bustling opening of the 'folle journée'.

From the logical tonal scheme of the Act II finale, it seems but a short step to decipher large-scale tonal progressions within particular acts. Hermann Abert discerns the following pattern in Act I:[6]

I	G major	Figaro, Susanna
	B flat major	Figaro, Susanna
	F major	Figaro
II	D major	Bartolo
	A major	Marcellina, Susanna
III	E flat major	Cherubino
	B flat major	Count, Basilio, Susanna
IV	G major	Chorus
	C major	Figaro

Here the keys are largely related by fifths and thirds, the shifts are dictated by entries of new characters or changes in the dramatic situation, and the act elaborates a large-scale V–I progression. These keys also establish relationships that occur elsewhere in the opera: for example, juxtapositions of G and B flat major appear in Act II (Nos. 11–12, and in the finale, No. 15.3–4) and Act IV (Nos. 24–5), while the end of Act III (duet in B flat, chorus in G, finale in C) parallels the end of Act I. One can go further still: Levarie notes the D major of the overture, the E flat major of much of Act II (a Neapolitan acting as a substitute subdominant), the A minor/major at the beginning and end of Act III (see No. 16 and the A minor fandango in the finale), and the D major of the Act IV finale, and views the opera as an extended I–♭II(=IV)–V–I progression.[7]

The Act IV finale does appear to resolve the tonal dissonances of the opera, just as it resolves the emotional dissonances of the Count and Countess and, as we have seen, the melodic and harmonic 'dissonances' of their previous material. Its tonal scheme is less dynamic than that of the Act II finale – D major/G major/(E flat major/B flat major)/G major/D major – but it does take up the tonal threads of the earlier acts. The middle E flat and B flat major episodes, marking the reconciliation of Figaro and Susanna, hark back to the prominent keys of the Act II finale, while the D and G major sections take us back to the very beginning of the opera. Here the D major of the overture, a 'public' statement of the frenetic activity to come, led to the G major of the first duet, a 'private' domestic scene between Figaro and Susanna. At the end of the Act IV finale, the process is reversed: we move from the G major of the 'private' reconciliation between the Count and the Countess to the D major of the 'public' chorus of rejoicing. The point is emphasised by the motivic links between the final chorus (note the running quavers and the triadic fanfares) and the overture. The 'folle journée' opens and closes in D and thus exists within a single tonal space.

However, this neat tonal resolution may mask a problem with the ending of the opera. A number of critics seem to sense some dissatisfaction with the last two acts of *Figaro*, feeling that they fail to live up to the promise of Acts I and II. It is true that the action becomes confused as da Ponte compresses Beaumarchais's fast-moving action into an even more restricted time-scale, that the succession of arias in Act IV creates an uneasy stasis, and that the focus shifts from what is ostensibly the main plot of the opera, Figaro's wedding, to the Countess and the Count. But the crux comes when da Ponte and Mozart are required to pay the price for dramatic and musical strategies apparently adopted earlier in the opera. Just as the ending of *Don Giovanni* is 'difficult' in its transition from the high drama of Giovanni's death to the final *buffo* chorus, so too is that of *Figaro*. In the play, the reconciliation between the Count and the Countess is carried out with the same levity as the rest of the action. The Countess, prompted in part by guilt over Chérubin, forgives the Count once more, and we are left with the impression that she will have to do so yet again before too long. However, da Ponte and Mozart had to decide whether such a casual ending was appropriate given their alterations to the play, and in particular their redefinition of the Countess.

They seem to have disagreed. Da Ponte's ending matches the play and maintains the comic pace. In keeping with a long-established tradition of sudden operatic dénouements, he provides a text that is perfunctory to an extreme:

Count:	Contessa, perdono.	Countess, forgive me.
Countess:	Più docile io sono	I am kind
	e dico di sì.	and say yes.
All:	Ah! tutti contenti	Ah! all happy
	saremo così.	shall we be thus.

However, Mozart's setting, magnificent in its serenity and translucence, suggests another course. The Countess no longer forgives the Count out of affection mixed with a little guilt. Instead, her act of forgiveness is the ultimate self-sacrifice, a moment of true nobility and perfect love. 'Porgi amor qualche ristoro' and 'Dove sono i bei momenti' have been building up to just this. It seems clear that in Mozart's eyes at least the Count can only reform. But having reached a point of such high drama, it is difficult to end in the comic manner. The final D major chorus runs the danger of sounding trite: Mozart has gone too far to pull back.

Beaumarchais attempts to preserve a neutral tone in his play. However, music, and especially Mozart's music, cannot be neutral. As the opera progresses, Mozart increasingly injects a new emotional intensity into the apparently gay events of the 'folle journée'. The Act II trio, 'Susanna or via sortite' (No. 13), and most especially the Count's vicious curse of his wife in the Act II finale (No. 15.1, bar 64, in a fearsome F minor), seem to mark points where the *buffo* comedy is taken over by a more elemental, almost frightening drama. From here to the transcendental reconciliation, Mozart articulates emotions that Beaumarchais may have felt were better left unsaid. Perhaps he saw too much in the play's high-spirited intrigue. But perhaps it is precisely this that makes *Le nozze di Figaro* an operatic masterpiece.

8 *Le nozze di Figaro: a brief performance history*

Both Lorenzo da Ponte and the Irish tenor Michael Kelly left accounts of the rehearsals and first performance of *Le nozze di Figaro.* Neither are particularly impartial, but their colourful prose captures the flavour of events. In his *Memorie*, da Ponte offers a delightful description of problems caused by the Act III finale (No. 22), with its march and fandango. Dances had recently been banned from the theatre in Vienna, and when the Lord Chamberlain and Director-in-Chief of the Court Theatres, Count Franz Xaver Rosenberg, learnt of the dance planned for Act III of *Figaro*, he ordered the scene to be removed. According to da Ponte, Mozart was furious and threatened to withdraw the opera, but the librettist saw the ban for what it was, a malicious attempt by Rosenberg, and perhaps da Ponte's rival, the librettist Giambattista Casti, to sabotage the endeavour. He was ready with a solution:

On that same day, the dress rehearsal of the opera was to take place. I went personally to tell the Emperor [Joseph II], who told me that he would be there at the appointed time. He did indeed come, and with him half the nobility of Vienna. Abbate [Casti] also appeared with him. The first [third?] act was performed to universal applause. At the end of the act, there is a dumbshow between the Count and Susanna, during which the orchestra plays and the dance is performed. But since His Excellency Do-it-all [Rosenberg] had taken out that scene, one saw only the Count and Susanna gesticulating, and, with the orchestra silent, it seemed just like a puppet show. 'What is this?', said the Emperor to Casti, who was sitting behind him. 'You should ask the poet', replied the Abbate, with a wicked smile. Therefore I was summoned, but instead of replying to the question put to me, I presented him [the Emperor] with my manuscript, in which I had replaced the scene. The Emperor read it and asked me why there was no dance. My silence led him to understand that some foul play was afoot. He turned to the Count [Rosenberg] and asked for an explanation, and he, half mumbling, said that the dance was missing because the theatre had no dancers. 'Are there any', he [the Emperor] said, 'in the other theatres?' They told him that there were. 'Good, then let da Ponte have as many as he needs.' In less than half an hour, 24 dancers, or rather players, had arrived, at the end of the second act the missing scene was repeated, and the Emperor proclaimed 'Now it's all right!'.[1]

Michael Kelly, the first Basilio and Don Curzio, concentrates instead on the success of the opera, while also casting light on his own performance, his views on the music, and his opinion of Mozart:

Of all the performers in this opera at that time, but one survives – myself. It was allowed that never was opera stronger cast. I have seen it performed at different periods in other countries, and well too, but no more to compare with its original performance than light is to darkness. All the original performers had the advantage of the instruction of the composer who transfused into their minds his inspired meaning. I never shall forget his little animated countenance, when lighted up with the glowing rays of genius; – it is as impossible to describe it, as it would be to paint sun-beams.

I called on him one evening; he said to me, 'I have just finished a little duet for my opera, you shall hear it.' He sat down to the piano, and we sang it. I was delighted with it, and the musical world will give me credit for being so, when I mention the duet, sung by Count Almaviva and Susan, 'Crudel perchè finora farmi languire così' [No. 16]. A more delicious morceau never was penned by man, and it has often been a source of pleasure to me to have been the first who heard it, and to have sung it with its greatly gifted composer. I remember at the first rehearsal of the full band, Mozart was on the stage with his crimson pelisse and gold-laced cocked hat, giving the time of the music to the orchestra. Figaro's song, 'Non più andrai, farfallone amoroso' [No. 9], Bennuci gave, with the greatest animation, and power of voice.

I was standing close to Mozart, who, *sotto voce*, was repeating, Bravo! Bravo! Bennuci; and when Bennuci came to the fine passage, 'Cherubino, alla vittoria, alla gloria militar', which he gave out with Stentorian lungs, the effect was electricity itself, for the whole of the performers on the stage, and those in the orchestra, as if actuated by one feeling of delight, vociferated Bravo! Bravo! Maestro. Viva, viva, grande Mozart. Those in the orchestra I thought would never have ceased applauding, by beating the bows of their violins against the music desks. The little man acknowledged, by repeated obeisances, his thanks for the distinguished marks of enthusiastic applause bestowed upon him.

Kelly goes on to report the success of the Act II finale ('that piece of music alone, in my humble opinion, if he had never composed any thing else good, would have stamped him as the greatest master of his art'), and the way in which he managed to persuade Mozart to allow him (as Don Curzio) to stutter in the Act III sextet ('which was Mozart's favourite piece of the whole opera'). Finally:

At the end of the opera, I thought the audience would never have done applauding and calling for Mozart; almost every piece was encored, which prolonged it nearly to the length of two operas, and induced the Emperor to issue an order on the second representation, that no piece of music should be encored. Never was any thing more complete, than the triumph of Mozart, and his 'Nozze di Figaro', to which numerous overflowing audiences bore witness.[2]

Kelly's claims for the enthusiastic reception of *Figaro* in Vienna may be justified, for within the next few days, Joseph II banned repetitions of ensembles as encores in the Viennese theatres 'to prevent the excessive duration of the operas'.[3] However, during the nine performances of *Figaro* in Vienna in 1786, audience reaction seems generally to have been mixed. According to Count Karl Zinzendorf, 'the opera bored me', although Franz Kazinczy recorded that 'Storace, the beautiful singer, enchanted eye, ear and soul. – Mozart directed the orchestra, playing his fortepiano; but the joy which this music causes is so far removed from all sensuality that one cannot speak of it. Where could words be found that are worthy to describe such joy?'[4] Perhaps the *Wiener Realzeitung* of 11 July 1786 best summed up general reactions to the opera:

Herr Mozart's music was generally admired by connoisseurs already at the first performance. . .The *public*, however. . .did not really know on the first day where it stood. It heard many a *bravo* from unbiassed connoisseurs, but obstreperous louts in the uppermost storey exerted their hired lungs with all their might to deafen singers and audience alike with their *St!* and *Pst!*; and consequently opinions were divided at the end of the piece. Apart from that, it is true that the first performance was none of the best, owing to the difficulty of the composition. But now, after several performances, one would be subscribing either to the *cabal* or to *tastelessness* if one were to maintain that Herr *Mozart's* music is anything but a masterpiece of art. It contains so many beauties, and such a wealth of ideas, as can be drawn only from the source of innate genius.[5]

In Prague, public reaction to *Figaro* seems to have been more spontaneous and enthusiastic. The opera was first performed there in late November or early December 1786 by Pasquale Bondini's opera company. According to the *Prager Oberpostamtszeitung* (12 December 1786):

No piece. . .has ever caused such a sensation as the Italian opera *Die Hochzeit des Figaro*, which has already been given several times here with unlimited applause by Bondini's resident company of opera virtuosi. . . Connoisseurs who have seen this opera in Vienna are anxious to declare that it was done much better here; and this is very likely, since the wind instruments, on which the Bohemians are well known to be decided masters, have a great deal to do in the whole piece; the duets for trumpet and horn please especially.[6]

Mozart arrived in Prague on 11 January 1787, and on the 15th he wrote excitedly to Baron Gottfried von Jacquin in Vienna, 'here they talk about nothing but "Figaro". Nothing is played, sung or whistled but "Figaro". No opera is drawing like "Figaro". Nothing, nothing but "Figaro".'[7] He attended a performance of the opera on 17 January and conducted it on the 22nd. Prague always seems to have been more sympathetic to Mozart than Vienna, and the success of *Figaro* led to the commission for *Don Giovanni*, first performed there on 29 October 1787.

Soon after the first performance of *Figaro*, the Viennese music-copying firms of Torricella and Lausch advertised full scores, piano scores and arrangements of the opera for string quartet: by mid-1787 one could also buy versions for string quintet, and six- or eight-part wind ensemble.[8] Such arrangements were a common means of disseminating operas in the late eighteenth century; indeed, this was often the way in which music-lovers came to know such works. Mozart himself was to poke fun at the vogue for wind arrangements as *Tafelmusik* in the banquet scene of the Act II finale of *Don Giovanni*, where a stage wind-band performs extracts from Vicente Martín y Soler's *Una cosa rara*, Giuseppe Sarti's *Fra i due litiganti il terzo gode*, and 'Non più andrai farfallone amoroso' (No. 9) from *Figaro*, the last to Leporello's comment 'Questa poi la conosco pur troppo' ('I know this all too well'). *Figaro* was performed in German by mid-1787 in Prague and then Donaueschingen, and from 1788 onwards, two German translations, one by Christian August Vulpius and a reputedly better one by Baron Adolf Knigge, were in use throughout Germany.[9] Knigge's translation, with spoken dialogue rather than recitative, apparently incorporated material from the original play and thus 'restored a number of amusing passages omitted in the Italian'.[10] In February 1789, 'Non più andrai farfallone amoroso' was also included in a *pasticcio* opera to a libretto by da Ponte, *L'ape musicale*.[11]

Figaro does not seem to have been performed in Vienna in 1787 or 1788; perhaps it was eclipsed by operas such as *Una cosa rara*. On 29 August 1789, however, Mozart revived it in the Burgtheater. There were some additions and revisions. Adriana Ferrarese del Bene (i.e. Francesca Gabrielli, da Ponte's mistress), the new Susanna, was given two new arias: 'Venite, inginocchiatevi' (No. 12) was replaced by 'Un moto di gioia', K579, and 'Deh vieni non tardar, oh gioia bella' (No. 27) by 'Al desio di chi t'adora', K577.[12] Apparently, 'Dove sono i bei momenti' (No. 19) was shortened and its second section slightly rewritten (see Plate 3). 'Vedrò mentre io sospiro' (No. 17) was also given a slightly extended second section and the vocal range was adapted upwards for the new Count (possibly Francesco Albertarelli, the first Vienna Don Giovanni).[13] Mozart always deemed it important to write according to the qualities of his singers and therefore provided new pieces where necessary in revivals of his operas 'so as to fit the costume to [the] figure'.[14] Both of del Bene's added arias seem to anticipate *Così fan tutte*: 'Un moto di gioia' is akin to the music associated with Despina (compare 'Una donna a quindici anni', No. 19, and the quartet 'La mano a me date', No. 22); and the virtuosic 'Al desio di chi t'adora', a rondò like the original aria which 'Deh vieni non tardar, oh gioia bella' replaced, reminds one of the music of del Bene's next great Mozart role, Fiordiligi. This revised *Figaro* was performed in Vienna 11 times in 1789, 14 times in 1790, and 3 times in 1791. After the performance on 9 February 1791, no opera by Mozart was performed in either of the court theatres in Vienna until the revival of *Figaro* at the Kärntnertortheater on 10 July 1798.

Opinions of *Figaro*, like opinions of Mozart in general, varied. Most critics agreed on the high quality of parts of the opera, but they often gave only qualified approval to the whole. According to the *Dramaturgische Blätter* of Frankfurt on Main (1788), 'Mozart's music has fine passages, but also familiar ideas and turns'.[15] The critic of the *Chronik von Berlin* (2 October 1790) praised the music, but noted: 'The only thing one missed was a manly tenor among the principal voices, and it is a great loss that Mozart composed his *Figaro* for a Court at a time when it had good basses but no good tenor'.[16] On 9 October 1790 the same journal raised another problem: 'this grand, heavenly music lies quite beyond the confines of the local public's perceptive faculty; for it cannot sing this through to itself afterwards, as it can with *Der Baum der Diana* and *Lilla*'.[17] This reflects criticisms often made of Mozart's music: that it was too artfully conceived and that the melodies and orchestrations were often too complex. His apparent over-use of wind instruments was frequently criticised, which may reflect the poor quality of wind players in most centres apart from Prague at the time. However, others noted that Mozart's music 'suits the characters and the sentiments of the singing personages, and for ear and heart alike is full of expression and truth',[18] and that *Figaro* 'is more theatrical than any other of his compositions for the stage. Faithful depiction of character, beautiful, spirited melodies, choruses [i.e. ensembles] that form an integral part of the action, above all a spirit of complaisance and

Plate 3 'Dove sono i bei momenti' (No. 19) from British Library, R.M. 22.i.5, possibly as performed in Vienna, 1789

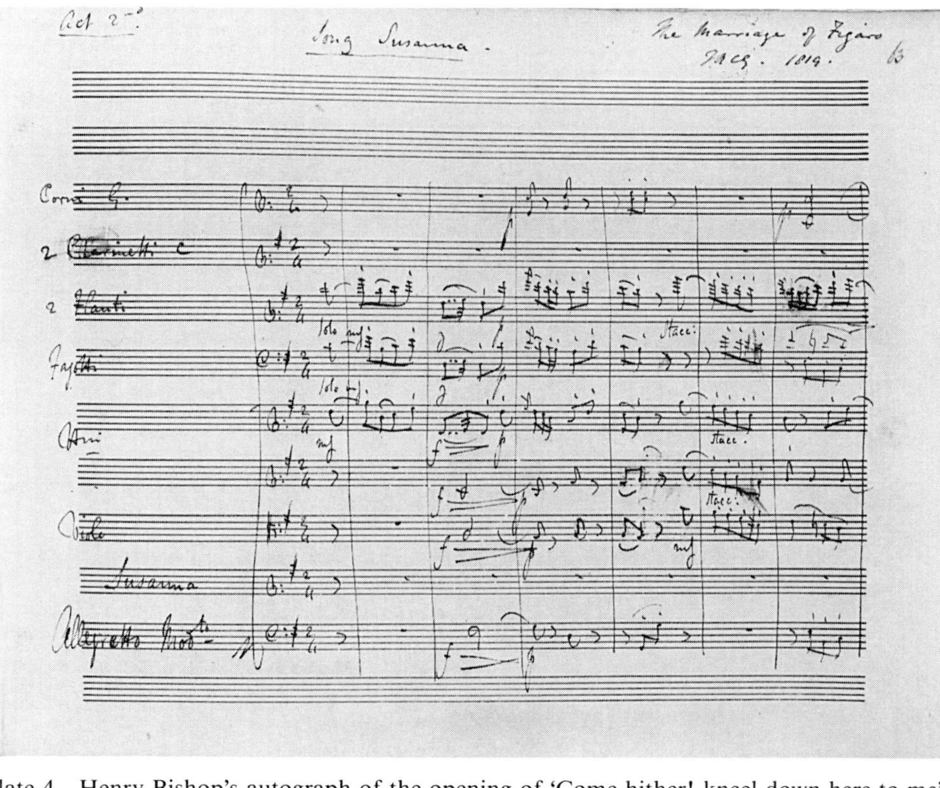

Plate 4 Henry Bishop's autograph of the opening of 'Come hither! kneel down here to me' ('Venite, inginocchiatevi', No. 12)

lightness, give it a worth by means of which it will always maintain its place on our lyric stage.'[19] Perhaps the most perceptive contemporary comment was by Bernhard Anselm Weber:

> It is what was to be expected of Mozart: great and beautiful, full of new ideas and unexpected turns, full of art, fire and genius. Now we are enchanted by beautiful, charming song; now we are made to smile at subtle, comic wit and fancy; now we admire the naturally conceived and superbly executed planning; now the magnificence and greatness of Art takes us by surprise. Where all this is united, it is bound to make its effect and to satisfy the sensitive hearer as well as the experienced and practised expert. Mozart is gifted with the happy genius that can blend art with nature and song with grace. Again he ventures on impetuous and fiery sallies, and how bold are his harmonies! In this opera, too, he shows that he possesses a true talent for the comic-dramatic style. . .[20]

Figaro moved south of the Alps in autumn 1787 with a performance in Monza in Lombardy.[21] Acts III and IV were reset to music by Angelo Tarchi (*c*1760–1814). Barbarina was cut out completely (Antonio is given the task of delivering the pin to the Count at the beginning of Act IV), and although the Count entered as usual in Act I scene 6, he first sang 'Voi che sapete' (Cherubino, No. 11) to slightly altered words before continuing in Mozart's recitative. This aria was then omitted in Act II. There were other changes to the libretto: the second stanza of the Countess's 'Dove sono i bei momenti' (No. 19) was omitted, and the texts of the Act III sextet and the duet in the Act III finale ('Amanti costanti') were slightly altered. Some nine months later, *Figaro* was performed in Florence at the Teatro della Pergola: Acts I and II on 12 June, and Acts III and IV on 16 June 1788.[22] Cherubino's 'Non so più cosa son, cosa faccio' (No. 6) was replaced by an aria for Susanna, 'Senza speme ognor s'aggira', possibly by Bartolomeo Cherubini; a section of the Act II finale was omitted ('Conoscete, signor Figaro', bars 398–466, as also seems to have occurred in Prague in 1786–7); and other sections of the recitative were cut. These performances at Monza and Florence were perhaps prompted by Joseph II recommending the opera to his brothers, Archduke Ferdinand, the governor of Lombardy, and Archduke Peter Leopold, Grand Duke of Tuscany. However, *Figaro* does not seem to have entered the regular Italian repertory. In 1792, an altered version of da Ponte's libretto, entitled *La serva onorata* was performed in Naples with music by Niccolò Piccinni (1728–1800), and the same text was set by Ferdinando Paer (1771–1839) for his *Il nuovo Figaro* (Parma, January 1794). Of course, the practice of adapting pre-existing libretti was nothing new. The next performance of Mozart's *Figaro* seems to have been in Turin in autumn 1811.

Figaro was probably first performed at the Paris Opéra on 20 March 1793, in a five-act version sung in French and with the recitatives replaced by Beaumarchais's original spoken dialogue.[23] It required no fewer than 40 rehearsals. Beaumarchais may have been involved in the production in an advisory role, although the verse translations of the arias and ensembles seem to have been done by one Notaris. In Act II, Cherubino sang both 'Voi che sapete' (No. 11) and, after 'Venite, inginocchiatevi' (No. 12), 'Auprès d'une fontaine', the original song which Beaumarchais had the page sing to the tune of 'Malbroug s'en va-t-en guerre'. Act III ended with the sextet, which was preceded by Basilio's 'In quegl'anni in cui val poco' (No. 25), and then Act IV began, like Act II, with the Countess alone. This act ended with Mozart's Act III finale, which was expanded: the fandango was replaced by a gavotte (possibly by Antoine Laurent Baudron (1742–1834), who had written the music for the 1784 performance of Beaumarchais's play); Figaro sang 'Les preuves les plus sûres' to the music of Don Giovanni's 'Metà di voi qua vadano' from *Don Giovanni* (No. 18); and Marcellina then sang 'Ces maîtres de nos âmes' to the music of Dorabella's 'È amore un ladroncello' from *Così fan tutte* (No. 28). This aria for Marcellina replaced 'Il capro e la capretta' (No. 24), which was omitted from the new Act V.

One review of the performance criticised the mixture of singing and speech, which was felt to more suitable to *opéra comique* than to a performance at the Opéra. However, the music received due praise:

> This comedy is embellished with the superb music of Mozart, a distinguished artist who died a year ago in Vienna in the service of the Emperor. The music bears the hallmark of the greatest masters; two finales are masterpieces, especially the one of the second act. Its genius, vigour and elegance are noteworthy, and we encourage lovers of fine music to go and hear this [finale] often, for it will particularly please them. The piece is produced with care, but it is too long, and although the trial scene in the third act has had to be omitted, there remain many cuts to be made in the dialogue, which would further tighten up the action.[24]

The length of the dialogue was a problem, and after the second performance on 22 March Beaumarchais consented to cut the play. He also advised that instrumental pieces should be written to begin each act and that more dances should be added. A new four-act version was produced. The new Act III now began with the sextet, followed by the duet between the Count and Susanna ('Crudel! perchè finora', No. 16), and the Count's and Basilio's arias (the latter moved to Act III in the first French version) were omitted. The finale to Act III was further expanded, with a more extended gavotte preceded by a movement based on *Les folies d'Espagne* (i.e. the bass pattern known as *la folia*). This revised version was performed on 15 April 1793, and repeated on 19 and 24 April before being withdrawn because of poor receipts at the box-office.

This hybrid *Figaro* was repeated on 1 September 1793 but was then revived (with some further cuts) only at the Théâtre de l'Opéra-Comique on 19 December 1807, at the same time as the Opéra was mounting an 'authentic' version of the opera in Italian (first performed on 23 December 1807). Both the Italian version and a French version by François Henri Joseph Castil-Blaze (first used at Nîmes in 1818 and Paris in 1826) continued to be performed in France and Belgium through the nineteenth century. There were also *pasticcio* reworkings of the play and the opera, including *Le page inconstant ou Honni soit qui mal y pense*, a 'ballet héroï-comique' (mid-1818), and *Figaro ou Le jour de noces*, a *pasticcio* after Beaumarchais, Mozart and Rossini, to a text by F. V. A. and L. C. A. d'Artois de Bournonville and with the music arranged by Felice Blangini (1781–1841), first performed at the Théâtre des Nouveautés on 16 August 1827.[25]

In London, music from Mozart's *Figaro* first became known through interpolations in other operas.[26] The English-speaking singers of the first performance, Nancy Storace and Michael Kelly, and Mozart's pupils Stephen Storace (1762–96) and Thomas Attwood (1765–1838), were important in bringing his music to the London stage. Nancy Storace and Francesco Benucci, the first Figaro, inserted 'Crudel! perchè finora' (No. 16) in a performance of Giuseppe Gazzaniga's *La vendemmia* (1778) at the King's Theatre, Haymarket, on 9 May 1789; Nancy Storace sang 'Deh vieni non tardar, oh gioia bella' (No. 27, plus Zerlina's 'Batti, batti, bel Masetto' from *Don Giovanni*, No. 13) in a *pasticcio*, *La villanella rapita*, first performed on 27 February 1790; 'Non più andrai farfallone amoroso' (No. 9) was included in Attwood's *The Prisoner* (18 October 1792); 'Che soave zeffiretto' (No. 20) was 'loudly encored' in Attwood's *Caernarvon Castle* (12 August 1793; it may also have been included in Storace's *The Siege of Belgrade*, 1 January 1791);[27] and 'Non so più cosa son, cosa faccio' (No. 6) was included in a performance of Pietro Alessandro Guglielmi's *La pastorella nobile* (1788) on 17 February 1801. 'Non più andrai farfallone amoroso' also has the distinction of being the Slow March of the Coldstream Guards (according to some, since 1787), and in 1824 it was turned into a virtuosic show-piece for Angelica Catalani (the first London Susanna). However, even though da Ponte was in London between late 1792 and 1805 – for a time he was librettist at the King's Theatre, Haymarket – a complete opera by Mozart was not performed there until 1806, when *La clemenza di Tito* was first staged at the King's Theatre, Haymarket, on 27 March. Between 1809 and 1811 there were amateur performances of *Don Giovanni*, *Le nozze di Figaro* and *Così fan tutte*. However, *Così fan tutte* was first staged professionally on 9 May 1811 (with the addition of 'Voi che sapete', sung by Guglielmo), *Die Zauberflöte*, in Italian, on 6 June 1811, *Le nozze di Figaro* on 18 June 1812, *Don Giovanni* on 12 April 1817, and *Die Entführung aus dem Serail* on 24 November 1821.[28]

The London première of *Le nozze di Figaro* (anticipated by a one-act *burletta* based on the opera first staged at the Pantheon on 2 May 1812) received the following announcement in *The Times*:

> There will be represented at this Theatre [the King's Theatre, Haymarket], THIS EVENING, June 18, and for the first time in this country, the celebrated Opera of LE MARIAGE DE FIGARO: the music by Mozart. To be performed by Madame Catalani [Susanna], Signor Fischer [the Count], Signor Naldi [Figaro], Signor Righi [Bartolo], Signor Miarteni [Basilio], Signor Di Giovanni [Antonio], Madame Bianchi [Marcellina], Madame Pucitta [Cherubino], Signora Luigia [?Calderini, Barbarina], and Mrs Dickons [the Countess], from the English stage, being her first appearance at this Theatre. [At the] End of the first Act will be revived (expressly for the occasion) the favourite popular Scotch ballet of PEGGY's LOVE: composed by M. Didelot. After the Opera, the grand national air of 'God save the King,' will be sung by Signor Tramezzani, who is anxious to give his assistance on this occasion. To conclude with the new Ballet of LA REINE DE GOLCONDE; composed by M. Didelot, and performed by Mons. Vestris and Madame Angiolini, Mons. Bourdin, Master Byrne, Miss Smith, Miss Twamley, Miss Peto, Misses Davis, and Mons. and Mad. Didelot, &c. In the course of the evening, a Poem, written for this occasion by an English Lady, will be recited by Mr. Elliston. All the above eminent performers have generously given their gratuitous assistance on this occasion. Doors to open at six, and the performance begin at seven o'clock.[29]

The performance was for the benefit of the Scottish Hospital, and with the addition of two ballets, the national anthem and a poem, it must have been a lengthy affair, even with the cuts that were undoubtedly made in the opera. Henry Robertson, writing in *The Examiner*, commented on the delay in bringing Mozart to the London stage, offered some perceptive insights into the opera, and made a revealing comparison between Mozart and Beethoven:

The works of MOZART, which have long lain dormant, and enjoyed the repose due to so many of our living manufacturers of music, have at length shone forth from the obscurity in which jealousy and bad taste had involved them. Till the last two or three years this great genius has been known chiefly as an instrumental writer, and might still have remained so, had not a society of amateurs, who were capable of perceiving where true merit was to be found, laudably exerted themselves to diffuse the delight his vocal works had given themselves. With this view, and aided by some tasteful professors, they brought forward the Opera of *Don Giovanni*, and followed it up successively with performances of two of his other productions, which required only to be heard, to ensure them a high reputation. Till they had gained this, none of the Opera Performers thought of reviving them, and of the four which have been performed at the King's Theatre, only one has been produced by the Manager – so little have the Public to thank Mr. Taylor for his endeavours on their behalf. The last which has been produced, *Le Nozze di Figaro*, is perhaps, altogether, the finest of his works. The subject is taken, with little alteration, from BEAUMARCHAIS's celebrated comedy of 'La Folle Journée', and, in its quick succession of incident, gives full scope to the fancy, which teemed with delightful combinations of sound, and sprung from subject to subject with inexhaustable freshness, vigour, and originality. Every air, and almost every close, has strong character of novelty, and seems carefully to shun resemblance to other authors; for even when the passages seem to lead to something we have heard before, a dexterous turn or an unexpected change redeems them from all charge of plagiarism. This attempt at constant novelty would be dangerous in unskilful hands, and might repress merit, or draw it into passages only original for their extravagance. Here, BEETHOVEN, with all his gigantic powers, his wonderful harmony, and splendid effects, seems to have failed; and without possessing the charms of melody that play so perpetually through the works of MOZART, he sacrifices our pleasure to our astonishment; gaining in novelty what he loses in feeling, and speaking to the ear rather than to the heart.[30]

Figaro was given eight times in 1812, and then revived in March 1813, June 1816, and February 1817. The 1817 revival, first staged on 1 February with an all-Italian cast, was given eleven performances and seems to have been a marked success. Afterwards, *The Times* was prompted to remark that *Figaro* was 'among all the works of Mozart that which combines in the greatest degree the two qualities of sprightliness and grandeur'.[31]

Figaro was first performed in English at Covent Garden on 6 March 1819 in a three-act version 'translated, altered and arranged. . .and the whole adapted to the English stage' by Henry Rowley Bishop (1786–1855), a prodigious composer and arranger of works designed to cater for the seemingly idiosyncratic tastes of English audiences.[32] The plot was drastically simplified, the recitative was replaced by spoken dialogue, the Count became a speaking role, and one character, Fiorello (appropriated from Rossini's *Il barbiere di Siviglia*) was added, in part to sing the Count's music. Other music was also reallocated: for example, the Countess sang 'Voi che sapete' (to the text 'Love ever leave me, peace to restore'). Bishop added his own arias, arranged music from other works by Mozart and, at one point, Rossini, and reworked those pieces from Mozart's score that remained. He supplied a new finale for Act I, incorporating part of 'Non più andrai farfallone amoroso' and some of the Act I finale of *Così fan tutte*, but in general the more complex action-ensembles were removed and played out in dialogue. It seems that these ensembles were deemed too complex for English ears, and the opera became more a succession of solo songs. In altering Mozart's music, Bishop tended to enlarge the orchestration and add instrumental music, including extra introductions and interpolations in the arias. He also regularised the formal structure of individual pieces. Thus both 'Se vuol ballare' (sung to 'Count Almaviva's a compound of evil') and 'Non so più cosa son, cosa faccio' became straightforward rondos. Similarly, 'Venite, inginocchiatevi', with its irregular phrases and asymmetrical organisation, was drastically recomposed (see Plate 4).

Bishop claimed that his intention was 'to improve our National taste for Music, by, at every opportunity, establishing the works of the immortal MOZART on the English stage'. Moreover:

> The obstacles, also, that arose in adapting the *Music* were innumerable! The reception, however, the Opera has met with, was at once gratifying and encouraging, has repaid every exertion, and forms a most important era in the Musical History of this country.[33]

Some critics agreed. According to an account in the *Theatrical Inquisitor*:

> The chief object in this piece, and that which doubtless gave birth to the drama in its novel form, was the music of Mozart's 'Nozze di Figaro' adapted to English words, and then introduced for the first time at a national theatre. In praise of this design it is impossible to say too much; because wherever good taste, and perhaps it may be said good sense, prevails, it must be a subject for sincere admiration. Mr. Bishop, to whom the credit is due of bringing it before the public, performed his task in a manner much beyond the fairest expectation, considering the difficulties he had to encounter. The piece was given out for repetition amidst the loudest and most unanimous applause.[34]

However, others were less enthusiastic:

> We must here take leave to lament, that *Mr. Bishop* should have omitted so

much of *Mozart's* music, to make room for his own: which latter, we beg to assure him, contrasts very disadvantageously with the original music of Figaro, though *he* perhaps may not be disposed to take our word for this salutary truth.

Similarly:

What are we to say to an adapter of *Mozart*, who for some of his pieces substitutes the airs about the street, and in others alters passages to suit the voice of the performer? Those passages were written to suit particular passions or emotions, not to be at the mercy of this or that incapacity. Their beauty also, and that of the context itself, depends upon preserving the context entire.[35]

This bowdlerised *Figaro* held the stage for some twenty years both in the London theatres and in the provinces (Edinburgh, July 1819; Portsmouth, April 1823; Newcastle, July 1823; Cambridge, 1 October 1825). 'Non più andrai farfallone amoroso' seems to have been restored in its entirety, but 'Voi che sapete' remained with the Countess, and Susanna was regularly given such 'airs about the street' as 'Home, Sweet Home' and 'I've Been Roaming'.[36]

Figaro was intermittently revived in Italian in London: in winter 1837–8 it was done at Covent Garden by 'a troop of fourth rate continental singers. . .under the controul of seven-and-twentyfifth-rate fiddlers and hornblowers'.[37] A performance of the unadulterated score in German (with spoken dialogue rather than recitative) by a visiting German troupe at Drury Lane in May 1841 seems to have been more successful. Perhaps this encouraged the demise of Bishop's score. On 15 April 1842, a new English version by Planché was given its first night at Covent Garden, conducted by Julius Benedict. Although there was again spoken dialogue rather than sung recitative, Planché's version was generally faithful to the original. The manager, Madame Vestris, who had earlier played Susanna and who was also well known for her shapely legs, played Cherubino, Adelaide Kemble (the daughter of Charles Kemble, the proprietor of the theatre) Susanna, Miss Rainforth the Countess, and Stretton the Count. The opera was done 'with great taste and care' and with splendid scenery, and the performance was generally praised. At last a good version of *Figaro* in English had reached the London stage.

Figaro was not the most popular of Mozart's operas in the nineteenth century. The diabolic overtones of *Don Giovanni* held far more attraction for the Romantics. For those who favoured Italianate vocal display, the complex ensembles and rich orchestrations of *Figaro* had little appeal. On the other hand, those Germans who demanded that opera should make grand philosophical statements on the human condition could not understand why Mozart dealt with such frivolous material which, as with *Così fan tutte*, only served to broadcast the loose morals of the eighteenth century. It is significant that when Otto Jahn produced his monumental study of Mozart in the 1850s, he felt it necessary to defend *Figaro* against the accusation of immorality.[38] Susanne Vill's performance statistics of *Figaro, Don Giovanni* and *Così fan tutte* in selected European theatres document the extent to which *Figaro* took second place to *Don Giovanni* in this period (Table 4). Also noteworthy is the general

Table 4 *Performances of Le nozze di Figaro, Don Giovanni and Così fan tutte at theatres in Cologne, Darmstadt, Dresden, Frankfurt, Hamburg, Karlsruhe, Munich, Prague and Vienna, 1790–1970*

	Figaro	Don Giovanni	Così fan tutte
1790/91–1799/1800	69	99	51
1800/01–1809/10	70	101	32
1810/11–1819/20	119	184	31
1820/21–1829/30	155	186	21
1830/31–1839/40	101	216	19
1840/41–1849/50	195	258	8
1850/51–1859/60	167	298	19
1860/61–1869/70	232	247	47
1870/71–1879/80	227	250	19
1880/81–1889/90	221	299	81
1890/91–1899/1900	272	276	47
1900/01–1909/10	303	203	28
1910/11–1919/20	315	237	61
1920/21–1929/30	560	355	157
1930/31–1939/40	339	251	131
1940/41–1949/50	635	316	207
1950/51–1959/60	654	447	390
1960/61–1969/70	674	534	450

Source: S. Vill (ed.), *'Così fan tutte': Beiträge zur Wirkungsgeschichte von Mozarts Oper* (Bayreuth, Mühl'scher Universitätsverlag, 1978), pp. 283–7. Vill presents statistics for five-year periods, and her details are not always complete for each city.

unpopularity of *Così fan tutte*, at least until the 1920s. Similarly, there seem to have been no performances of *Figaro* at Covent Garden between 1849 and 1866.[39] Of course, the opera was not entirely neglected, and 'Voi che sapete' or 'Deh vieni non tardar, oh gioia bella' remained popular in Victorian drawing rooms. But on the whole, the times seem to have been out of sympathy with the opera.

Only with the twilight of Romanticism did *Figaro* gain ground. This was accompanied by a revaluation of the composer. Even in 1915, Frederick Niecks, Reid Professor of Music at Edinburgh University, felt it necessary to counter the nineteenth-century view that Mozart was simply a facile melodist: 'In fact, Mozart at his best was not a mere purveyor of pleasing tunes, but a divine master, great as a craftsman and great as a tone poet.' He also justified Mozart's ensembles against accusations of artificiality and a lack of dramatic credibility, arguing against the trend of neglecting such ensembles in favour of his arias and duets: 'Mozart may be cited as one of those who in utilizing aria and *ensemble* have not only not weakened the dramatic truth and force, but have infinitely increased them.'[40] It is significant that Niecks's defence is conducted in Wagnerian terms, and also that Mozart's ensemble technique is increasingly seen as an important aspect of his art. However, the tide was already turning. In the 1906 Salzburg Festival, Gustav Mahler conducted a performance of *Figaro* that created 'an imperishable memory. . .This was the ideal *Figaro* in its enchanting grace, its lightwinged conversational tone and the incomparable balance of the whole ensemble. No one who was present on that occasion can ever forget it.'[41]

If Mahler (and later Franz Schalk at Vienna and Bruno Walter at Salzburg) fostered a new view of *Figaro* in Austria and Germany, the credit for doing so in England perhaps belongs to Thomas Beecham and Edward Dent. The famous Beecham revivals of Mozart's operas in 1910, and then a remarkable production at Drury Lane in the summer of 1917 (produced by Nigel Playfair and designed by Hugo Rumbold) set new standards for performances of *Figaro* in English: critics particularly noted the bold and novel approach to the production and the exceptionally clear enunciation of the singers.[42] Dent's masterly study of Mozart's operas was published in 1913, and his splendid translation of the libretto to *Figaro* (prepared in 1915) was used in a series of performances at the Old Vic beginning on 15 January 1920, initiating a distinguished set of Mozart productions involving the collaboration of Dent, the producer Clive Carey, and the conductor Charles Corri. The recitatives were replaced by spoken dialogue, and the Act III sextet and much of the Act IV finale were cut. But Carey took advantage of a cast that was almost entirely new to the opera to build up a carefully rehearsed performance that returned to the spirit and practice of eighteenth-century comedy: according to Dent, 'we were determined to avoid the Dresden China prettiness with which Mozart was almost always staged in the German court theatres'.[43] Carey also insisted that the words should always be heard, even in the most complex ensembles. The result was a fine realisation of the opera that played to houses 'packed from stalls to gallery'.[44]

Under the influence of the neo-classical revival, the time was ripe for Mozart to be viewed no longer from a Romantic perspective. To do so, however, required, as Clive Carey knew, much more rehearsal time than was common in most repertory opera houses, and also a greater commitment to teamwork than that to which many opera virtuosi were accustomed. The ideal *Figaro*, then, requires ideal conditions, and it is to John Christie's credit that he provided such conditions at Glyndebourne: *Figaro* inaugurated the annual festival of opera at Glyndebourne in May 1934. The producer, Carl Ebert, and the conductor, Fritz Busch, were given unparalleled opportunities to work long and hard with their cast and the orchestra, building up the production detail by detail. Busch taught his audience, not to mention a younger generation of conductors, 'that the Mozart of the operas never was pretty even if he might be delicate: that his vein of ardour, of passionate vigour could only be served by playing and singing intensely, not at all by mere precision. . .that orchestral detail must be made vivid if Mozart's conception of his characters. . .was to be made plain in performance'. His readings were 'of almost bucolic humour, of masculine directness'.[45] As for the production, critics noted the penetrating interaction of music and drama (the effectiveness of the ensembles was again singled out for comment) and generally approved the fact that the opera was not done as usual in English or German – neither language is particularly well suited to Mozart's vocal lines in *Figaro* – but instead in the original Italian, where the relationship of word and music could come through forcefully, and for many for the first time. The argument of whether *Figaro* should be done in translation, for the sake of audience comprehension, or in Italian, for the sake of the music, continues today.

Some six years after the Glyndebourne performance, *Figaro* was revived at the New York Metropolitan Opera. The work has had a mixed history there. It was first performed by the company on 31 January 1894 (ten years after the house was opened), and there had been some memorable performances over the turn of the century, whether in New York or on tour (three performances in San Francisco in the 1901–2 season were particular successes).[46] Mahler also conducted *Figaro* in New York and Boston in 1909. But in the 1920s and 1930s the opera suffered from the Metropolitan's emphasis on nineteenth-century grand opera, and particularly Wagner: there were no performances of *Figaro* between the first and second world wars. It was revived (sung in Italian) on 20 February 1940 in a production by Herbert Graf, with sets by Jonel Jorgulesco and conducted by Ettore Panizza, and it is significant that B. H. Haggin and Alfred Frankenstein, in essays prefacing a radio broadcast of the Metropolitan's *Figaro* on 7 December 1940, had to warn listeners to expect something different from Wagnerian opulence.[47] Graf had already produced the opera in Philadelphia and at the 1937 Maggio Musicale Festival in Florence. He sought to restore the printed and manuscript stage directions in the copy of the 1786 libretto housed in the Library of Congress, aiming 'to express the atmosphere of the refined, courtly rococo comedy of Beaumarchais. . .as seen through the warm humanity and grace of Mozart's music'.[48] This did not meet with total approval: Olin Downes in the *New York Times* noted, perhaps unfortunately to our eyes, that the production ignored 'the purity of traditions established through many years on many stages'. But Downes was struck by the same features that so distinguished the Glyndebourne production, the 'unified dramatic and musical ensemble' and the 'spirit and authority' of the performance, and he owned that it was 'one of the Metropolitan's most earnest and brilliant achievements of many seasons. . .The public will discover from this performance that Mozart is not a cold classic of a former age.'[49]

In the post-war years, a remarkable group of singers nurtured by the Vienna Staatsoper, including Lisa Della Casa, Hilde Gueden, Erich Kunz, Irmgard Seefried and Elisabeth Schwarzkopf, established themselves as the principal Mozart singers of their generation and brought new insights to *Figaro* whether at home or on tour (for example, in London and New York). Moreover, the introduction of long-playing records in the late 1940s made their and other fine interpretations of the opera available to a wide public: Erich Kleiber's 1955 recording is still justly regarded as a classic. But to judge by reviews, many productions of *Figaro* through the 1950s seem to have lacked the sense of adventure and discovery that was so much a feature of the pre-war revivals. Glyndebourne continued to set the standard for Mozart, and it was occasionally matched by other houses. However, the impression is that the new styles of performance were gradually becoming as staid as the old as *Figaro* became a standard repertory piece. To some extent, the problem lay with current perceptions of the opera. Frankenstein lauded *Figaro* for 'its romantic vivacity, its comic freshness, its music of moonlight and garlands', and Graf sought to emphasise its 'refined, courtly rococo comedy'. This courtly image of *Figaro* was reinforced by contemporary stage designs, whether Jorgulesco's, which did such sterling service at the Metropolitan (they were used through the 1950s), or Oliver Messel's sets for Glyndebourne (1955) and the Metropolitan (1959). *Figaro* ran the danger of becoming ossified as Viennese rococo kitsch.

The trend in the early 1960s, however, was to re-think the opera. If the most remarkable aspect of *Figaro* productions in the first half of the century had been to discover Mozart anew, now it was time to seek out Beaumarchais and accordingly to exploit the social and political tensions of the opera. Lucchino Visconti's production (premièred in Rome in the 1963–4 season, with sets by Visconti and Filippo Sanjust, and conducted by Carlo Maria Giulini) turned away from Austrian and British traditions by putting the opera back in a southern Mediterranean setting and placing strong emphasis both on the political undercurrents of the plot and on the real-life qualities of the characters. Visconti 'staged the opera with an unfailingly theatrical point of view – one that brought out the passionate skepticism in Mozart instead of the creampuff melancholy'.[50] Oscar Schuh's new production of *Figaro* at Covent Garden (1963, designed by Teo Otto, conducted by Georg Solti) was praised, despite Solti's too-fast speeds, for allowing the audience 'to savour its structural complexity, its tough intellectual fibre and its emotional seriousness'.[51] Even the Ebert production at Glyndebourne was re-worked so that 'the contempt which the servants feel for the characters and qualities of their noble masters, and equally the contempt with which they are treated by them, was more strikingly expressed than in any earlier post-war production',[52] while revolution was also a prominent feature of the new production by Gustav Rudolf Sellner (designed by Michael Raffenelli, conducted by Karl Böhm) premièred at the Salzburg Festival in 1962.

This exploration of the sources for *Figaro* was matched by an

Plate 5 'Voi che sapete' (No. 11), Act II scene 3: set by Oliver Messel, Glyndebourne 1955

attempt to discover 'what Mozart really meant', the title of an essay by Charles Mackerras prefacing John Bletchley's new production at Sadler's Wells (1965, using the Dent translation).[53] Mackerras, who conducted the performance, adopted the re-ordering of Act III (placing the Countess's 'Dove sono i bei momenti' before the sextet), restored Marcellina's and Basilio's Act IV arias, and added ornamentation, including appoggiaturas in the recitatives (now thought to be indispensable) and decoration in the arias in part modelled on Henry Bishop's score (somewhat more controversial, although many critics now favour some such ornamentation, including a cadenza in 'Dove sono i bei momenti'). It is revealing of the times, however, that Bletchley was criticised for underplaying the social and satirical implications of the opera,[54] even if more than one listener remarked that he was 'hearing Mozart's *Figaro* as if for the first time'.[55]

The trend of 'politicising' *Figaro* continued in the 1970s. John Copley's production for Covent Garden (1971, designed by Stefanos Lazaridis, conducted by Colin Davis) exploited the social and sexual tensions of the opera to the full, being 'fertile, busy, and keenly observant of the text and its implications'.[56] Jean-Pierre Ponnelle's production at Salzburg (1972, designed by Ponnelle, conducted by Herbert von Karajan), with its ravishing sets, rivalled the Covent Garden performance in perception, even if some critics found it unduly serious and solemn.[57] Peter Hall's fine production at Glyndebourne (1973, designed by John Bury, conducted by John Pritchard) was praised by Stanley Sadie as 'no vivacious frolic. It almost entirely avoids the kind of horseplay and comic business in which many *Figaro* productions abound; and it has a marvellously clear and sharp sense of what the opera is really about. . .' The production stressed firmly the social conflicts which motivate the opera, and the whole was 'a compliment to an audience's intelligence'.[58] Likewise, Michael Geliot produced *Figaro* for the Welsh National Opera (1977, designed by Alexander MacPherson, conducted by György Fischer, with a new translation by Geliot himself)[59] in a way 'evidently designed to emphasize the political and sexual realism that is an undoubted element in the plot'.[60]

But although most critics approved of this deeper exploration of the social tensions underlying *Figaro*, one can also sense a certain unease. Alberto Pironti felt unhappy with Visconti's emphasis on satire and social protest, elements 'which, although clearly present in Beaumarchais's comedy, should properly disappear in Mozart's

Plate 6 Act II scene 8 (above), Act III scene 5 (below): production and set by Jean-Pierre Ponnelle, Salzburg 1972

Plate 7 'Riconosci in questo amplesso' (No. 18), Act III scene 5: production by Peter Hall, Glyndebourne 1973

opera, where everything is transformed in an enchanting atmosphere of unreality, where military life with its "marching through the mud" and "concerts of bombards and cannons" seems no more than an amusing fairytale'.[61] Few critics have hankered so strongly after Frankenstein's 'moonlight and garlands', but many seem to feel that things might have gone a little too far. David Fallows notes that a setting of *Figaro* that is too overtly Spanish contrasts awkwardly with the 'solidly Viennese qualities' of Mozart's music,[62] and both Richard Evidon (reviewing a revival of the Copley production at Covent Garden) and Winton Dean (reviewing Geliot's Welsh National Opera production) sense that 'political' readings of the opera might fail to take account of Mozart's transformation and indeed transcendence of Beaumarchais's play.[63] Stanley Sadie, too, warns of the danger 'that the comedy and wit that properly belong to *Figaro* might seem alien and intrusive',[64] and he suggests that in Hall's production (in its 1981 revival) the social and sexual tensions were perhaps 'a shade overstressed'.[65] Thus he has some praise for Jonathan Miller's production for the English National Opera (1978, designed by Patrick Robertson and Rosemary Vercoe, conducted by Charles Groves) – 'the production is sparing of class-consciousness, at least among the principals, and still more so of specifically revolutionary feeling. . .which is unfashionable and welcome' – even if he is ambivalent about the apparent conservatism of the result.[66] Perhaps the tide is turning yet again.

As we have seen, one of the problems facing a modern opera house mounting *Figaro* is the amount of rehearsal needed to secure a good production. Another is the opera's scale. The point is emphasised by the list of works staged at the Metropolitan Opera during the week that included the revival of *Figaro* in 1940 (19–24 February): *Götterdämmerung*, *Manon*, *Aida*, *Parsifal*, *La Bohème*, *Lohengrin*, *Otello* and *Das Rheingold*. Clearly *Figaro* is of a different order, and the mixed fortunes of the opera at the Metropolitan, and even Covent Garden for a time in the 1950s, suggest that it has difficulties for a large theatre. Thus many British devotees of the opera will perhaps remember more fondly productions exploiting the greater intimacy of the Glyndebourne or Sadler's Wells theatres, or even the scaled-down productions taken on tour in the provinces. The touring version of Peter Hall's Glyndebourne production was a remarkable success, turning the disadvantages of small provincial theatres into a positive asset.[67] Even the village-hall performances with piano mounted for many years by the late-lamented 'Opera for All' company had an impact far greater than one would expect from the available resources. However, the intimacy required for *Figaro* does make the opera singularly effective in television broadcasts. Both the American National Broadcasting Company and West German television broadcast *Figaro* in the 1950s, and the British Broadcasting Corporation has since done good service for the opera (for example, televising an uncut Glyndebourne performance in 1963, and commissioning its own production by Basil Coleman, conducted by Charles Mackerras, in 1974). Peter Hall's 1973 Glyndebourne production was also televised by the independent Southern Television. Similarly, Ponnelle has done an impressive television film version (1976, first transmitted by the BBC on 7 March 1981). Some disliked it intensely; others found it revelatory.[68]

There remains the question of why *Figaro* appears to have struck such a chord with post-war audiences. What makes the opera so attractive? For some it will be the tremendous wealth of comic invention in the plot: Cherubino discovered in the chair, Susanna appearing in the dressing-room doorway, the gardener entering with a broken pot of carnations, Figaro rediscovering his long-lost parents, the Count searching through the garden only to seduce the 'wrong' woman. Witness, too, Basilio's malicious irony in the Act I trio, Figaro's witty defeat of the Count in the Act II finale, the *double entendres* of the seduction duet at the beginning of Act III, and the misunderstandings of much of Act IV. Seldom do we find an opera so richly endowed with comic effects, indeed so much an embodiment of the spirit of comedy.

For others, *Figaro* will be attractive for the depth and essential humanity of its characters. These characters may be derived from the comic stereotypes of the *commedia dell'arte*, but Beaumarchais, da Ponte and Mozart endow them with a new life: these are real people with whom we can identify. We may not like the Count, but we can perhaps understand how he is trapped by a code of feudal ethics and even sympathise with his deep attraction to Susanna (that it is deep seems clear from the opening of Act III) and with his being perpetually defeated by Figaro, Susanna and, worse still, Cherubino. Susanna is more than just the typical comic servant (compare Zerlina in *Don Giovanni* and Despina in *Così fan tutte*): she is a real woman who, by the end of the opera, transcends all boundaries. Figaro has all the strengths and weaknesses of Everyman: he is both attractive and infuriating, cunning yet naïve; despite all his bravado he is eventually beaten at his own game, but even then he comes out on top. The Countess occupies prime place in our attentions because of her depth and intensity of feeling, as well as her sacrifices to her love for the Count. Then there is Cherubino, in action, word and music the epitome of a youth awaking to love, and Marcellina, the frustrated spinster, and Bartolo, the pompous doctor, reunited through their long-lost son. Even the cynical Basilio is shown (if we hear his Act IV aria) to have a place in the opera's rich canvas of humanity.

For others still, the appeal of *Figaro* will lie in its comments on the appearances and realities of the world. Figaro and Susanna may be of a lower social standing than the Count and the Countess, but through Beaumarchais's wit and Mozart's music the servants are the equal of their masters. Indeed, by the end of the opera Figaro and the Count are reduced to the same level of jealous posturing at the supposed infidelities of their women, while the Countess and Susanna are each able to take the other's part. But this concerns more than just the difference or no between social classes. Rather, the opera is also about relationships between man and man, woman and woman, and above all man and woman. Both Figaro and the Count, despite their differences of class and outlook, are imprisoned by an institutionalised sense of male dominance. It is through Susanna and the Countess that they learn the perils of male power-play and come to a higher understanding of the strength and value of a woman's love. And it is through this understanding that all the characters in the opera realise, in the final hymn, the essential oneness of man and woman in the search for and attainment of human happiness.

But above all, it is Mozart's music that makes *Figaro* a great opera. We can admire the skill of Beaumarchais's play and the craftsmanship of da Ponte's libretto, and appreciate their vital contribution to the whole. We can acknowledge the rich fabric of the action, and the crucial social, moral and emotional issues which it raises. But in the end it is Mozart who, through his music, breathes life into the characters and their situations. The main aim of this Handbook has been to explore and explain Mozart's response to the drama, and thus our own ideal response to his music. If *Figaro* appeals to us today, it is ultimately because of the masterly achievement of a great opera composer.

Notes

1 Introduction

1 See Mozart's letter to his father, Vienna, 17 March 1781, given in E. Anderson (ed.), *The Letters of Mozart and His Family*, 3rd edn (London, Macmillan, 1985), pp. 713–14.
2 Mozart to the Abbé Bullinger, Paris, 7 August 1778, in *ibid.*, p. 594; compare Mozart's letter to his father of 6 May 1781 in *ibid.*, pp. 736–7.
3 Michael Kelly, *Reminiscences*, ed. R. Fiske (London, Oxford University Press, 1975), p. 100.
4 Mozart to his father, Vienna, 2 June 1781, given in Anderson (ed.), *The Letters of Mozart and His Family*, p. 739.
5 Much of the account below relies on D. Heartz, 'Setting the Stage for Figaro', *The Musical Times*, 127 (1986), 256–60.
6 Mozart to his father, Vienna, 26 September 1781, given in Anderson (ed.), *The Letters of Mozart and His Family*, p. 769.
7 *Ibid.*, p. 832. Speculation about these singers, and the fate of the German opera, appears in a number of Mozart's letters in early 1783, for example, see the letter to his father of 12 March, *ibid.*, pp. 841–2, and to Professor Anton Klein, 21 May, *ibid.*, pp. 890–1.
8 Kelly, *Reminiscences*, p. 97.
9 Quoted in Heartz, 'Setting the Stage for Figaro', p. 257. Lord Mount-Edgcumbe had similar things to say of Nancy Storace, see his *Musical Reminiscences of an Old Amateur for Fifty Years from 1773 to 1823* (London, W. Clarke, 1824), pp. 63–4: 'She had a harshness in her countenance, a clumsiness of figure, a coarseness in her voice, and a vulgarity of manner, that totally unfitted her for the serious opera, which she never attempted. But her knowledge of music was equal to any thing, and she could sing well in every style. . .In her own particular line on the stage, she was unrivalled, being an excellent actress, as well as a masterly singer.'
10 The most recent and best biography of Lorenzo da Ponte is S. Hodges, *Lorenzo da Ponte: The Life and Times of Mozart's Librettist* (London, Granada, 1985).
11 Mozart to his father, Vienna, 5 February 1783, given in Anderson (ed.), *The Letters of Mozart and His Family*, p. 839.
12 *Ibid.*, pp. 847–8.
13 Taken as a whole, however, the specification is closer to the cast of *Don Giovanni* and *Così fan tutte*.
14 Mozart to his father, Vienna, 21 May 1783, given in Anderson (ed.), *The*

Letters of Mozart and His Family, p. 849. See also his letter of 6 December 1783, *ibid.*, p. 862: 'the more comic an Italian opera is the better'.

15 Mozart to his father, Vienna, 21 June 1783, in *ibid.*, p. 853.

16 Mozart to his father, Vienna, 10 February 1784, in *ibid.*, p. 867.

17 Mozart to his father, Vienna, 6 December 1783, in *ibid.*, p. 861. Here he also voices his concern about the plot: 'I must tell you, however, that my only reason for not objecting to this goose story altogether was because two people of greater insight and judgment than myself have not disapproved of it, I mean yourself and Varesco.'

18 A. Einstein, *Mozart: His Character – His Work*, reprint edn (London, Panther, 1971), p. 434.

19 Given in Anderson (ed.), *The Letters of Mozart and His Family*, p. 855.

20 Einstein, *Mozart: His Character – His Work*, p. 442.

21 Leopold Mozart to his daughter, Salzburg, 11 November 1785, given in Anderson (ed.), *The Letters of Mozart and His Family*, p. 893.

22 See D. Heartz, 'Constructing *Le Nozze di Figaro*', *Journal of the Royal Musical Association*, 112/1 (1987), 77–98. This important essay discusses many aspects of *Figaro*, including its links with Paisiello.

23 Leopold Mozart to his daughter, Salzburg, 28 April 1786, given in Anderson (ed.), *The Letters of Mozart and His Family*, p. 897.

2 Mozart and the *opera buffa* tradition

1 These totals are calculated from the lists of Viennese opera performances in O. Michtner, *Das alte Burgtheater als Opernbühne* (Vienna, Hermann Böhlaus, 1970), pp. 470–502.

2 Fracasso's two arias in da capo form have a truncated rather than full da capo repeat.

3 The authorship of the libretto of *La finta giardiniera* is uncertain. The text has often been attributed to Raniero de Calzabigi and/or Marco Coltellini. More recently, Giuseppe Petrosellini has been suggested, see Mozart, *La finta giardiniera*, ed. R. Angermüller and D. Berke, in *Wolfgang Amadeus Mozart: Neue Ausgabe sämtlicher Werke*, II/5/8 (2 vols., Kassel, Bärenreiter, 1978), vol. 1, pp. viii–ix.

4 T. de Wyzewa and G. de Saint-Foix, *Wolfgang Amédée Mozart: sa vie musicale et son oeuvre* (5 vols., Paris, Desclée de Brouwer, 1936–46), vol. 2, p. 198.

5 E. J. Dent, *Mozart's Operas: A Critical Study*, 2nd edn (London, Oxford University Press, 1947), pp. 108–9.

6 Confusingly, bipartite arias containing repeated material in both sections were sometimes called 'rondò'. These rondos should not be confused with others with a single refrain. See D. Heartz, 'Mozart and His Italian Contemporaries: *La clemenza di Tito*', *Mozart-Jahrbuch* (1978–9), 275–93, p. 281, for comments on the use of bipartite rondos in *opere serie* of the 1780s.

7 See S. Levarie, *Mozart's 'Le nozze di Figaro': A Critical Analysis*, reprint edn (New York, Da Capo Press, 1977), pp. 44–5.

8 See Paisiello's correspondence of the years 1781–2 now housed in the library of the Società di Storia Patria, Naples (Catalogue No. XXXI.c.13).

9 Indeed, Michael Kelly speaks of *Figaro* as being in two acts, see his *Reminiscences*, p. 132.

10 A similar three-bar phrase with 'snatched' ending appears at the start of the first aria in J. Mysliveček's *Olimpiade* (1778), see the music in M. F. Robinson, *Naples and Neapolitan Opera* (Oxford, Clarendon Press, 1972), p. 144. Compare, too, the opening vocal phrase of Ramiro's aria 'Va pur ad altri in braccio' (No. 26) in Act III of Mozart's *La finta giardiniera*.

11 Dent, *Mozart's Operas*, pp. 106–8. The similarities between the opening motives of Bartolo's aria 'Veramente ho torto, è vero' in Act II scene 9 of *Il barbiere di Siviglia* and Figaro's 'Non più andrai farfallone amoroso' (No. 9) in *Figaro* suggest that Mozart was influenced by Paisiello here as well.

12 Levarie, *Mozart's 'Le nozze di Figaro'*, p. 88.

13 For instance, in the opening Allegro section of the Act III finale of *Il barbiere* and in Gafforio's aria 'Queste son lettere' from Act I scene 6 of *Il re Teodoro in Venezia* (1784).

3 Beaumarchais, da Ponte and Mozart: from play to opera

1 A useful survey of Beaumarchais's life and works is given in P.-A. C. de Beaumarchais, *'The Barber of Seville' and 'The Marriage of Figaro'*, trans. J. Wood (Harmondsworth, Penguin, 1964), pp. 11–35. A standard study is still L. de Loménie, *Beaumarchais et son temps: études sur la société en France au XVIIIe siècle d'après des documents inédits* (2 vols., Paris, Michel Lévy, 1856).

2 For the original text, see P.-A. C. de Beaumarchais, *Théâtre: 'Le barbier de Séville', 'Le mariage de Figaro', 'La mère coupable'*, ed. R. Pomeau (Paris, Garnier-Flammarion, 1965), p. 132. The translation of this extract is taken from G. Schmidgall, *Literature as Opera* (New York, Oxford University Press, 1977), p. 90.

3 L. da Ponte, *Memorie*, ed. G. Gambarin and F. Nicolini, Scrittori d'Italia, vols. 81–2 (2 vols., Bari, Laterza, 1918), vol. 1, pp. 110–11. Joseph II had indeed encouraged a ban of the play on 31 January 1785, see his memorandum given in O. E. Deutsch, *Mozart: A Documentary Biography*, trans. E. Blom, P. Branscombe and J. Noble (London, Adam & Charles Black, 1965), p. 235. If we are to believe da Ponte's statement that this ban occurred only 'a few days earlier', then Mozart could have approached the librettist with his idea of turning *Le mariage de Figaro* into an opera in February or March 1785, i.e. earlier than is currently assumed. However, da Ponte's *Memorie* is not the most reliable of sources. Indeed, it seems possible that he fabricated this entire interview with the Emperor. These and other important questions on the genesis of *Figaro* are raised in Heartz, 'Setting the Stage for Figaro' and 'Constructing *Le Nozze di Figaro*'.

4 Da Ponte, *Memorie*, vol. 1, p. 111.

5 Translated in Deutsch, *Mozart: A Documentary Biography*, pp. 273–4.

6 *Ibid.*, p. 329.

7 This and subsequent translations from the play are taken from Beaumar-

chais, *'The Barber of Seville' and 'The Marriage of Figaro'*, trans. Wood, and the page numbers refer to this edition (which lacks scene divisions). References to scenes in the play or libretto use the following code where convenient: B = play, dP = libretto, followed by the act and scene. Thus B: III.5 is Act III scene 5 of the play.

8 Marceline's comments in B:III.16 were also cut by the actors of the Comédie-Française at the first and subsequent performances.

9 Beaumarchais, *'The Barber of Seville' and 'The Marriage of Figaro'*, trans. Wood, p. 29–31.

10 From the preface to *Le mariage*, Beaumarchais, *Théâtre*, p. 127.

11 *Ibid.*, p. 120.

12 *Ibid.*, p. 118.

13 J.-V. Hocquard, *'Le nozze di Figaro' de Mozart* (Paris, Aubier Montaigne, 1979), pp. 5–6, quoting from Mozart's letters to his father of 16 and 20 June 1781 from Vienna, given in Anderson (ed.), *The Letters of Mozart and His Family*, pp. 746, 747.

14 The scene divisions in Table 2 are taken from Mozart, *Le nozze di Figaro*, ed. R. Gerber, reprint edn (London, Eulenburg, 1983), which matches the libretto as given in L. da Ponte, *Tre libretti per Mozart: 'Le nozze di Figaro', 'Don Giovanni', 'Così fan tutte'*, ed. P. Lecaldano (Milan, Rizzoli, 1956). L. Finscher's edition in *Wolfgang Amadeus Mozart: Neue Ausgabe sämtlicher Werke*, II/5/16 (2 vols., Kassel, Bärenreiter, 1973) differs slightly in Acts II and IV, and the vocal score edited by E. J. Dent (London, Boosey & Hawkes, 1947) does not have scene divisions. The numbering of the arias, ensembles, etc., follows Gerber and Dent: Finscher gives the chorus 'Giovani liete' (No. 8) a new number on its second appearance, and thus the numbers thereafter are each increased by one.

15 Da Ponte, *Memorie*, vol. 1, p. 125.

16 *Ibid.*, vol. 1, pp. 97–8, translated in Dent, *Mozart's Operas*, pp. 104–5.

17 The translation here is my own. It is somewhat more literal and less elegant than Wood's (p. 117).

18 Although 'Se vuol ballare' and its preceding recitative correspond to Figaro's equivalent scene in the play (B:I.2), the text for the cavatina draws its origins from a line given to Figaro at the end of B:II.2: 'et puis dansez, Monseigneur' ('and then – dance, Your Lordship', trans. p. 133). A fragment of 'Se vuol ballare' returns at the equivalent of this point in the opera (dP:II.2).

19 From the preface to *Le mariage*, Beaumarchais, *Théâtre*, pp. 118–19.

20 *Ibid.*, p. 119.

4 Synopsis

1 The slow section was removed from the autograph score: its beginning, now excised, can be seen reproduced in Mozart, *Le nozze di Figaro*, ed. Finscher, vol. 1, p. xxiii. On the pacing of the overture, see Wagner's comments in R. Wagner, *Prose Works*, trans. W. A. Ellis (8 vols., London, Kegan Paul & Co., 1892–9), vol. 8, p. 208 (from Wagner's essay 'Künstler und Kritiker, mit Bezug auf einen besonderen Fall' published in the *Dresdener Anzeiger*, 14 August 1846): 'With particular reference to *Figaro* I

have gathered most authentic intimations, especially from the late Director of the Prague Conservatoire, Dionys Weber (an exclusive admirer of Mozart); as eye-and-ear-witness of the first production of *Figaro* and its antecedent rehearsals by Mozart himself, this gentleman informed me how the master could never get the overture, for instance, played fast enough to please him, and how, to maintain its unflagging swing, he constantly urged on the pace wherever consistent with the nature of the theme.'

2 For scene divisions and numberings, see Chapter 3, note 14. The tempo markings follow Mozart, *Le nozze di Figaro*, ed. Finscher: I have not differentiated between those markings present in the autograph in Mozart's hand and those justified on other grounds. Text incipits give the complete first line: the orthography generally follows Finscher, although I have added some punctuation.

3 See the perceptive discussion of this duet in F. Noske, 'Verbal to Musical Drama: Adaptation or Creation?', *Themes in Drama*, 3 (1981), 143–52.

4 For the use of dance patterns in *Figaro*, see F. Noske, 'Social Tensions in "Le Nozze di Figaro"', *Music & Letters*, 50 (1969), 45–62, also as '*Le nozze di Figaro*: Social Tensions' in F. Noske, *The Signifier and the Signified: Studies in the Operas of Mozart and Verdi* (The Hague, Martinus Nijhoff, 1977), pp. 18–38 (to which all subsequent references will be made); W. J. Allanbrook, *Rhythmic Gesture in Mozart: 'Le nozze di Figaro' and 'Don Giovanni'* (Chicago, University of Chicago Press, 1983).

5 For the rustic connotations of $\frac{6}{8}$ and G major, see D. Heartz, 'The Creation of the Buffo Finale in Italian Opera', *Proceedings of the Royal Musical Association*, 104 (1977–8), 67–78, p. 69.

6 According to a stage direction in B:II.4: 'The Countess, seated, holds the music to follow it. Suzanne is behind her armchair and plays an introduction looking at the music over her mistress's shoulders. The little page is in front of her, with downcast gaze. This pose is precisely as in the fine print after Vanloo called *La conversation espagnole*.' See Beaumarchais, *Théâtre*, p. 162.

7 On the fandango, see Noske, '*Le nozze di Figaro*: Social Tensions', pp. 36–7. Brian Trowell points out that a $\frac{6}{8}$ version of the melody is given in Sir John Hawkins's *A General History of the Science and Practice of Music* (London, 1776), see his letter to the editor, *Music & Letters*, 50 (1969), 427–8, where he quotes Hawkins's comment that the dance was usually performed with 'a variety of the most indecent gesticulations that can be conceived'. According to Trowell, the suggestive overtones of the genre point up the events onstage. However, Noske, letter to the editor, *Music & Letters*, 51 (1970), 346, argues that the 'refined eroticism' of Mozart's fandango, in $\frac{3}{4}$ rather than $\frac{6}{8}$, is rather more aristocratic. This is not the only melody in *Figaro* which seems to have been borrowed from or via Gluck: 'Signori, di fuori' (No. 15.4) derives from a *vaudeville* tune in *Le chinois poli en France* (Paris, 1754; arranged by Gluck for Vienna in 1756), see Heartz, 'Constructing *Le Nozze di Figaro*', pp. 87–8. As Professor Heartz remarks, a 'rustic' *vaudeville* is entirely appropriate for Figaro's rustic pipers.

8 In the edition of the libretto printed by G. N. de Kurzbek (Vienna, 1786; followed by Finscher in the *Neue Mozart-Ausgabe*), Act IV scenes 1-4 take place in a 'gabinetto', i.e. a small room (other sources say a corridor); see also H. Graf, 'Der 4. Akt des Figaro', *Mozart-Jahrbuch* (1968–70), 95–8. The scene-change to the garden is then made at the end of Marcellina's 'Il capro e la capretta' (No. 24) for the entrance of Barbarina in scene 5. A number of arguments support this scheme, which is also closer to the play, although there is a strong tradition of staging the whole of Act IV in the garden.
9 Allanbrook, *Rhythmic Gesture in Mozart*, pp. 145–8, 157–94.
10 W. J. Allanbrook, 'Pro Marcellina: The Shape of "Figaro", Act IV', *Music & Letters*, 63 (1982), 69–84.
11 The autograph of the recitative is missing and it is not clear exactly what Cherubino should be singing. In the 1786 libretto, he is given 'La la la la la la la la lera' and then the text of the first stanza of 'Voi che sapete' (with the first line as 'Voi che intendete'). In the copy of this libretto that survives in the Library of Congress, Washington, this stanza is marked to be cut. The 'la' repetition would fit the first line of 'Non so più cosa son, cosa faccio'. Finscher and Gerber give Cherubino one 'la' less, which can just about be made to fit the first two lines of 'Voi che sapete'. This is what Dent suggests, and Dent's solution seems the most feasible.
12 Gerber and Dent also have Bartolo and Don Curzio enter here, and hereafter Dent indicates that Basilio's line should be doubled by Don Curzio, and Antonio's by Bartolo. This makes sense if one is not having Basilio and Don Curzio, and Antonio and Bartolo, each played by one singer, as occurred at the first performance. There is also some disagreement about what Barbarina and Marcellina should sing from here to the end. In bars 389–94, Finscher has Barbarina doubling Susanna and Marcellina doubling Cherubino, Gerber has Barbarina doubling Susanna and no indication for Marcellina, and Dent has Barbarina and Marcellina both doubling Cherubino. In bars 430–513, Finscher and Dent have Marcellina and Barbarina doubling Cherubino, and Gerber has Marcellina doubling Cherubino and no indication for Barbarina.
13 In addition to the changes discussed below, there may have been another duet for the Countess and Susanna before, or replacing, 'Che soave zeffiretto' (No. 20), see L. von Köchel *et al.*, *W. A. Mozarts Werke. . . Supplement: Revisionsbericht* (Leipzig, Breitkopf & Härtel, 1889), p. 82. This duet might have contained the temporary disagreement between Susanna and the Countess in B:IV.3, but see A. Tyson, 'Some Problems in the Text of *Le nozze di Figaro*: Did Mozart Have a Hand in Them?', *Journal of the Royal Musical Association*, 112/1, (1987), 99–131, p. 129. There may also have been a change in the order of Figaro's and Susanna's arias in Act IV, see A. Tyson, '*Le nozze di Figaro*: Lessons from the Autograph Score', *The Musical Times*, 122 (1981), 456–61.
14 From Mozart, *Le nozze di Figaro*, ed. Finscher, vol. 2, pp. 638–41. The rondò is briefly discussed in Tyson, '*Le nozze di Figaro*: Lessons from the Autograph Score', pp. 460–1, where it is suggested that the substitution of 'Deh vieni non tardar, oh gioia bella' was made at a late stage. 'Non tardar, amato bene' uses similar locutions to 'Non temer, amato bene',

K490, an additional aria for Idamante in *Idomeneo* (Act II scene 1) written for the performance in Vienna in March 1786 (the text was set again for the concert-aria *Ch'io mi scordi di te*, K505). Its eight-syllable lines and three strophes are typical of rondò texts.

15 Köchel, *W. A. Mozarts Werke. . .Supplement: Revisionsbericht*, pp. 87–8, and Mozart, *Le nozze di Figaro*, ed. Finscher, vol. 2, p. 641.

16 Mozart, *Le nozze di Figaro*, ed. Finscher, vol. 1, p. xix. Even before completing *Figaro*, Mozart seems to have had second thoughts about 'Aprite, presto aprite'. He began another duet for Susanna and Cherubino in its place, see the sketch in Köchel, *W. A. Mozarts Werke. . .Supplement: Revisionsbericht*, p. 80, and Mozart, *Le nozze di Figaro*, ed. Finscher, vol. 2, p. 631. An (authentic?) replacement recitative for this duet also survives, see Mozart, *Le nozze di Figaro*, ed Finscher, vol. 1, pp. xiv, xix. These and other textual problems in the opera are discussed in S. Anheißer, 'Die unbekannte Urfassung von Mozarts Figaro', *Zeitschrift für Musikwissenschaft*, 15 (1933), 301–17; and most important, A. Tyson, 'Some Problems in the Text of *Le nozze di Figaro*'.

17 R. Moberly and C. Raeburn, 'Mozart's "Figaro": The Plan of Act III', *Music & Letters*, 46 (1965), 134–6.

18 Tyson, '*Le nozze di Figaro*: Lessons from the Autograph Score', *passim*. Tyson makes the point (p. 460) that if Cherubino's 'Se così brami' were intended to be in G major, the descending circle of fifths would begin at the first number in Act III in the suggested revised order, although he argues that this tonal scheme is not a strong point in favour of changing the present layout of the act.

5 Verse and music in *Le nozze di Figaro*

1 Leopold Mozart to his daughter, Salzburg, 11 November 1785, given in Anderson (ed.), *The Letters of Mozart and His Family*, p. 893.

2 See the work-lists in R. Angermüller, 'Da Ponte, Lorenzo', in S. Sadie (ed.), *The New Grove Dictionary of Music and Musicians* (20 vols., London, Macmillan, 1980), vol. 5, pp. 236–8, and S. Hodges, *Lorenzo da Ponte: The Life and Times of Mozart's Librettist*, pp. 226–35.

3 Mozart sets this line as 'Oh cielo! dunque ha sentito'. Having 'cielo' for 'ciel' gives the line one syllable too many, but Mozart may have wished to give greater force to the Count's exclamation.

4 It was not unknown for Mozart to compose music for an aria and then commission a text, see the comments in his letter to his father, Vienna, 26 September 1781, in Anderson (ed.), *The Letters of Mozart and His Family*, pp. 768–70. In a slightly different context, Friedrich Lippmann has discussed the extent to which line-lengths influence the construction of Mozart's vocal melodies, see 'Mozart und der Vers', *Analecta Musicologica*, 18 (1978), 107–37.

5 Similarly, No. 6 may originally have been planned to be in rondo form with an extended coda. There is a sketch for a second episode in A flat major (on the text of the second quatrain) following on from the first return of the A section in bars 38–51, see Köchel, *W. A. Mozarts Werke. . .*

Supplement: Revisionsbericht, p. 79. Such an episode would have required a second return of the A section. Mozart, however, changed his mind, leaving A flat major for his setting of 'Parlo d'amor vegliando'.

6 Siegmund Levarie remarks on the hidden artfulness apparent even in the text of 'Voi che sapete': by taking two lines as one and ignoring the final repeat of the first strophe, the verse becomes a fourteen-line sonnet, see *Mozart's 'Le nozze di Figaro'*, p. 81. Several commentators have noticed the allusions to Canto XIX of Dante's *Vita nuova*, 'Donna che avete intelletto d'amor'. Similarly, 'Il capro e la capretta' (No. 24) contains echoes of Ariosto, *Orlando furioso*, V.1, and the beginning of No. 28.3 (Figaro: 'Tutto è tranquillo e placido') evokes Homer, *Odyssey*, VIII.266ff.

7 The verse in the first finale of *Don Giovanni* is in regular metrical and rhyming patterns. However, there is an example in *Don Giovanni* of recitative verse being set within a concerted item: Don Giovanni's and Leporello's interjections in Elvira's 'Ah! chi mi dice mai' (No. 3).

8 On the interaction of verse structure and musical structure in the *opera buffa* finale, see Heartz, 'The Creation of the Buffo Finale in Italian Opera'. Heartz establishes some useful precedents for da Ponte and Mozart.

9 Anderson (ed.), *The Letters of Mozart and His Family*, pp. 659ff.

10 Da Ponte, *Memorie*, vol. 1, p. 98. See also da Ponte's letter in verse to Giambattista Casti given in A. Marchesan, *Della vita e delle opere di Lorenzo da Ponte* (Treviso, Turazza, 1900), p. 205.

11 Mozart to his father, Vienna, 13 October 1781, in Anderson (ed.), *The Letters of Mozart and His Family*, p. 773; J. Kerman, *Opera as Drama*, (New York, Vintage Books, 1956), p. 108.

12 Da Ponte, *Memorie*, vol. 1, pp. 101–2.

6 *Opera buffa* and the Classical style: the Act I trio

1 The most cogent study of the musical problems to be discussed in the first part of this chapter is C. Rosen, *The Classical Style: Haydn, Mozart, Beethoven* (London, Faber, 1971), see pp. 57–98, 228–325. My ideas on the 'comic' qualities of the Classical style also owe something to J. D. Drummond, *Opera in Perspective* (London, Dent, 1980), pp. 193–222.

2 Given in Rosen, *The Classical Style*, p. 96.

3 C. Burney, *A General History of Music from the Earliest Ages to the Present Period (1789)*, ed. F. Mercer, reprint edn (2 vols., New York, Dover, 1957), vol. 2, p. 917.

4 Bars 29–36 are *on* the dominant of F major/minor, they are not *in* F minor. Similarly, bars 23–6 are, at least at first, *on* the dominant of B flat major/minor, not *in* B flat minor. Inflections above a dominant pedal do not necessarily indicate the mode (major or minor) to which that pedal will resolve.

5 A similar bass progression can be found in the last movement of Mozart's A major String Quartet, K464 (composed in January 1785), where there is again a prominent subdominant episode in the Development section.

The fact that Basilio's 'Ah, del paggio quel ch'ho detto / era solo un mio sospetto' ('Ah, what I said about the page was only my suspicion') is stated in E flat major may also be a reference to Cherubino's 'Non so più cosa son, cosa faccio' (No. 6), with which it shares the same key and motivic similarities (and see p. 116 and Ex. 18)

7 Music and drama in *Le nozze di Figaro*

1 Schoenberg provided some perceptive remarks on this section of the Act II finale in his essay 'Brahms the Progressive' (1947), now in A. Schoenberg, *Style and Idea*, ed. L. Stein, rev. edn (London, Faber, 1984), pp. 398–441, see pp. 411–13. Massimo Mila also points out that the first accompaniment pattern that appears in bars 167–8 is related to the music of 'Solo ai nomi d'amor, di diletto' in Cherubino's 'Non so più cosa son, cosa faccio' (No. 6, bars 16–18), see his *Lettura delle 'Nozze di Figaro': Mozart e la ricerca della felicità* (Turin, Einaudi, 1979), p. 99.
2 Siegmund Levarie points out this 'search' for *g''* and its effect on the rest of the Countess's music in his *Mozart's 'Le nozze di Figaro'*, pp. 75–80, 155–61. According to Tyson, 'Some Problems in the Text of *Le nozze di Figaro*', pp. 128–9, 'Porgi amor qualche ristoro' may have been a late addition.
3 Levarie, *Mozart's 'Le nozze di Figaro'*, pp. 137–43, 249–51. The descending D major scale occurs three times, in bars 114 (as in Ex. 15), 141 and 144. Its final appearance is followed by triplet quaver flourishes that once again fill in the space of the octave. These triplet quavers were a late addition, see Köchel, *W. A. Mozarts Werke. . .Supplement: Revisionsbericht*, p. 81.
4 The decision to use this triadic melody in the final cadence of 'Deh vieni non tardar, oh gioia bella' was taken late, see the original conclusion of the aria excised from the autograph score in Köchel, *W. A. Mozarts Werke. . .Supplement: Revisionsbericht*, p. 88. On opening phrases becoming closing phrases, see Rosen, *The Classical Style*, p. 78.
5 F. Noske, 'Musical Quotation as a Dramatic Device: The Fourth Act of "Le Nozze di Figaro"', *The Musical Quarterly*, 54 (1968), 185–98, also as '*Le nozze di Figaro*: Musical Quotation as a Dramatic Device', in Noske, *The Signifier and the Signified: Studies in the Operas of Mozart and Verdi*, pp. 3–17.
6 In the preface to Mozart, *Le nozze di Figaro*, ed. Gerber, pp. xviii–xxi, where Abert also discusses the tonal schemes of Acts II–IV. Some important comments on keys in *Figaro* are also made in Heartz, 'Constructing *Le Nozze di Figaro*'.
7 Levarie, *Mozart's 'Le nozze di Figaro'*, pp. 233–45.

8 *Le nozze di Figaro*: a brief performance history

1 Da Ponte, *Memorie*, vol. 1, pp. 119–20. My translation differs slightly from Deutsch, *Mozart: A Documentary Biography*, p. 547.
2 Kelly, *Reminiscences*, pp. 131–2. Kelly adds his own note: 'I was not aware at that time of what I have since found to be the fact, that those

who labour under the defect of stuttering while speaking, articulate distinctly in singing. That excellent bass, Sedgwick, was an instance of it; and the beautiful Mrs. Inchbald, the authoress, another.'

3 Deutsch, *Mozart: A Documentary Biography*, p. 275. At the second performance of *Figaro*, five numbers had to be repeated, and at the third, seven. It is possible that the length of the opera, for which da Ponte apologised in his preface (see above, p. 36), led to cuts being made in one or more of the Viennese performances. The copy of the 1786 edition of the libretto that survives in the Library of Congress, Washington, which is also linked to the 1786 performances by noting the singers against the list of *dramatis personae*, contains a number of excisions made at an unknown date. As well as Cherubino's Act III aria 'Se così brami', the reprise of 'Voi che sapete' in Act IV, and some brief passages of recitative, 'Non so più cosa son, cosa faccio' (No. 6), the C major section of the Act II finale (No. 15.4, bars 398–466, Count: 'Conoscete, Signor Figaro'), and perhaps 'Via resti servita' (No. 5) are also scored out. Some of these cuts were also made in the Prague performances, see below, note 6, and also Tyson, 'Some Problems in the Text of *Le nozze di Figaro*'.

4 Deutsch, *Mozart: A Documentary Biography*, pp. 274 (Zinzendorf, 1 May 1786), 276 (Kazinczy). Mozart directed the first two performances of *Figaro* on 1 and 3 May; then Joseph Weigl took over.

5 *Ibid.*, p. 278. Leopold Mozart referred to the cabals ranged against *Figaro*, particularly by Salieri and his allies, in a letter to his daughter, Salzburg, 28 April 1786, in Anderson (ed.), *The Letters of Mozart and His Family*, p. 897, see above, p. 10. Franz Xaver Niemetschek wrote in 1808 that at the first performance of *Figaro*, the singers made deliberate mistakes 'out of hatred, envy and low cabals, in the intention of bringing about the opera's downfall', Deutsch, *Mozart: A Documentary Biography*, p. 506.

6 Deutsch, *Mozart: A Documentary Biography* pp. 280–1. On the success of *Figaro* in Prague, see also Leopold Mozart to his daughter, Salzburg, 12 January 1787, in Anderson (ed.), *The Letters of Mozart and His Family*, p. 902. The performance was conducted by Johann Josef Strobach. On the evidence of the score of Acts I and II of *Figaro* now surviving in Donaueschingen, which may relate to one or more Prague performances, there seem to have been some cuts made, including the omission of 'Conoscete, signor Figaro' in the Act II finale and Nos. 5 and 6 (see above, note 3). No. 5 was replaced by a new cavatina for Marcellina, 'Signora mia garbata', edited in A. Einstein, 'Eine unbekannte Arie der Marcelline', *Zeitschrift für Musikwissenschaft*, 13 (1930–1), 200–5. It is now thought that this is unlikely to be by Mozart, see L. von Köchel, *Chronologisch-thematisches Verzeichnis sämtlicher Tonwerke Wolfgang Amadé Mozarts*, 6th edn, ed. F. Giegling, A. Weinmann and G. Sievers (Wiesbaden, Breitkopf & Härtel, 1964), pp. 541–2, and Mozart, *Le nozze di Figaro*, ed. Finscher, vol. 1, pp. xiii–xiv, although the aria does bear a passing resemblance to Sandrina's 'Noi donne poverine' (No. 4) in Mozart's *La finta giardiniera*.

7 Anderson (ed.), *The Letters of Mozart and His Family*, p. 903.

8 Deutsch, *Mozart: A Documentary Biography*, pp. 275, 276–7, 293–4.

Lausch's piano score, advertised on 1 July 1786, omitted Nos. 4, 5 and 24. It is not clear whether this relates to cuts in the Vienna performances, see above, note 3. Printed editions of *Figaro* came later, with partial vocal scores appearing in the early 1790s and the first complete vocal scores appearing in the middle of this decade, see P. Hirsch, 'More Early Mozart Editions', *The Music Review*, 3 (1942), 38–45, and Köchel, *Chronologisch-thematisches Verzeichnis*, pp. 545–6. The first print of part of *Figaro* may well have been the edition of 'Crudel! perchè finora' (No. 16) 'as sung in Gazzaniga's "La Vendemmia" by Sig[r]. Benucci & Sig[ra] Storace' issued in 1789 by Birchall & Andrews in London.

9 Details (incomplete) of performances of *Figaro* are given in A. Loewenberg, *Annals of Opera, 1597–1940*, 2nd edn (New York, Rowman & Littlefield, 1970), cols. 425–9. However, according to Köchel, *Chronologisch-thematisches Verzeichnis*, p. 546, the first performance in St Petersburg was on 31 July 1815, if not before, and the first performance in New York on 3 May 1823 (in English; it was first performed there in Italian on 1 November 1858). Details of German translations, beginning with the one issued by Kurzbek contemporaneously with his first edition of the Italian libretto (Vienna, 1786), are given in Köchel, *Chronologisch-thematisches Verzeichnis*, p. 545. The first recorded performance of Knigge's translation is at Lübeck on 18 May 1788, see Deutsch, *Mozart: A Documentary Biography*, p. 315 (Köchel, *Chronologisch-thematisches Verzeichnis*, p. 545, lists only the Hanover performance on 18 May 1789), and that of the Vulpius translation at Frankfurt, 11 October 1788, see Deutsch, *Mozart: A Documentary Biography*, p. 329.

10 See Knigge's comments in his *Dramaturgische Blätter*, Hanover, 1789, given in Deutsch, *Mozart: A Documentary Biography*, pp. 343–5. It seems that Knigge translated the arias, etc., and his daughter, Philippine, the dialogue.

11 Deutsch, *Mozart: A Documentary Biography*, pp. 335–7. A *pasticcio* is a dramatic entertainment produced by compiling pieces from two or more operas, often by different composers. There may or may not be a convincing dramatic thread. Adriana Ferrarese del Bene, the 1789 Susanna, sang in *L'ape musicale*. Mozart also arranged 'Non più andrai farfallone amoroso' as the first of the five Contredanses, K609 (1791).

12 Given in Mozart, *Le nozze di Figaro*, ed. Finscher, vol. 2, pp. 597–617. A copy of 'Al desio di chi t'adora' in the British Library, Add. MS 14396, contains an autograph cadenza by Mozart, reproduced in A. H. King, *A Mozart Legacy: Aspects of the British Library Collections* (London, British Library, 1984), p. 30.

13 Tyson, 'Some Problems in the Text of *Le nozze di Figaro*', pp. 122–8. The 1789 revisions were adopted in the production by the Welsh National Opera (cond. Mackerras) premièred on 10 June 1987. For the Count's aria, see M. Raeburn and C. Raeburn, 'Mozart Manuscripts in Florence', *Music & Letters*, 40 (1959), 334–40, including a transcription taken from the Lausch copy of *Figaro* in Florence, Conservatorio di Musica Luigi Cherubini, A 262. Another manuscript in the Conservatorio di Musica Luigi Cherubini (636.8) contains a new accompanied recitative to precede 'Non più andrai farfallone amoroso', headed 'Benucci'. Einstein sug-

gested that Mozart composed this recitative to provide a concert version of the aria for Benucci shortly before or after the first performance of *Figaro*, see Köchel, *Chronologisch-thematisches Verzeichnis*, pp. 542–4, which includes a transcription. However, its authenticity is not entirely proven, see Raeburn and Raeburn, 'Mozart Manuscripts in Florence', p. 337.

14 Leopold Mozart to his wife, Milan, 24 November 1770, commenting on his son's reluctance to write an aria without knowing the singer, see Anderson (ed.), *The Letters of Mozart and His Family*, p. 171, and note the similar comments in *ibid.*, p. 497.

15 Deutsch, *Mozart: A Documentary Biography*, p. 329.

16 *Ibid.*, pp. 372–3. This reports the first performance of *Figaro* (in German) in Berlin on 14 September 1790.

17 *Ibid.*, p. 373. *Der Baum der Diana* is Martín y Soler's *L'arbore di Diana* (1787), and *Lilla*, Soler's *Una cosa rara* (1786), which had been sung in German from 1789 and 1788 respectively.

18 *Ibid.*, p. 377, from the *Annalen des Theaters*, Berlin 1791, reporting the first performance of *Figaro* in Mannheim on 24 October 1790.

19 *Ibid.*, p. 464, from the *Hamburgische Theaterzeitung*, 7 July 1792.

20 *Ibid.*, pp. 344–5, from Baron Adolf Knigge's *Dramaturgische Blätter*, Hanover 1789, reporting a performance of *Figaro* in Hanover on 18 May.

21 Raeburn and Raeburn, 'Mozart Manuscripts in Florence', pp. 335–6; see also A. Einstein, 'Mozart and Tarchi', *The Monthly Musical Record*, 65 (1935), 127, also given in A. Einstein, *Essays on Music*, ed. R. Leavis, rev. edn (London, Faber, 1958), pp. 191–4. Tarchi's setting of the 'letter'-duet has been rediscovered, see C. Sartori, 'Lo "Zeffiretto" di Angelo Tarchi', *Rivista Musicale Italiana*, 56 (1954), 233–40.

22 Raeburn and Raeburn, 'Mozart Manuscripts in Florence', p. 336; Deutsch, *Mozart: A Documentary Biography*, p. 317.

23 S. Dudley, 'Les premières versions françaises du *Mariage de Figaro* de Mozart', *Revue de Musicologie*, 69 (1983), 55–83, gives full details and transcriptions of some of the new music.

24 *Ibid.*, p. 61, quoting an anonymous critic in the *Affiches, annonces et avis divers ou Journal général de France* of 22 March 1793.

25 F. Gaiffe, *Le mariage de Figaro* (Paris, Société française d'éditions littéraires et techniques, 1942), pp. 118–40, discusses these and other adaptations of Beaumarchais's play and Mozart's opera. See also Loewenberg, *Annals of Opera*, col. 427. At the Théâtre de l'Opéra-Comique, *Figaro* continued to be performed with Beaumarchais's dialogue until 1970, see *Opera*, 22 (1971), 904.

26 H. Beard, 'Figaro in England: Productions of Mozart's Opera, and the Early Adaptations of it in England Before 1850', *Maske und Kothurn*, 10 (1964), 498–513, is the source of much of the information given here.

27 Deutsch, *Mozart: A Documentary Biography*, p. 385.

28 For an amusing account of *Die Entführung*, see A. Einstein, 'The First Performance of Mozart's *Entführung* in London', *The Music Review*, 7 (1946), 154–60, also in Einstein, *Essays on Music*, pp. 207–16. For amateur performances, see C. Raeburn, 'Mozart's Operas in England', *The Musical Times*, 97 (1956), 15–17.

29 *The Times*, No. 8630, Thursday 18 June 1812, p. [2]. The missing member of the cast is Morandi, who played Don Curzio.

30 *The Examiner*, 12 July 1812, given in W. C. Smith, *The Italian Opera and Contemporary Ballet in London 1789–1820: A Record of Performances and Players with Reports from the Journals of the Time* (London, The Society for Theatre Research, 1955), pp. 116–17. Robertson goes on to praise the singing of Catalani and Mrs Dickons, whose performances are also noted by Lord Mount-Edgcumbe, see his *Musical Reminiscences of an Old Amateur*, pp. 101, 112. However, according to Mount-Edgcumbe Catalani 'detested Mozart's music, which keeps the singer too much under the controul of the orchestra, and too strictly confined to time, which she is apt to violate', *ibid.*, p. 101.

31 Beard, 'Figaro in England', p. 504.

32 The libretto was 'printed for John Miller, Burlington Arcade, Piccadilly' in 1819: it cost two shillings and sixpence. A vocal score was printed 'by Goulding, D'Almaine, Potter, & Co. 20, Soho Square; & to be had at 7, Westmorland Str.[t] Dublin', price fifteen shillings. Copies of both survive in the British Library, London. British Library, Add. MS 27712, contains Bishop's autograph of much of his music for the adaptation. According to the 1819 libretto, the cast was: Count, Mr Jones; Fiorello, Mr Durusett; Figaro, Mr Liston; Basil, Mr I. Isaacs; Antonio, Mr Fawcett; Sebastian, Mr Comer; Cherubino, Miss Beaumont; Countess, Mrs Dickons; Susanna, Miss Stephens; Barbarina, Mrs Liston; Marcellina, Mrs Sterling. New verse had been provided by Isaac Pocock and Louise Costello, the dances were choreographed by Mr Noble, and the opera was produced by Mr Fawcett.

33 From Bishop's 'Advertisement' to the printed libretto of 1819, pp. [iii], iv.

34 Given in R. Northcott, *The Life of Sir Henry R. Bishop* (London, The Press Printers, 1920), p. 49.

35 Both extracts given in Beard, 'Figaro in England', p. 506, with no reference to the original sources.

36 See the review in *The Times*, No. 13463, Saturday 15 December 1827, and Beard, 'Figaro in England', pp. 507–11. 'Home, Sweet Home' was by Bishop and was used as the theme-song of his opera *Clari, or The Maid of Milan* (1823).

37 Beard, 'Figaro in England', p. 512. Berlioz had similar comments to make after a visit to England in 1852, see his *Evenings with the Orchestra*, trans. J. Barzun, reprint edn (Chicago, University of Chicago Press, 1973), p. 356: 'I am once again back from London. This time, except for two women singers, I heard nothing there by way of music but what was rather painful. At Her Majesty's Theatre [Haymarket] I saw a performance of Mozart's *Figaro* that was trombonized, ophicleided – in a word, copper-bottomed like a ship of the line. That is an English habit. Neither Mozart, nor Rossini, nor Weber, nor Beethoven has managed to escape *re-instrumentation*. Their orchestra is not sufficiently spicy, and it is deemed imperative to remedy the defect. Besides, if the theatres have regular performers on the trombone, ophicleide, bass drum, triangle, and cymbals, they are obviously not hired to twiddle their thumbs. This is an old story and it would seem about time to drop it.'

38 O. Jahn, *The Life of Mozart*, trans. P. D. Townsend (3 vols., London, Novello, Ewer & Co., 1882, 1891), vol. 3, pp. 72–117.
39 H. Rosenthal, *Two Centuries of Opera at Covent Garden* (London, Putnam, 1958), pp. 679–803, gives details of the repertoire at Covent Garden from 1847–1957. See also H. Rosenthal, 'Mozart at Covent Garden', *The Musical Times*, 122 (1981), 473–4.
40 F. Niecks, 'The Second Finale in Mozart's "Le Nozze di Figaro"', *The Monthly Musical Record*, 45 (1915), 186–8, 217–19.
41 Julius Korngold writing in the *Neue Freie Presse* in 1926, quoted in P. Hirsch, 'The Salzburg Mozart Festival, 1906: Reminiscences of an Amateur', *The Music Review*, 7 (1946), 149–53, p. 153, and see also R. Werba, 'Mahlers Wiener Mozart-Taten (VI): Die Hochzeit des Figaro', *Wiener Figaro*, 45 (1978), 19–24. Mahler composed a recitative setting of Beaumarchais's trial scene for insertion into Act III, and made other additions and alterations, see G. K. Kende, 'Gustav Mahlers Wiener "Figaro"', *Österreichische Musikzeitschrift*, 26 (1971), 295–302.
42 E. J. Dent, 'The Modern Cult of Mozart', *Opera Annual*, 2 (1955–6), 13–18. These Mozart performances are also discussed in Beecham's autobiography, *A Mingled Chime* (New York, Putnam, 1943).
43 E. J. Dent *A Theatre for Everybody: The Story of the Old Vic and Sadler's Wells* (London, Boardman, 1945), p. 87.
44 See the review in *The Times*, No. 42310, Saturday 17 January 1920.
45 J. Pritchard, 'Conducting Mozart', *Opera Annual*, 2 (1955–6), 26–34, p. 27. In *Opera Annual*, 5 (1958–9), 34–44, Roy Henderson, the first Glyndebourne Count, reminisces on the 1934 *Figaro*. See also *The Musical Times*, 125 (1984), 253–65, part of a special issue (May 1984) on the 50th anniversary of opera at Glyndebourne.
46 I. Kolodin, *The Story of the Metropolitan Opera, 1883–1950* (New York, Knopf, 1953): Q. Eaton, *Opera Caravan: Adventures of the Metropolitan on Tour, 1883–1956* (New York, Farrar, Straus & Cudahy, 1957). Kolodin gives full details of the season-by-season repertoire of the Metropolitan.
47 *Metropolitan Opera News*, 5 (1940–41), No. 7, pp. 21, 22.
48 As reported in the *New York Times*, Sunday 18 February 1940, Section 9, p. 7. The first performance of the *Figaro* revival is reviewed by Olin Downes, Wednesday 21 February, p. 15, and there is further commentary (and photographs) in the Sunday 25 February issue.
49 Reviewing the second performance of *Figaro* at the Metropolitan on 26 February, the *New York Times*, Tuesday 27 February, p. 17.
50 *Metropolitan Opera News*, 33 (1968–9), No. 1, p. 34, reviewing the Rome Opera production of *Figaro* as toured to New York on 22 June 1968. Visconti's production was careful to mark the passing of time through the 'folle journée' of the opera, with Act I in the morning, Act II at midday, Act III in the afternoon, and Act IV in the evening, moving (rather improbably) to sunrise at the dawning reconciliation of the Count and Countess.
51 Edmund Tracey in *The Musical Times*, 104 (1963), 489; see also Jeremy Noble in *The Musical Times*, 105 (1964), 521. This was the first time since 1914 that *Figaro* had been sung in Italian at Covent Garden.

52 *Opera*, 13 (1962), Festival issue, pp. 40–2, reviewing a performance at Glyndebourne on 24 May 1962.
53 In *Opera*, 16 (1965), 240–6. This material is also presented in a slightly different format in *Metropolitan Opera News*, 34 (1969–70), No. 24, pp. 24–5.
54 By Winton Dean in *The Musical Times*, 106 (1965), 449–50; see also *Opera*, 16 (1965), 448–50.
55 *The Musical Times*, 107 (1966), 137, reviewing a revival of the Sadler's Wells *Figaro* on 30 December 1965.
56 Stanley Sadie in *The Musical Times*, 113 (1972), 60–2; see also *Opera*, 23 (1972), 6–10.
57 For example, Hugh Ottaway in *The Musical Times*, 113 (1972), 1000.
58 Sadie in *The Musical Times*, 114 (1973), 821–2; see also Pierluigi Petrobelli in *The Musical Times*, 115 (1974), 681–2.
59 Geliot reports on his new translation in *The Musical Times*, 118 (1977), 907–8: 'But finally my reason for wishing to undertake a new version is my somewhat bleaker view of the piece than seems to be shared by others. This is surely the harshest, most painful comedy we have ever laughed at.'
60 Dean in *The Musical Times*, 119 (1978), 66.
61 *Opera*, 15 (1964), 596–7.
62 *The Musical Times*, 117 (1976), 243, reviewing a revival of the Copley *Figaro* at Covent Garden, 8 January 1976.
63 Respectively, *The Musical Times*, 116 (1975), 162–3; 119 (1978), 66.
64 *The Musical Times*, 125 (1984), 404, reviewing the 1984 revival of Hall's Glyndebourne production.
65 *The Musical Times*, 122 (1981), 492.
66 *The Musical Times*, 120 (1979), 56.
67 See Joseph Kerman's review of the Glyndebourne Touring Company at Oxford in 1973, *The Musical Times*, 114 (1973), 1260.
68 For a negative review, see Harold Rosenthal in *Opera*, 32 (1981), 537–8.

Select bibliography

Allanbrook, W. J., 'Metric Gesture as a Topic in *Le Nozze di Figaro* and *Don Giovanni*', *The Musical Quarterly*, 67 (1981), 94–112.

'Pro Marcellina: The Shape of "Figaro", Act IV', *Music & Letters*, 63 (1982), 69–84.

Rhythmic Gesture in Mozart: 'Le nozze di Figaro' and 'Don Giovanni', Chicago, University of Chicago Press, 1983.

Anderson, E., ed., *The Letters of Mozart and His Family*, 3rd edn, London, Macmillan, 1985.

Angermüller, R., and Berke, D., eds., Mozart, *La finta giardiniera*, in *Wolfgang Amadeus Mozart: Neue Ausgabe sämtlicher Werke*, II/5/8, 2 vols., Kassel, Bärenreiter, 1978.

Anheißer, S., 'Die unbekannte Urfassung von Mozarts Figaro', *Zeitschrift für Musikwissenschaft*, 15 (1933), 301–17.

Beard, H. R., 'Figaro in England: Productions of Mozart's Opera, and the Early Adaptations of it in England Before 1850', *Maske und Kothurn*, 10 (1964), 498–513.

Beaumarchais, P.-A. C. de, *Théâtre: 'Le barbier de Séville', 'Le mariage de Figaro', 'La mère coupable'*, ed. R. Pomeau, Paris, Garnier-Flammarion, 1965.

'The Barber of Seville' and 'The Marriage of Figaro', trans. J. Wood, Harmondsworth, Penguin, 1964.

Beecham, T., *A Mingled Chime*, New York, Putnam, 1943.

Berlioz, H., *Evenings with the Orchestra*, trans. J. Barzun, reprint edn, Chicago, University of Chicago Press, 1973.

Brophy, B., *Mozart the Dramatist*, New York, Harcourt, Brace & World, 1964.

'"Figaro" and the Limitations of Music', *Music & Letters*, 51 (1970), 26–36.

'Da Ponte and Mozart', *The Musical Times*, 122 (1981), 454–6.

Brown, B. A., 'Beaumarchais, Mozart and the Vaudeville: Two Examples from "The Marriage of Figaro"', *The Musical Times*, 127 (1986), 261–5.

Burney, C., *A General History of Music from the Earliest Ages to the Present Period (1789)*, ed. F. Mercer, reprint edn, 2 vols., New York, Dover, 1957.

Da Ponte, L., *Le nozze di Figaro: comedia per musica tratta dal francese in quattro atti*, Vienna, G. N. de Kurzbek, [1786].

Memorie, ed. G. Gambarin and F. Nicolini (Scrittori d'Italia, 81–2), 2 vols., Bari, Laterza, 1918.
Tre libretti per Mozart: 'Le nozze di Figaro', 'Don Giovanni', 'Così fan tutte', ed. P. Lecaldano, Milan, Rizzoli, 1956.
Dent, E. J., *Mozart's Operas: A Critical Study*, 2nd edn, London, Oxford University Press, 1947.
A Theatre for Everybody: The Story of the Old Vic and Sadler's Wells, London, Boardman, 1945.
'The Modern Cult of Mozart', *Opera Annual*, 2 (1955–6), 13–18.
Dent, E. J., ed., Mozart, *Le nozze di Figaro*, vocal score with translation, London, Boosey & Hawkes, 1947.
Deutsch, O. E., *Mozart: A Documentary Biography*, trans. E. Blom, P. Branscombe and J. Noble, London, Adam & Charles Black, 1965.
Döhring, S., 'Die Arienformen in Mozarts Opern', *Mozart-Jahrbuch* (1968–70), 66–76.
Drummond, J. D., *Opera in Perspective*, London, Dent, 1980.
Dudley, S., 'Les premières versions françaises du *Mariage de Figaro* de Mozart', *Revue de Musicologie*, 69 (1983), 55–83.
Eaton, Q., *Opera Caravan: Adventures of the Metropolitan on Tour, 1883–1956*, New York, Farrar, Straus & Cudahy, 1957.
Einstein, A., 'Eine unbekannte Arie der Marcelline', *Zeitschrift für Musikwissenschaft*, 13 (1930–1), 200–5.
'Mozart and Tarchi', *The Monthly Musical Record*, 65 (1935), 127, also in Einstein, *Essays on Music*, pp. 191–4.
Mozart: His Character – His Work, reprint edn, London, Panther, 1971.
'The First Performance of Mozart's *Entführung* in London', *The Music Review*, 7 (1946), 154–60, also in Einstein, *Essays on Music*, pp. 207–16.
Essays on Music, ed. R. Leavis, rev. edn, London, Faber, 1958.
Finscher, L., ed., Mozart, *Le nozze di Figaro*, in *Wolfgang Amadeus Mozart: Neue Ausgabe sämtlicher Werke*, II/5/16, 2 vols., Kassel, Bärenreiter, 1973.
Fitzlyon, A., *The Libertine Librettist: A Biography of Mozart's Librettist Lorenzo da Ponte*, London, Calder, 1955.
Gaiffe, F., *Le mariage de Figaro*, Paris, Société française d'éditions littéraires et techniques, 1942.
Gerber, R., ed., Mozart, *Le nozze di Figaro*, with preface by H. Abert, reprint edn, London, Eulenburg, 1983.
Gianturco, C., *Mozart's Early Operas*, London, Batsford, 1981.
Goldin, D., 'Mozart, da Ponte e il linguaggio dell'opera buffa' in M. T. Muraro, ed., *Venezia e il melodramma nel settecento, II*, Florence, Olschki, 1981, pp. 213–77.
'Da Ponte librettista fra Goldoni e Casti', *Giornale Storico della Letteratura Italiana*, 158 (1981), 396–408.
'Aspetti della librettistica italiana fra 1770 e 1830', *Analecta Musicologica*, 21 (1982), 128–91.
Graf, H., 'Der 4. Akt des Figaro', *Mozart-Jahrbuch* (1968–70), 95–8.
Greither, A., *Die sieben großen Opern Mozarts: Versuche über das Verhältnis der Texte zur Musik*, 3rd edn, Heidelberg, Verlag Lambert Schneider, 1977.

Heartz, D., 'The Creation of the Buffo Finale in Italian Opera', *Proceedings of the Royal Musical Association*, 104 (1977–8), 67–78.
'Mozart and His Italian Contemporaries: *La clemenza di Tito*', *Mozart-Jahrbuch* (1978–9), 275–93.
'Setting the Stage for Figaro', *The Musical Times*, 127 (1986), 256–60.
'Constructing *Le Nozze di Figaro*', *Journal of the Royal Musical Association*, 112/1 (1987), 77–98.
Hirsch, P., 'More Early Mozart Editions', *The Music Review*, 3 (1942), 38–45.
'The Salzburg Mozart Festival, 1906: Reminiscences of an Amateur', *The Music Review*, 7 (1946), 149–53.
Hocquard, J.-V., *'Le nozze di Figaro' de Mozart*, Paris, Aubier Montaigne, 1979.
Hodges, S., *Lorenzo Da Ponte: The Life and Times of Mozart's Librettist*, London, Granada, 1985.
Jahn, O., *The Life of Mozart*, trans. P. D. Townsend, 3 vols., London, Novello, Ewing & Co., 1882, 1891.
John, N., ed., *The Marriage of Figaro* (English National Opera Guide, 17), London, Calder, 1983.
Kelly, M., *Reminiscences*, ed. R. Fiske, London, Oxford University Press, 1975.
Kende, G. K., 'Gustav Mahlers Wiener "Figaro"'. *Österreichische Musikzeitschrift*, 26 (1971), 295–302.
Kerman, J., *Opera as Drama*, reprint edn, New York, Vintage Books, 1956.
King, A. H., *A Mozart Legacy: Aspects of the British Library Collections*, London, British Library, 1984.
Köchel, L. von, *et al.*, *W. A. Mozarts Werke. . .Supplement: Revisionsbericht*, Leipzig, Breitkopf & Härtel, 1889.
Chronologisch-thematisches Verzeichnis sämtlicher Tonwerk Wolfgang Amadé Mozarts, 6th edn, ed. F. Giegling, A. Weinmann and G. Sievers, Wiesbaden, Breitkopf & Härtel, 1964.
Köhler, K.-H., 'Mozarts Kompositionsweise: Beobachtungen am Figaro-Autograph', *Mozart-Jahrbuch* (1967), 31–45.
'Figaro-Miscellen: einige dramaturgische Mitteilungen zur Quellensituation', *Mozart-Jahrbuch* (1968–70), 119–31.
Kolodin, I., *The Story of the Metropolitan Opera, 1883–1950*, New York, Knopf, 1953.
Kunze, S., *Mozarts Opern*, Ditzingen, Philipp Reclam, 1984.
Landon, H. C. R., and Mitchell, D., eds., *The Mozart Companion*, London, Faber, 1956.
Levarie, S., *Mozart's 'Le nozze di Figaro': A Critical Analysis*, reprint edn, New York, Da Capo Press, 1977.
Liebner, J., *Mozart on the Stage*, London, Calder & Boyars, 1972.
Lippmann, F., 'Mozart und der Vers', *Analecta Musicologica*, 18 (1978), 107–37.
Loewenberg, A., *Annals of Opera, 1597–1940*, 2nd edn, New York, Rowman & Littlefield, 1970.
Loménie, L. de, *Beaumarchais et son temps: études sur la société en France au XVIIIe siècle d'après des documents inédits*, 2 vols., Paris, Michel Lévy, 1856.

Lorenz, A., 'Das Finale in Mozarts Meisteropern', *Die Musik*, 29 (1927), 621–32.

Mackerras, C., 'What Mozart Really Meant', *Opera*, 16 (1965), 240–6 (and see correspondence in *ibid.*, pp. 462–4, 542, 612–13).

Mann, W., *The Operas of Mozart*, London, Cassell, 1977.

Marchesan, A., *Della vita e delle opere di Lorenzo da Ponte*, Treviso, Turazza, 1900.

Michtner, O., *Das alte Burgtheater als Opernbühne*, Vienna, Hermann Böhlaus, 1970.

Mila, M., *Lettura delle 'Nozze di Figaro': Mozart e la ricerca della felicità*, Turin, Einaudi, 1979.

Moberly, R. B., *Three Mozart Operas: 'Figaro', 'Don Giovanni', 'The Magic Flute'*, London, Gollancz, 1967.

Moberly, R. [B.], and Raeburn, C., 'Mozart's "Figaro": The Plan of Act III', *Music & Letters*, 46 (1965), 134–6.

Mount-Edgcumbe, Richard, 2nd Earl of, *Musical Reminiscences of an Old Amateur for Fifty Years from 1773 to 1823*, London, W. Clarke, 1824.

Mozart, W. A., *La finta giardiniera*, edition: see Angermüller and Berke.

Le nozze di Figaro, editions: see Dent; Finscher; Gerber.

Letters: see Anderson; Deutsch.

Newman, E., *More Opera Nights*, London, Putnam, 1954.

Niecks, F., 'The Second Finale in Mozart's "Le Nozze di Figaro"', *The Monthly Musical Record*, 45 (1915), 186–8; 217–19.

Northcott, R., *The Life of Sir Henry R. Bishop*, London, The Press Printers, 1920.

Noske, F., 'Musical Quotation as a Dramatic Device: The Fourth Act of "Le Nozze di Figaro"', *The Musical Quarterly*, 54 (1968), 185–98, also as '*Le nozze di Figaro*: Musical Quotation as a Dramatic Device', in Noske, *The Signifier and the Signified: Studies in the Operas of Mozart and Verdi*, pp. 3–17.

'Social Tensions in "Le Nozze di Figaro"', *Music & Letters*, 50 (1969), 45–62, also as '*Le nozze di Figaro*: Social Tensions', in Noske, *The Signifier and the Signified: Studies in the Operas of Mozart and Verdi*, pp. 18–38.

Letter to the Editor, *Music & Letters*, 51 (1970), 346.

The Signifier and the Signified: Studies in the Operas of Mozart and Verdi, The Hague, Martinus Nijhoff, 1977.

'Verbal to Musical Drama: Adaptation or Creation?', *Themes in Drama*, 3 (1981), 143–52.

Osborne, C., *The Complete Operas of Mozart*, reprint edn, London, Gollancz, 1986.

Pritchard, J., 'Conducting Mozart', *Opera Annual*, 2 (1955–6), 26–34.

Raeburn, C., 'Mozart's Operas in England', *The Musical Times*, 97 (1956), 15–17.

Raeburn, M., and Raeburn, C., 'Mozart Manuscripts in Florence', *Music & Letters*, 40 (1959), 334–40.

Reiss, G., 'Die Thematik der Komödie in *Le Nozze di Figaro*', *Mozart-Jahrbuch* (1965–6), 164–78.

Robinson, M. F., *Naples and Neapolitan Opera*, Oxford, Clarendon Press, 1972.
Rosen, C., *The Classical Style: Haydn, Mozart, Beethoven*, London, Faber, 1971.
Rosenthal, H., *Two Centuries of Opera at Covent Garden*, London, Putnam, 1958.
'Mozart at Covent Garden', *The Musical Times*, 122 (1981), 473–4.
Ruf, W., *Die Rezeption von Mozarts "Le nozze di Figaro" bei den Zeitgenossen* (Beihefte zum Archiv für Musikwissenschaft, 16), Wiesbaden, Franz Steiner Verlag, 1977.
Sadie, S., ed., *The New Grove Dictionary of Music and Musicians*, 20 vols., London, Macmillan, 1980.
Sartori, C., 'Lo "Zeffiretto" di Angelo Tarchi', *Rivista Musicale Italiana*, 56 (1954), 233–40.
Scheel, H. L., '" Le Mariage de Figaro" von Beaumarchais und das Libretto der "Nozze di Figaro" von Lorenzo Da Ponte', *Die Musikforschung*, 28 (1975), 156–73.
Schenk, E., 'Zur Tonsymbolik in Mozarts "Figaro"', *Neues Mozart-Jahrbuch*, 1 (1941), 114–34.
Schmidgall, G., *Literature as Opera*, New York, Oxford University Press, 1977.
Schoenberg, A., 'Brahms the Progressive', in A. Schoenberg, *Style and Idea*, ed. L. Stein, rev. edn, London, Faber, 1984, pp. 398–441.
Schoffman, N., 'Vocal Sonata Forms of Mozart', *Current Musicology*, 28 (1979), 19–29.
Singer, I., *Mozart & Beethoven: The Concept of Love in Their Operas*, Baltimore, Johns Hopkins University Press, 1977.
Smith, P. J., *The Tenth Muse: A Historical Study of the Opera Libretto*, London, Gollancz, 1971.
Smith, W. C., *The Italian Opera and Contemporary Ballet in London 1789–1820: A Record of Performances and Players with Reports from the Journals of the Time*, London, The Society for Theatre Research, 1955.
Trowell, B., Letter to the Editor, *Music & Letters*, 50 (1969), 427–8.
Tyson, A., '*Le nozze di Figaro*: Lessons from the Autograph Score', *The Musical Times*, 122 (1981), 456–61.
'Some Problems in the Text of *Le nozze di Figaro*: Did Mozart Have a Hand in Them?', *Journal of the Royal Musical Association*, 112/1 (1987), 99–131.
Vill, S., ed., *'Così fan tutte': Beiträge zur Wirkungsgeschichte von Mozarts Oper*, Bayreuth, Mühl'scher Universitätsverlag, 1978.
Wagner, R., *Prose Works*, trans. W. A. Ellis, 8 vols., London, Kegan Paul & Co., 1892–9.
Werba, R., 'Mahlers Wiener Mozart-Taten (VI): Die Hochzeit des Figaro', *Wiener Figaro*, 45 (1978), 19–24.
Westrup, J. A., 'Cherubino and the G Minor Symphony', in H. van Thal, ed., *A Fanfare for Ernest Newman*, London, Barker, 1955, pp. 181–91.
Wyzewa, T. de, and Saint-Foix, G. de, *Wolfgang Amédée Mozart: sa vie musicale et son oeuvre*, 5 vols., Paris, Desclée de Brouwer, 1936–46.

Discography

MALCOLM WALKER

all recordings are in stereo unless otherwise stated

symbols

(m) mono recording (4) cassette version (CD) Compact Disc version

A Count Almaviva; *C* Countess Almaviva; *S* Susanna; *F* Figaro; *Ch* Cherubino; *M* Marcellina; *Bas* Don Basilio; *Bar* Dr Bartolo; *Barb* Barbarina; *Ant* Antonio; *Cur* Don Curzio

Complete

1934/5 (omits recitatives and Nos. 8, 23–25) Henderson *A*; Rautawaara *C*; Mildmay *S*; Domgraf-Fassbaender *F*; Helletsgruber *Ch*; Willis *M*; Nash *Bas*; Tajo, Allin *Bar*; W. Radford *Barb*; Dunlop *Ant*; Jones *Cur* / Glyndebourne Festival Chorus and Orch / Busch
Classics for Pleasure (m) CFP117/118
Turnabout (m) THS65081/3

1937 (live performance: Salzburg Festival) Stabile *A*; Rautawaara *C*; Réthy *S*; Pinza *F*; Novotná *Ch*; Cravcenco *M*; Wernick *Bas*; Lazzari *Bar*; Komarek *Barb*; Madin *Ant*; Nessi *Cur* / Vienna State Opera Chorus; VPO / Walter
Bruno Walter Society (m) RR801

1938 (Radio Stuttgart broadcast: in German) Ahlersmayer *A*; Teschemacher *C*; Cebotari *S*; Schoeffler *F*; Kolniak *Ch*; Waldenau *M*; Vessely *Bas*; Böhme *Bar*; Frank *Barb*; Fiedler *Ant*; Buchta *Cur* / Stuttgart Radio Chorus and Orch / Böhm
Preiser (m) HF1–3

1940 (live performance: Metropolitan Opera House, New York) Brownlee *A*; Rethberg *C*; Sayão *S*; Pinza *F*; Novotná *Ch*; Petina *M*; De Paolis *Bas*; Baccaloni *Bar*; M. Farrell *Barb*; L. D'Angelo *Ant*; Garris *Cur* / Metropolitan Opera Association Chorus and Orch / Panizza
EJS (m) EJS118

1940 (live performance: Metropolitan Opera House, New York) Brownlee *A*; Rethberg *C*; Albanese *S*; Pinza *F*; Novotná *Ch*; Petina *M*; De Paolis *Bas*; Baccaloni *Bar*; M. Farrell *Barb*; L. D'Angelo *Ant*; Garris *Cur* / Metropolitan Opera Association Chorus and Orch / Panizza
Metropolitan Opera (m) MET1

1944 (live performance: Metropolitan Opera House, New York) Brownlee

A; Steber *C*; Sayão *S*; Pinza *F*; Novotná *Ch*; Petina *M*; De Paolis *Bas*; Baccaloni *Bar*; M. Farrell *Barb*; L. D'Angelo *Ant*; Garris *Cur* / Metropolitan Opera Association Chorus and Orch / Walter
Bruno Walter Society (m) BWS808

1949 (live performance: Metropolitan Opera House, New York) Brownlee *A*; Steber *C*; Sayão *S*; Tajo *F*; Novotná *Ch*; Turner *M*; De Paolis *Bas*; Baccaloni *Bar*; Bollinger *Barb*; Alvary *Ant*; Chabay *Cur* / Metropolitan Opera Association Chorus and Orch / Busch
CLS (m) MDTP021/3

1950 (omits recitatives) London *A*; Schwarzkopf *C*; Seefried *S*; Kunz *F*; Jurinac *Ch*; Höngen *M*; Majkut *Bas*, *Cur*; Rus *Bar*; Schwaiger *Barb*; Felden *Ant* / Vienna State Opera Chorus, VPO / Karajan
EMI (m) 1C 147 01751/3M
CBS (US) (m) SL114

1951 Bruscantini *A*; Gatti *C*; Noni *S*; Tajo *F*; Gardino *Ch*; Truccato-Pace *M*; Mercuriali *Bas*; Corena *Bar*; Sciutti *Barb*; Dalamangas *Ant*; Ponz de Leon *Cur* / Italian Radio Chorus and Orch, Milan / Previtali
Cetra (m) LPS3219

1952 (in German) Anonymous artists, Leipzig State Opera Chorus and Orch / von Herten
Royale (m) 1502/4

1953 (live performance: Salzburg Festival) Schoeffler *A*; Schwarzkopf *C*; Seefried *S*; Kunz *F*; Gueden *Ch*; S. Wagner *M*; Klein *Bas*; Koréh *Bar*; Maikl *Barb*; Pernerstorfer *Ant*; Majkut *Cur* / Vienna State Opera Chorus, VPO / Furtwängler
Fonit-Cetra (m) FE27
Discocorp (m) IGI343

1954 (live performance: Teatro alla Scala, Milan) Petri *A*; Schwarzkopf *C*; Seefried *S*; Panerai *F*; Jurinac *Ch*; Villa *M*; Pirino *Bas*; Maionica *Bar*; Adani *Barb*; Calabrese *Ant*; Nessi *Cur* / Teatro alla Scala Chorus and Orch / Karajan
Cetra (m) LO70 (3)

1955 Poell *A*; Della Casa *C*; Gueden *S*; Siepi *F*; Danco *Ch*; Roessl-Majdan *M*; M. Dickie *Bas*; Corena *Bar*; Felbermayer *Barb*; Pröglhöf *Ant*; Meyer-Welfing *Cur* / Vienna State Opera Chorus, VPO / E. Kleiber
Decca 417 315-1D03 (4) 417 315-4D02
London OSA1402 (4) OSA5-1402

1955 Calabrese *A*; Jurinac *C*; Sciutti *S*; Bruscantini *F*; Stevens *Ch*; M. Sinclair *M*; Cuénod *Bas*; Wallace *Bar*; J. Sinclair *Barb*; Griffiths *Ant*; McCoshan *Cur* / 1955 Glyndebourne Festival Chorus and Orch / Gui
EMI EX290017-3
Victor (US) (m) LM6401

1955 (live performance: Aix-en-Provence Festival) Rehfuss *A*; Stich-Randall *C*; Streich *S*; Panerai *F*; Lorengar *Ch*; Gayraud *M*; Cuénod *Bas*; Ignal *Barb* / 1955 Aix-en-Provence Festival Chorus, Paris Conservatoire Orch / Rosbaud
Pathé (m) 2C 127 16312/4M
Vox (m) OPBX1653

1956 Schoeffler *A*; Jurinac *C*; Streich *S*; Berry *F*; Ludwig *Ch*; Malaniuk *M*;

Majkut *Bas*; Czerwenka *Bar*; Schwaiger *Barb*; Donch *Ant*; M. Dickie *Cur* / Vienna State Opera Chorus, Vienna SO / Böhm
Philips (m) 6707 006
Epic (m) LC6022

1957 (live performance: Salzburg Festival) Fischer-Dieskau *A*; Schwarzkopf *C*; Seefried *S*; Kunz *F*; Ludwig *Ch*; S. Wagner *M*; M. Dickie *Bas*; G. Stern *Bar*; Felbermayer *Barb*; Pernerstorfer *Ant*; Majkut *Cur* / Vienna State Opera Chorus, VPO / Böhm
Melodram (m) MEL709

1959 London *A*; Della Casa *C*; Peters *S*; Tozzi *F*; Elias *Ch*; S. Warfield *M*; Carelli *Bas*, *Cur*; Corena *Bar*; Felbermayer *Barb*; Pantscheff *Ant* / Vienna State Opera Chorus, VPO / Leinsdorf
Decca ECS743/5
RCA (US) LSC6408

1959 Waechter *A*; Schwarzkopf *C*; Moffo *S*; Taddei *F*; Cossotto *Ch*; Gatta *M*; Ercolani *Bas*, *Cur*; Vinco *Bar*; Fusco *Barb*; Cappuccilli *Ant* / Philharmonia Chorus and Orch / Giulini
EMI SLS5152 (4) TC-SLS5152
Angel SCL3608 (4) 4X3X3608

1960s (in Russian) Zakharov *A*; Rozhdestvenskaya *C*; Kazantieva *S*; Abranov *F* / Moscow Radio Chorus and Orch / Sanderling
Melodiya M10–36437/42

1960 Fischer-Dieskau *A*; Stader *C*; Seefried *S*; Capecchi *F*; Toepper *Ch*; Bennsingen *M*; Kuen *Bas*; Sardi *Bar*; Schwaiger *Barb*; Wieter *Ant*; Lenz *Cur* / Berlin RIAS Chorus, Berlin RSO / Fricsay
DG 2728 004

1963 (live performance: Salzburg Festival) Fischer-Dieskau *A*; Gueden *C*; Sciutti *S*; Evans *F*; Lear *Ch*; P. Johnson *M*; van Kesteren *Bas*; Lagger *Bar*; B. Vogel *Barb*; Frese *Ant*; Vantin *Cur* / Vienna State Opera Chorus, VPO / Maazel
Movimento Musica (m) 03.025

1964 (in German) Prey *A*; Gueden *C*; Rothenberger *S*; Berry *F*; Mathis *Ch*; Burmeister *M*; Schreier *Bas*; Ollendorf *Bar*; Ronisch *Barb*; Vogel *Ant*; Forster *Cur* / Dresden State Opera Chorus, Dresdener Staatskapelle / Suitner
Seraphim SIC6002
EMI 1C 183 30159/61

1967 Fischer-Dieskau *A*; Janowitz *C*; Mathis *S*; Prey *F*; Troyanos *Ch*; Johnson *M*; Wohlfahrt *Bas*; Lagger *Bar*; Vogel *Barb*; Hirte *Ant*; Vantin *Cur* / German Opera Chorus and Orch, Berlin / Böhm
DG 2740 108 (4) 3371 005
DG (US) 2711 007 (4) 3371 005
(CD) 416 370–2PH3

1968 (live performance) Petri *A*; Jurinac *C*; Stratas *S*; Bruscantini *F*; Berganza *Ch* / chorus and orch / Mehta
Legendary Recordings LR206 (3)

1970 Bacquier *A*; Söderström *C*; Grist *S*; Evans *F*; Berganza *Ch*; Burmeister *M*; Hollweg *Bas*; Langdon *Bar*; M. Price *Barb*; Grant *Ant*;

Brookmeier *Cur* / Alldis Choir, New Philharmonia Orch / Klemperer
EMI SLS955
EMI 1C 157 02134/7

1970 Wixell *A*; Norman *C*; Freni *S*; Ganzarolli *F*; Minton *Ch*; Casula *M*; Tear *Bas*; Grant *Bar*; L. Watson *Barb*; Hudson *Ant* / BBC Chorus, BBC SO / C. Davis
Philips 6707 014 (4) 7699 055

1974 (live performance: Salzburg Festival) Krause *A*; Harwood *C*; Freni *S*; van Dam *F*; von Stade *Ch*; Berbié *M*; Sénéchal *Bas*; Montarsolo *Bar*; Schary *Barb*; Kelemen *Ant*; Caron *Cur* / Vienna State Opera Chorus, VPO / Karajan
Estro Armonico EA10

1976 Fischer-Dieskau *A*; Harper *C*; Blegen *S*; Evans *F*; Berganza *Ch*; Finnila *M*; Fryatt *Bas*; McCue *Bar*; Gale *Barb*; Donnelly *Ant*; Robertson *Cur* / Alldis Choir, ECO / Barenboim
EMI 2C 165 02856/9
Pantheon (US) 1913

1979 Krause *A*; Tomowa-Sintow *C*; Cotrubas *S*; van Dam *F*; von Stade *Ch*; Berbié *M*; Zednik *Bas*; Bastin *Bar*; Barbaux *Barb*; Kelemen *Ant*; Equiluz *Cur* / Vienna State Opera Chorus, VPO / Karajan
Decca D132D4
London OSA1443

1981 Allen *A*; Te Kanawa *C*; Popp *S*; Ramey *F*; von Stade *Ch*; Berbié *M*; Tear *Bas*; Moll *Bar*; Kenney *Barb*; Tadeo *Ant*; Langridge *Cur* / London Opera Chorus, LPO / Solti
Decca D267D4 (4) K267K42 (CD) 410 150–2DH3
London LDR74001 (4) 74001 (CD) 410 150–2LH3

1985 Raimondi *A*; Popp *C*; Hendricks *S*; van Dam *F*; Baltsa *Ch*; Palmer *M*; Baldin *Bas*; Lloyd *Bar*; Pope *Barb*; Maxwell *Ant*; Jenkins *Cur* / Ambrosian Opera Chorus, Academy of St Martin-in-the-Fields / Marriner
Philips 416 370–1PH3 (4) 416 370–4PH3 (CD) 416 370–2PH3

1986 Hynninen *A*; M. Price *C*; Battle *S*; Allen *F*; Murray *Ch*; Nicolesco *M*; Ramirez *Bas*; Rydl *Bar*; Pace *Barb*; De Grandis *Ant*; Gavazzi *Cur* / Vienna State Opera Concert Choir, VPO / Muti
EMI EX270576-3 (4) EX270576-5 (CD) in preparation

Excerpts/highlights

1937 (in Swedish) Forsell *A*; Hertzberg *C*; Forsell *F* / Royal Opera Orch, Stockholm / Sandberg
EJS (m) EJS349

1940 – Nos. 1, 9, 10, 11, 13, 14, 16, 20, 26, 27
Cehanovsky *A*; Della Chiesa *C*; Dickey *S*; Cordon *F*; Browning *Ch* / Publishers Service SO / Steinberg
RCA (US) (m) CAL227

1947 Tomei *A*; Gatti *C*; Labia *S*; Neroni *F*; Elmo *Ch*; Biasini *Bar* / Rome Opera House Chorus and Orch / Questa
Royale (m) 1210

1952 – Ov; Nos. 6, 9, 10, 11, 12, 19, 22 (part), 26, 27 (in German)
Metternich *A*; Kupper *C*; Trötschel *S*; Griendl *F*; Stader *Ch* / various orch and conductors
DG (m) LPEM19066

c1953 Pease *A*; Troxell *C*; Hunt *S*; Sgarro *F* / orch / Walther
Royale (m) 1636

1955 – Ov; Nos. 2, 3, 6, 7, 9, 11, 14 (part), 16, 17, 20, 26, 27, 28 (part)
Driessen *A*; Opawsky *C*; van der Graaf *S*; Jongsma *F*; Meyer *Ch* / chorus, Netherlands PO / Goehr
Musical Masterpieces Society (m) MMS2020
Classics Club (m) X76

1955 Singher *A*; Amara *C*; Conner *S*; Tozzi *F*; Miller *Ch*; Glaz *M*; De Paolis *Bas*; Baccaloni *Bar*; Cundari *Barb*; Carelli *Cur* / Metropolitan Opera Association Chorus and Orch / Rudolf
Metropolitan Opera (m) MET315

1955–6 (in German) Kohn *A*; Grümmer *C*; Berger *S*; Prey *F*; Köth *Ch*; Frick *Bar* / Berlin PO, Berlin SO, North-West German PO / Klobucar, Schüchter
EMI 1C 047 28574

1960s (in German) Wenglor; Ebers; Lauhofer; Adam / Berlin State Opera Orch / Stein
Eterna 720 197

1960s (in German) Wenglor; Rose; Koziel; Prentzlow; Adam; Neukirch / Berlin State Opera Orch / Apelt
Eterna 820449

1960s (in German) Ebers; Lani; H. Schreier; Pease; Lehmann / Berlin SO / Martin
CBS S51095

1960 (in French) Giovinetti; Berton; Blanc; Sautereau / Lamoureux Orch / Fournet
DG (m) LPEM19468

1960 (in German) Fischer-Dieskau *A*; Stader *C*; Streich *S*; Berry *F*; Steffek *Ch* / Berlin PO / Leitner
DG 2535 279 (4) 3335 279

1961 (in German) Müszely *C*; Wenglor *S*; Röth-Ehrang *F*; Exner *Ch* / German Opera Chorus and Orch / Lange
Ariola-Eurodisc 75875ZR
Marble Arch (m) MAL807

1962 Pease *A*; Ebers *C*; Rizzoli *S*; Berry *F*; Steiner *Ch* / Hamburg Radio SO / Zillig
Musica e Lettera MEL8006
CMS/Summit 112

1965 - Nos. 2, 3, 6, 9, 10, 11, 16, 17, 19, 20, 26, 27
Jedlicka *A*; Harper *C*; Miljakovič *S*; Holeček *F*; Yachmi *Ch* / Vienna Opera Orch / Wallberg
Concert Hall SMSA2586

1968 (live performance) Gobbi *A*; Ligabue *C*; Sciutti *S* / Rome Opera Orch / Giulini
MRF (m) MRF25

Replacement arias

recordings listed are those with orchestra

Un moto di gioia, K579

1953 Stader / Bavarian Radio SO / Lehmann
DG (m) EPL30458

1979 Gruberová / Vienna CO / G. Fischer
Decca D251D5
Decca SXL7000 (4) KSXC7000
London OS26662 (4) OS5 26662

1984 Baker / Scottish CO / Leppard
Erato NUM75176 (4) MCE75176
(CD) ECD88090

1985 Battle / RPO / Previn
EMI EL270406-1 (4) EL270406-4
(CD) CDC7 47355-2

Al desio di chi t'adora, K577

1975 M. Price / LPO / Lockhart
RCA (UK) GL12124 (4) GK12124
RCA (US) AGL1 2124 (4) AGK1 2124

1979 Berganza / Vienna CO / G. Fischer
Decca D251D5
Decca SXL7001 (4) KSXC7001

1984 Baker / Scottish CO / Leppard
Erato NUM75176 (4) MCE75176
(CD) ECD88090

Index

Abert, Hermann, 119, 156 n. 6
Adamberger, Johann Valentin, 4
Albertarelli, Francesco, 126
Allanbrook, Wye Jamison, 152 n. 4, 153 nn. 9, 10
Anfossi, Pasquale, 12, 16, 22, 26, 32
  Il curioso indiscreto, additions by Mozart, 9; *La finta giardiniera*, compared with Mozart, 16–22, 28
Angermüller, Rudolph, 149 n. 3, 154 n. 2
Arco, Count Georg Anton Felix von, 38
Ariosto, Ludovico, 155 n. 6
Attwood, Thomas, 131

Bach, Carl Philipp Emanuel, 2, 88
Bach, Johann Sebastian, 2, 92
Baudron, Antoine Laurent, 130
Beaumarchais, Pierre-Augustin Caron de, ix, 33, 38, 130, 131, 150 n. 1
  L'autre Tartuffe ou La mère coupable, 34, 46
  Le barbier de Séville ou La précaution inutile, ix, 6, 33, 34, 42, 51, 108; *see also* Paisiello, *Il barbiere di Siviglia*; Rossini, *Il barbiere di Siviglia*
  La folle journée ou Le mariage de Figaro, ix, 6, 24, 33, 34, 34–5, 42, 130, 133, 139, 147, 150–1 n. 7, 151 n. 8; characterisation, 45, 47, 48, 120, 121, 146; the Countess, 45–7, 48, 120–1; Leopold Mozart's views on, 75; music in, 42, 46, 82, 84, 130; performances banned in Paris, 34, and in Vienna, 26, 35–6, 150 n. 3; political content, 25, 26, 34, 35, 36, 37–8; preface, 35, 46, 48, 150 n. 2, 151 nn. 10, 11, 12, 19, 20; structure, 35, 43, 44, 75, 84, 88, 95, 120; success, 34, 34–5; translations, 35; see also *Le nozze di Figaro*, and Beaumarchais
Beecham, Thomas, 137, 161 n. 42
Beethoven, Ludwig van, 132, 133, 160 n. 37
Benedict, Julius, 135
Benucci, Francesco, 5, 6, 6–7, 10, 123, 131, 157–8 n. 8, 158–9 n. 13
Berlin, x, see also *Le nozze di Figaro*, performances
Berlioz, Hector, 160 n. 37
Bertati, Giovanni, 75
Bianchi, Francesco, 12
  La villanella rapita, additions by Mozart, 9
Bishop, Henry Rowley, 128, 133–5, 135, 142, 160 nn. 32, 33, 36
Blangini, Felice, 131
Bletchley, John, 142
Böhm, Karl, 140, 168, 170
Bonaparte, Napoleon, 38
Bondini, Pasquale, 124
Bournonville, F. V. A. d'Artois de, 131
Bournonville, L. C. A. d'Artois de, 131
Bullinger, Abbé Joseph, 1, 148 n. 2
Burney, Charles, 88, 92, 155 n. 3
Bury, John, 142
Busch, Fritz, 138, 168, 169
Bussani, Dorotea, 10
Bussani, Francesco, 5, 10, 37, 73

Calzabigi, Raniero de, 149 n. 3
Carey, Clive, 137, 138
Casanova, Giovanni Jacopo (Giacomo), 5
Casti, Giambattista, 122, 155 n. 10
Castil-Blaze, François Henri Joseph, 131
Catalani, Angelica, 132, 160 n. 30
Catherine II (Empress), 25
Chaulnes, Duc de, 33
Cherubini, Bartolomeo, 129
Christie, John, 138
Cimarosa, Domenico, 3, 12
  Giannina e Bernardone, 28–30
Coleman, Basil, 146
Colloredo, Hieronymus (Archbishop of Salzburg), 1, 38
Coltellini, Marco, 15, 149 n. 3
commedia dell'arte, 2, 9, 14, 35, 109, 146
Copley, John, 142, 145
Corri, Charles, 138
Costello, Louise, 160 n. 32

da capo aria, 3, 14, 16, 102, 107, 149 n. 2
Dante Alighieri, 155 n. 6
Da Ponte, Lorenzo (Bishop of Ceneda), 5
Da Ponte, Lorenzo (Emmanuele Conegliano; librettist), ix, 5–6, 6, 8, 9, 35, 125, 132

complaints against composers and singers, 42, 85, 87, 155 n. 10
skills as librettist, ix, 75, 78–9, 80, 82, 85, 87, 147
views on finales, 43–4, 84
works (other than *Le nozze di Figaro*): *L'ape musicale*, 125, 158 n. 11; *Il burbero di buon cuore*, 9–10, 75; *Il dissoluto punito o sia il Don Giovanni*, 75; *Gli equivoci*, 75; *Memorie*, 35–6, 42, 43–4, 85, 87, 122–3, 150 nn. 3, 4, 151 nn. 15, 16, 155 nn. 10, 12, 156 (Ch. 8) n. 1; *Il ricco d'un giorno*, 8; *La serva onorata* (anonymous adaptation of *Le nozze di Figaro*), 129; *Lo sposo deluso*(?), 8; *Una cosa rara o sia Bellezza ed onestà*, 36, 42, 75; *see also* Martín y Soler, *Una cosa rara*; Mozart, *Così fan tutte*, *Don Giovanni*; *Le nozze di Figaro*, libretto
Davis, Colin, 142, 171
Dean, Winton, 145, 162 nn. 54, 60
Del Bene, Adriana Ferrarese (Francesca Gabrielli), 125, 158 n. 11
Della Casa, Lisa, 139, 169, 170
Dent, Edward J., xi, 23, 28, 72, 137, 138, 142, 149 n. 5, 150 n. 11, 151 nn. 14, 16, 153 nn. 11, 12, 161 nn. 42, 43
Deutsch, Otto Erich, 150 nn. 3, 5, 6, 156 (Ch. 8) n. 1, 157 nn. 3, 4, 5, 6, 157–8 n. 8, 158 nn. 9, 10, 11, 159 nn. 15, 16, 17, 18, 19, 20, 22, 27
Dickons, Maria, 132, 160 nn. 30, 32
Donaueschingen, 157 n. 6; see also *Le nozze di Figaro*, performances
Downes, Olin, 139, 161 nn. 48, 49
Dresden, 5; see also *Le nozze di Figaro*, performances
Durazzo, Count Giacomo, 4
Duschek (Dušek), František Xaver, 10
Duschek (Dušek), Josephine, 10

Ebert, Carl, 138, 140
Edinburgh, 137; see also *Le nozze di Figaro*, performances
Einstein, Alfred, 8, 9, 149 nn. 18, 20, 157 n. 6, 158–9 n. 13, 159 nn. 21, 28
Evidon, Richard, 145

Fallows, David, 145
Ferdinand (Archduke of Lombardy), 129
Finscher, Ludwig, xi, 72, 151 n. 14, 151–2 n. 1, 152 n. 2, 153 nn. 11, 12, 153–4 n. 14, 154 nn. 15, 16, 157 n. 6, 158 n. 12
Fischer, György, 142
Fischer, Johann Ignaz Ludwig, 3
Florence, 158–9 n. 13; see also *Le nozze di Figaro*, performances
Frankenstein, Alfred, 139, 140, 145
Frankfurt on Main, 37, 126; see also *Le nozze di Figaro*, performances

Galitzin, Prince Dimitri Michaelovich, 4
Galuppi, Baldassare, 3
Gazzaniga, Giuseppe, 12, 131, 157–8 n. 8
Geliot, Michael, 142, 145, 162 n. 59
Gerber, Rudolf, xi, 72, 151 n. 14, 153 nn. 11, 12
Giulini, Carlo Maria, 140, 170, 173
Gluck, Christoph Willibald von, 64, 152 n. 7
Glyndebourne Opera House, 138, 161 n. 45, 168, 169; see also *Le nozze di Figaro*, performances
Goëzman de Thurne, Louis-Valentin, 33
Goldoni, Carlo, 3, 15, 35, 75, 85
Gottlieb, Anna, 10, 64–5
Graf, Herbert, 139, 140, 153 n. 8
Groves, Charles, 145
Gueden, Hilde, 139, 169, 170
Guevara, Luis Vélez de, 75
Guglielmi, Pietro Alessandro, 12, 131

Hagenauer, Ignaz, 4
Haggin, B. H., 139
Hall, Peter, 142, 144, 145, 146, 162 n. 64
Handel, George Frideric, 2, 92
Hawkins, John, 152 n. 7
Haydn, Joseph, x, 2, 92
Heartz, Daniel, xii, 148 nn. 5, 9, 149 nn. 22, 6, 150 n. 3, 152 nn. 5, 7, 155 n. 8
Henderson, Roy, 161 n. 45
Hofmannsthal, Hugo von, 47
Homer, 155 n. 6

Jacquin, Baron Gottfried von, 125
Jahn, Otto, 136, 161 n. 38
Jorgulesco, Jonel, 139, 140
Joseph II (Emperor), 5, 6, 10, 122–3, 129
bans encores in Burgtheater, 124, 157 n. 3
dislikes *opera seria*, 11
establishes German opera in Vienna, 3, 11
forbids performance of *Le mariage de Figaro* in early 1785, 26, 35–6, 150 n. 3
reinstates Italian opera in Vienna, 4–5, 5, 6, 11

Karajan, Herbert von, 142, 169
Kazinczy, Franz, 124, 157 n. 4
Kelly, Michael, 4, 5, 10, 37, 122, 123, 131
Reminiscences, 1–2, 4–5, 123–4, 150 n. 9, 156–7 n. 2
Kemble, Adelaide, 135
Kemble, Charles, 135
Kerman, Joseph, 87, 162 n. 67
Kleiber, Erich, 139, 169
Klein, Professor Anton, 148 n. 8
Knigge, Baron Adolf, 125, 158 nn. 9, 10, 159 n. 20
Knigge, Philippine, 158 n. 10
Köchel, Ludwig (Ritter) von, 72, 153 n. 13, 154 nn. 15, 16, 154–5 n. 5, 156 nn. 3, 4, 157 n. 6, 157–8 n. 8, 158 n. 9, 158–9 n. 13

Kraków, x
Kunz, Erich, 139, 169, 170
Kurzbek, Giuseppe Nob. de, 153 n. 8, 158 n. 9

La Harpe, Jean François de, 75
Laschi, Luisa, 10, 72
Lausch, Laurent, 125, 157–8 n. 8, 158–9 n. 13
Lazaridis, Stefanos, 142
Lecaldano, Paolo, xi, 151 n. 14
Levarie, Siegmund, 30, 118, 119, 149 n. 7, 150 n. 12, 155 n. 6, 156 nn. 2, 7
Lippmann, Friedrich, 154 n. 4
London, 36, 158 n. 12, 160 n. 32
  Coliseum (English National Opera), 145
  Covent Garden, 133, 135, 137, 140, 142, 145, 161 nn. 39, 51, 162 n. 62
  Drury Lane, 135, 137
  King's Theatre, Haymarket, 6, 131, 132–3, 160 n. 37
  Old Vic, 137–8
  Pantheon, 132
  Sadler's Wells, 142, 145, 162 n. 55
  see also *Le nozze di Figaro*, performances
Louis XVI (King of France), 34, 38

Mackerras, Charles, 142, 146, 158–9 n. 13
MacPherson, Alexander, 142
Mahler, Gustav, 136, 139, 161 n. 41
Mandini, Maria, 10
Mandini, Stefano, 5, 10
Mannheim, 1; see also *Le nozze di Figaro*, performances
Martín y Soler, Vicente, 5, 11, 12, 35–6
  L'arbore di Diana, 12, 126, 159 n. 17; *Il burbero di buon cuore*, 9–10; *Una cosa rara*, 12, 23, 36, 42, 125, 126, 159 n. 17
Massenet, Jules, 145
Mazzolà, Caterino, 5
Messel, Oliver, 140, 141
Metastasio, Pietro, 85
Mila, Massimo, 156 (Ch. 7) n. 1
Miller, Jonathan, 145
Moberly, Robert, 72–3, 154 n. 17
Molière, Jean-Baptiste Poquelin de, 33, 34
Mount-Edgcumbe, Richard, 2nd Earl of, 148 n. 9, 160 n. 30
Mozart, Anna Maria, 1
Mozart, Leopold, x, 1, 3, 4, 6, 7, 8, 9, 10, 75, 149 nn. 17, 21, 23, 154 n. 1, 157 n. 5, 158 n. 9, 159 n. 14
Mozart, Wolfgang Amadeus, 12
  and counterpoint, 92
  and Prague, 124–5
  and Salzburg, ix–x, 1–2, 38
  and the Classical style, 88–95
  arrival in Vienna, ix–x, 1–2; attempts to establish himself as an opera composer, 3, 4, 6–10, 11, 12–13, 26; rivalry, 6, 10, 12–13, 122–3, 124, 157 n. 5
  features of operatic style, 3–4, 13, 15–16, 22, 22–3, 32, 41, 48, 57; aria forms, 16, 22; characterisation, 3–4, 15–16, 22–3; influence of instrumental music, 9, 32, 90–5; use of instruments, 3–4, 22, 32; use of tonality, 3–4, 9; see also *Le nozze di Figaro*
  letters, 1, 3, 3–4, 4, 6, 7, 8, 38, 85, 87, 125, 148 nn. 1, 2, 4, 6, 7, 11, 12, 148–9 n. 14, 149 nn. 15, 16, 17, 19, 151 n. 13, 154 n. 4
  views on librettists and opera, x, 2, 3–4, 6, 7, 75–6, 80, 85, 87, 126, 148–9 n. 14, 154 n. 4, 159 n. 14
  works (other than *Le nozze di Figaro*): 'Al desio di chi t'adora' (K577, for *Figaro*, Vienna 1789), 125, 158 n. 12, 173; *Ch'io mi scordi di te* (K505, *see also* 'Non più, tutti ascoltai. . .Non temer, amato bene', K490), 153–4 n. 14; *La clemenza di Tito* (K621), 132; *Così fan tutte* (K588), ix, 8, 11, 49, 96, 113, 126, 130, 132, 134, 136–7, 146, 148 n. 13; 'Dite almeno in che mancai' (K479, for Bianchi, *La villanella rapita*), 9; *Don Giovanni* (K527), ix, 8, 9, 12, 26, 49, 67, 75, 84, 113, 120, 125, 126, 130, 131, 132, 133, 135, 136, 146, 148 n. 13, 155 n. 7; *Die Entführung aus dem Serail* (K384), x, 3–4, 8, 11, 49, 85, 132, 159 n. 28; *La finta giardiniera* (K196), 13, 16–22, 23, 24, 149 nn. 2, 3, 150 n. 10, 157 n. 6; *La finta semplice* (K51/46a), 2, 13, 15, 15–16, 23; Five Contredanses (K609, including arrangement of 'Non più andrai farfallone amoroso'), 158 n. 11; *Idomeneo* (K366), x, 1, 3, 6, 7, 10, 84, 85, 106–7, 107, 153–4 n. 14; 'Mandina amabile' (K480, for Bianchi, *La villanella rapita*), 9; 'No, che non sei capace' (K419, for Anfossi, *Il curioso indiscreto*), 9; 'Non più, tutti ascoltai. . . Non temer, amato bene' (K490, for *Idomeneo*, Vienna 1786, see also *Ch'io mi scordi di te*, K505), 10, 153–4 n. 14; *L'oca del Cairo* (K422), 7–8, 149 n. 17; Piano Quartet in G minor (K478), 90–5; 'Per pietà, non ricercate' (K420, for Anfossi, *Il curioso indiscreto*), 9; *Der Schauspieldirektor* (K486), 9, 10; 'Spiegarti non poss'io' (K489, for *Idomeneo*, Vienna 1786), 10; *Lo sposo deluso* (K430/424a), 8; String Quartet in A major (K464), 155–6 n. 5; 'Un moto di gioia' (K579, for *Figaro*, Vienna 1789), 30, 125, 126, 173; 'Vorrei spiegarti, oh dio' (K418, for Anfossi, *Il curioso indiscreto*), 9; *Die Zauberflöte* (K620), 49, 64, 132
Munich, 1, 13; see also *Le nozze di Figaro*, performances
Mysliveček, Josef, 150 n. 10

Naples, 25, 88
New York, 6

Metropolitan Opera, 138–9, 140, 145, 161 n. 46, 168, 169, 172
see also *Le nozze di Figaro*, performances
Niecks, Friedrich (Frederick), 137, 161 n. 40
Niemetschek, Franz Xaver, 157 n. 5
Noble, Jeremy, 161 n. 51
Noske, Frits, 116, 152 nn. 3, 4, 7, 156 n. 5
Notaris (author), 130
Le nozze di Figaro (K492), ix, 7, 8, 9, 11, 13, 23
and Beaumarchais, x, 25, 26, 35, 35–48, 75, 120–1, 131, 139, 142, 145, 161 n. 41; dialogue of play restored in later performances, 125, 130, 133–4, 135, 159 n. 25; differences in characterisation, 36–7, 39, 45–8, see also *Le nozze di Figaro*, characters, Countess; selection of episodes for arias and ensembles, 36, 41, 42–5, 84, 151 n. 18; treatment of 'political' content, 25, 26–7, 36, 37–8, 39, 47–8, 140–5, 147, 151 n. 8; see also *Le nozze di Figaro*, libretto
arias, 23, 24, 25, 44–5, 105–6, 107, 110, 111–12, 113–15, 137; ensembles, 8, 9, 23, 25, 50, 52, 56, 57, 95, 105, 109–10, 113, 126, 130, 134, 137, 138; finales, 26, 57, 66, 84–5; recitatives, 60–1, 62, 66, 83, 95, 106; see also *Le nozze di Figaro*, separate items
casting, 10, 36–7, 49, 73, 153 n. 12
composition, 7, 9–10, 35–6, 64–5, 68–74, 85, 90, 150 n. 3, 153 n. 13, 153–4 n. 14, 154 n. 16, 154–5 n. 5, 156 nn. 2, 3, 4, 157 n. 3; excised Act III arietta for Cherubino, 68, 70, 154 n. 18, 157 n. 3; 'Giunse il momento alfine. . .Non tardar, amato bene', 71–2, 126, 153–4 n. 14; middle section for overture, 8, 49, 151–2 n. 1; order of Act III, 72–4, 142
counterpoint, 92–4, 96, 109–10
critical reaction: at first performance, 10, 122–4, 157 n. 5; in Austria and Germany, 124, 125, 126–9, 136, 137, 138; in London, 132–3, 134–5, 135; in Paris, 130; in Prague, 124–5, 157 n. 6; in nineteenth century, 135–7; in twentieth century, 137–46; see also *Le nozze di Figaro*, reviews and announcements
dance and march patterns, 38, 51, 54, 57, 58, 63, 64, 66–7, 67, 78, 84, 106–7, 122–3, 152 n. 7; other aspects of metre, 53, 62, 64, 66, 67, 78, 152 n. 7
early editions and arrangements, 125, 157–8 n. 8, 158 n. 11
influences on, 8, 28–30; Paisiello's *Il barbiere di Siviglia*, 6–7, 9, 24–6, 28, 149 n. 22, 150 nn. 11, 13
later cuts and additions, 125–6, 127, 153 n. 11, 157 nn. 3, 6, 157–8 n. 8; accompanied recitative for No. 9, 158–9 n. 13; 'Al desio di chi t'adora' (K577, replacement for No. 27, Vienna 1789), 125, 158 n. 12, 173; replacement recitative for No. 14, 154 n. 16; 'Signora mia garbata' (replacement for No. 5, Prague ?1786), 157 n. 6; 'Un moto di gioia' (K579, replacement for No. 12, Vienna 1789), 30, 125, 126, 173; *see also* Bishop; Cherubini; Mahler; *Le nozze di Figaro*, performances; Tarchi
libretto: collaboration with Mozart, 35, 41, 42, 75–6, 84, 85, 120–1; da Ponte translates Beaumarchais, 35–6, 36, 39–41, 43, 44–5, 75; preface, 36; selection of arias and ensembles, 36, 41, 42–5, 84–5, 105–6, 151 n. 18; verse structure, x, 27, 36, 41, 75–87, 107, 154 n. 4; in arias, 27, 80–2, 155 n. 6; in ensembles, 82–4; in finales, 84–6, 107, 155 n. 8; in recitatives, 78–80; musical implications followed or not, 78, 80, 81–2, 83, 84, 84–5, 85, 103, 154 n. 3
manuscripts, x–xi, 71–2, 74, 127, 128, 151–2 n. 1, 152 n. 2, 153 nn. 11, 13, 153–4 n. 14, 154 n. 16, 154–5 n. 5, 156 nn. 2, 3, 4, 157 nn. 3, 6, 158 n. 12, 158–9 n. 13
orchestration, 30, 32, 50, 51, 52, 55, 56, 56–7, 57, 58, 59, 66, 68, 78, 95, 97, 106, 107–8, 113, 114, 116, 124, 126, 138, 160 nn. 30, 37
pacing, 24, 41, 50, 57, 95, 97–8, 102–4, 105–8, 118–19, 151–2 n. 1
pastoral elements, 62, 64, 66
performance problems, 72–4, 142, 153 nn. 8, 11, 12
performances, x, 136–7, 158 n. 9; 1786 première in Vienna, 10, 122–4, 157 nn. 3, 4; 1789 revival in Vienna, 30, 125–6, 127, 158 n. 12, 158–9 n. 13; other performances in Belgium, 131; Berlin, 159 n. 16; Boston, 139; Cambridge, 135; Cardiff (Welsh National Opera), 142, 145, 158–9 n. 13, 162 n. 59; Cologne, 136; Darmstadt, 136; Donaueschingen, 125; Dresden, 136; Edinburgh, 135; Florence, 129, 139; Frankfurt on Main, 37, 136, 158 n. 9; Glyndebourne (Glyndebourne Opera House), 138, 139, 140, 141, 142, 144, 145, 146, 162 n. 64; Hamburg, 136, 159 n. 19; Hanover, 158 nn. 9, 10, 159 n. 20; Karlsruhe, 136; London, 131–5, 137, 137–8, 139, 140, 142, 145, 157–8 n. 8, 160 nn. 29, 30, 32, 37, 161 n. 51, 162 nn. 55, 62; Lübeck, 158 n. 9; Mannheim, 159 n. 18; Monza, 129, 159 n. 21; Munich, 136; Newcastle-upon-Tyne, 135; New York, 138–9, 139, 140, 158 n. 9; Nîmes, 131; Oxford, 162 n. 67; Paris, 130–1, 159 n. 25; Philadelphia, 139; Portsmouth, 135; Prague, 124–5, 125, 129, 136, 157 nn. 3, 6; Rome, 140; St Petersburg, 158 n. 9; Salzburg, 137, 140, 142, 143; San Francisco, 139;

Le nozze di Figaro, (*cont.*)
Turin, 129; Vienna, 12, 124, 126, 136, 157 nn. 3, 4, 157–8 n. 8; see also *Le nozze di Figaro*, reviews and announcements
recordings and broadcasts, 139, 146, 168–73
reviews and announcements, 129, 134, 134–5, 135, 137, 139, 139–40, 160 n. 37, 161 n. 41; *Affiches, annonces et avis divers ou Journal général de France* (Paris), 130, 159 n. 24; *Annalen des Theaters* (Berlin), 126, 159 n. 18; *Chronik von Berlin*, 126; *Dramaturgische Blätter* (Frankfurt on Main), 37, 126; *Dramaturgische Blätter* (Hanover), 129, 159 n. 20; *The Examiner* (London), 132–3, 160 n. 30; *Hamburgische Theaterzeitung*, 126–9, 159 n. 19; *Metropolitan Opera News* (New York), 139, 140, 161 nn. 47, 50, 162 n. 53; *The Musical Times* (London), 140, 142, 145, 161 n. 51, 162 nn. 54, 55, 56, 57, 58, 59, 60, 62, 63, 64, 65, 66, 67; *The New York Times*, 139, 161 nn. 48, 49; *Opera* (London), 142, 142–5, 146, 159 n. 25, 162 nn. 52, 53, 61, 68; *Prager Oberpostamtszeitung*, 124; *The Theatrical Inquisitor* (London), 134; *The Times* (London), 132, 133, 138, 160 nn. 29, 36, 161 n. 44; *Weiner Realzeitung*, 124; *see also* da Ponte, *Memorie*; Kelly, *Reminiscences*; *Le nozze di Figaro*, critical reaction
tonality, 27, 50, 56, 57, 59, 60, 61, 64, 73–4, 98, 100–3, 108, 110–13, 114, 114–15, 118–20, 154 n. 18, 155 n. 4, 155–6 n. 5, 156 nn. 2, 3, 6; sonata form, 49, 84, 99–104, 107
translations, 125, 130–1, 133–5, 135, 137, 138, 142, 158 n. 9, 159 n. 16, 162 n. 59
'two-act' structure, 26, 150 n. 9
unity, 115–20, 155–6 n. 5, 156 n. 1
Le nozze di Figaro, characters, 9, 26–7, 36, 45, 47–8, 64, 92–4, 96, 105, 108–15, 126, 146–7, 147
Bartolo, 27, 49, 51, 80, 94, 103, 108, 109, 110, 118, 147; compared with the Count, 81, 113–15
Basilio, 49, 65, 96, 100, 102, 103–4, 110, 147
Cherubino, 27–8, 46–7, 49, 52, 53, 56, 63, 64, 68, 79, 80, 82, 106, 108, 109, 116, 146, 147, 153 n. 11, 155 n. 6
Count, 26, 38, 39–41, 49, 60–1, 79, 82–3, 94, 95–6, 99, 100, 103, 107, 108, 108–9, 109, 109–10, 110, 111, 113, 114–15, 118, 119–21, 129, 134, 146, 147; compared with Bartolo, 81, 113–15
Countess, 7, 49, 72, 103, 107, 108, 109, 110, 115, 118, 119–21, 147; new emphasis on, 39, 45–8, 54, 62, 109, 110–13, 120–1; relationship with Cherubino, 46–7, 116, 120–1
Don Curzio, 49, 94, 103, 109–10, 123
Figaro, 8, 26, 37–8, 39, 47, 49, 50, 54, 63, 66, 76–8, 80, 94, 95, 103, 108, 108–9, 109, 110, 116, 116–18, 118, 119, 120, 146–7, 147
Marcellina, 7, 26, 37, 47, 49, 65, 94, 103, 108, 109, 110, 118, 147
Susanna, 7, 8, 26, 39–41, 47, 49, 50, 66, 72, 82–3, 95, 96, 97, 103, 107, 108, 109, 109–10, 110, 111, 112, 116, 118, 119, 146, 147
Le nozze di Figaro, separate items
Overture, 8, 49, 105, 118, 119, 120, 151–2 n. 1
No. 1, 49–50, 105, 106, 108, 109, 116–17, 118, 120
No. 2, 50, 105, 106, 108
No. 3, 45, 50–1, 51, 76–8, 80, 81, 83, 105, 106, 116, 118, 134, 151 n. 18
No. 4, 8, 27, 51, 80, 81, 82, 106, 113, 113–14, 157–8 n. 8
No. 5, 24, 51, 106, 108, 116–17, 118, 157 nn. 3, 6, 157–8 n. 8
No. 6, 44–5, 52, 80, 80–1, 81, 106, 113, 116–17, 129, 131, 134, 153 n. 11, 154–5 n. 5, 155–6 n. 5, 156 n. 1, 157 nn. 3, 6
No. 7, 43, 52–3, 79, 83–4, 95–104, 106, 116–17, 118, 119, 146, 155 n. 4, 155–6 n. 5
No. 8/8a, 53, 106, 116, 119, 151 n. 14
No. 9, 45, 54, 80, 81, 82, 106, 113, 116, 119, 123, 125, 131, 131–2, 134, 135, 150 n. 11, 158 n. 11, 158–9 n. 13
No. 10, 45, 54, 80, 105, 106, 109, 110–11, 112, 113, 116, 119, 121, 156 n. 2
No. 11, 27–8, 28, 42, 46, 52, 55, 68, 80, 82, 105, 106, 116, 119, 129, 130, 132, 134, 135, 137, 141, 153 n. 11, 155 n. 6, 157 n. 3
No. 12, 30–2, 42, 55, 80, 81, 105, 106, 107, 116–17, 119, 125, 128, 130, 134
No. 13, 56, 72, 102–3, 105, 106, 107, 111, 116, 121
No. 14, 56–7, 72, 154 n. 16
No. 15, 28–30, 43–4, 57–9, 64, 83, 85–6, 95, 105, 106, 107–8, 108, 109, 110, 111, 116, 116–17, 118–19, 119, 121, 123, 129, 130, 146, 152 n. 7, 156 n. 1, 157 nn. 3, 6
No. 16, 9, 41, 60, 82–3, 106, 116, 119, 123, 130, 131, 146, 157–8 n. 8
No. 17, 27, 45, 60–1, 73, 80, 81, 106, 113, 113–14, 114–15, 125–6, 130, 156 n. 3, 158–9 n. 13
No. 18, 61, 73, 83, 84, 92–4, 103, 106, 107, 108, 109–10, 116, 118, 123, 129, 130, 138, 142, 144
No. 19, 45, 47, 62, 73, 80, 81, 106, 111–12, 113, 121, 125, 127, 129, 142
No. 20, 42, 62, 64, 73, 106, 112, 119, 131, 153 n. 13, 159 n. 21

No. 21, 63, 106, 116, 119
No. 22, 42, 43, 63–4, 84, 107, 116, 118, 119, 122–3, 129, 130, 130–1, 152 n. 7
No. 23, 64–5, 80, 106, 116
No. 24, 43, 65, 80, 81, 105, 106, 113, 119, 130, 142, 153 n. 8, 155 n. 6, 157–8 n. 8
No. 25, 43, 65, 80, 81, 105, 106, 113, 119, 130, 142
No. 26, 45, 66, 80, 81, 105, 106, 113, 116, 118, 153 n. 13
No. 27, 66, 71–2, 80, 105, 113, 116–17, 118, 125, 131, 137, 153 n. 13, 153–4 n. 14, 156 n. 4
No. 28, 42, 43, 47, 66–8, 69, 83, 84, 105, 112–13, 115, 116, 118, 119, 119–21, 130, 138, 147, 153 n. 12, 155 n. 6

opera buffa, 2–3, 88, 102; and the Classical style, 3, 88–95, 155 n. 1; popular in Vienna, 6–7, 11–12
arias, 13, 14, 16, 23, 24, 25; ensembles, 13, 23, 25; finales, 13–14, 15, 23, 43–4, 155 n. 8
based on plays, 25
characters, 13, 14–15, 26, 109
conventions, 13, 42–3, 108–9, 113, 120, 152 n. 5; in 1760s, 13–15; in 1770s–80s, 23–4, 26, 27; clichés, 27, 57, 150 n. 10; demands of singers, 42–3
influenced by *opera seria*, 14, 26–7, 150 n. 10
libretto and *poesia per musica*, 39, 43, 76, 78–9, 80, 82, 84–5
orchestration, 30, 57
pacing, 2–3, 102, 105; two-act structure, 23, 26
opéra comique, 3, 33, 130
Opera for All, 145–6
opera seria, 2, 46, 50, 60–1, 88, 102, 107; unpopular in Vienna, 11
influences on *opera buffa*, 14, 26–7, 150 n. 10
Ottaway, Hugh, 162 n. 57
Otto, Teo, 140

Paer, Ferdinando
Il nuovo Figaro, 129
Paisiello, Giovanni, 3, 12, 24, 26, 30, 32, 149 n. 8
Il barbiere di Siviglia, ix, 6, 9, 12, 24–6, 35; influence on *Le nozze di Figaro*, 6, 9, 24–6, 28, 149 n. 22, 150 nn. 11, 13
Il re Teodoro in Venezia, 9, 12, 150 n. 13
Panizza, Ettore, 139, 168
Paris, 1, 9, 37
Opéra, 130–1, 131
Théâtre de l'Opéra-Comique, 131, 159 n. 25
Théâtre des Nouveautés, 131
Théâtre Français, 33, 34
see also *Le nozze di Figaro*, performances
Pergolesi, Giovanni Battista
La serva padrona, 2
Peter Leopold (Archduke, Grand Duke of Tuscany), 129
Petrobelli, Pierluigi, 162 n. 58
Petrosellini, Giuseppe, 149 n. 3
Pezzl, Johannes, 5
Piccinni, Niccolò, 3, 22, 26
La buona figliuola, 15; *La serva onorata*, to an adaptation of *Le nozze di Figaro*, 129
Pironti, Alberto, 142
Planché, James Robinson, 135
Playfair, Nigel, 137
Pocock, Isaac, 160 n. 32
Ponnelle, Jean-Pierre, 142, 143, 146
Prague, 124–5, 126; see also *Le nozze di Figaro*, performances
Pritchard, John, 142, 161 n. 45
Puccini, Giacomo, 145

Quinault, Philippe, 75

Raeburn, Christopher, 72–3, 154 n. 17, 158–9 n. 13, 159 nn. 21, 22, 28
Raffenelli, Michael, 140
Rainforth, Miss (singer), 135
Rautenstrauch, Johann, 35
Robertson, Henry, 132–3, 160 n. 30
Robertson, Patrick, 145
Robinson, Michael F., x, xi, 150 n. 10
Rome, 15; see also *Le nozze di Figaro*, performances
rondò (bipartite aria), 16, 24, 71–2, 149 n. 6, 153–4 n. 14
Rosenberg (Orsini-Rosenberg), Count Franz Xaver Wolf, 4, 9, 122–3
Rosenthal, Harold, 161 n. 39, 162 n. 68
Rossini, Gioachino, 131, 134, 160 n. 37
Il barbiere di Siviglia, 134
Rumbold, Hugo, 137

Sadie, Stanley, 142, 145, 162 nn. 56, 58
St Petersburg, 24, 35; see also *Le nozze di Figaro*, performances
Salieri, Antonio, 5, 6, 10, 12, 157 n. 5
Axur, Re d'Ormus, 12; *Il ricco d'un giorno*, 8; *La scuola degli gelosi*, 5
Salzburg, 1–2, 13, 38; Festival, 137, 140, 142, 168, 169, 170, 171; see also *Le nozze di Figaro*, performances
Sanjust, Filippo, 140
Sarti, Giuseppe, 12
Fra i due litiganti il terzo gode, 12, 28, 125
Scarlatti, Domenico, 88
Schalk, Franz, 137
Schoenberg, Arnold, 156 n. 1
Schuh, Oscar, 140
Schwarzkopf, Elisabeth, 139, 169, 170
Seefried, Irmgard, 139, 169, 170
Sellner, Gustav Rudolf, 140
Shakespeare, William, 75

Singspiel, 3
Solti, Georg, 140, 171
sonata form, 89–90, 94, 99, 102, 107; used in *Le nozze di Figaro*, 49, 84, 99–104, 107
Stephanie, Gottlieb, 3
Storace, Anna (Nancy), 5, 10, 72, 124, 131, 148 n. 9, 157–8 n. 8
Storace, Stephen, 12, 131
Strauss, Richard
  Der Rosenkavalier, 47
Stretton (singer), 135
Strobach, Johann Josef, 157 n. 6
Swieten, Baron Gottfried van, 2, 92

Tarchi, Angelo, 129, 159 n. 21
Taylor, William, 133
Torricella, Christoph, 125
Tracey, Edmund, 161 n. 51
Trowell, Brian, 152 n. 7
Tyson, Alan, xi, xii, 73–4, 153 n. 13, 153–4 n. 14, 154 nn. 16, 18, 156 n. 2, 157 n. 3, 158–9 n. 13

Van Loo, Charles André, 152 n. 6
Varesco, Abbate Giambattista, 6, 7, 149 n. 17
Venice, 5
Vercoe, Rosemary, 145
Verdi, Giuseppe, 145
Vestris, Lucia Elizabeth, 135
Vienna, 1, 13, 35, 36, 37; attractions of, 1–2; *opera buffa* popular in, 6–7, 11–12
  Burgtheater, 2, 3, 6, 8, 9, 11–12, 23, 36, 122, 124, 125, 157 n. 3; German opera in, 3, 11, 148 n. 7; Italian opera in, 3, 4–5, 5, 6, 6–7, 148 n. 7; repertoire, 11–12
  Kärtnertortheater, 126
  Staatsoper, 139, 169, 170, 171
  see also *Le nozze di Figaro*, performances
Vill, Suzanne, 136
Visconti, Lucchino, 140, 142, 161 n. 50
Vulpius, Christian August, 125, 158 n. 9

Wagner, Richard, 137, 139, 145, 151–2 n. 1
Walter, Bruno, 137, 168, 169
Weber, Bernhard Anselm, 129
Weber, Carl Maria von, 160 n. 37
Weber, Dionys, 151–2 n. 1
Weigl, Joseph, 12, 157 n. 4
Wetzlar von Plankenstern, Baron Raimund, 36

Zinzendorf, Count Karl, 124, 157 n. 4